MADE IN AMERICA

Rafer Johnson, 1960 decathlon gold medalist, signifies the opening of Games.

MADE IN AMERICA

HIS OWN STORY

Peter Ueberroth

with Richard Levin and Amy Quinn

WILLIAM MORROW AND COMPANY, INC.
New York

Library of Congress Catalog Card Number: 85-72089

ISBN: 0-688-05882-5

Printed in the United States of America

First Edition

1 2 3 4 5 6 7 8 9 10

BOOK DESIGN BY BERNARD SCHLEIFER

To Ginny and our children, Vicki, Heidi, Keri, and Joe, as well as to:

—seventy-two thousand fellow employees and volunteers

—forty million Americans who stood by the roadsides to cheer on the Olympic torch

—and the athletes of the world who made the 1984 Olympic Games so special

FOREWORD

WINSTON CHURCHILL ONCE SAID: "Some see private enterprise as the predatory target to be shot, others as a cow to be milked, but few are those who see it as a sturdy horse pulling the wagon."

I am among those few. During my five years as president of the Los Angeles Olympic Organizing Committee, a private committee formed to stage the Games of the XXIIIrd Olympiad, I, with the help of seventy-two thousand courageous staff and volunteers, channeled the strength of private enterprise to change the face of sport and organize the Olympic Games—the greatest sporting event in the world—as it had never been done before.

From the beginning people said private enterprise would not step forward. But from the beginning I said, doomsayers be damned. The Olympics was the perfect vehicle to join the public and private sectors in a partnership. It had all the right elements: youth, healthy competition, tradition, drama, and a worldwide audience. It was an opportunity for private enterprise to enhance itself and show what is good about mankind.

When I took the job of organizing the 1984 Olympic Games in 1979, the doomsayers—the media as the representatives of the general public—presented the world with a list of reasons for why we'd fail. They said the people of the United States wouldn't welcome the athletes of the world, that we weren't hospitable. They said Americans were too selfish to volunteer, and, if they did, the system wouldn't work. They said the games would be a killing ground for terrorists. More specifically they said Los Angeles was a crime-ridden community plagued by suffocating smog and snarled traffic. Finally they said a private organizing committee couldn't raise the necessary funds and support to stage a Games worthy of its competitors. Over and over they reminded me of the terrorism of Munich and the billion-dollar financial debacle that left a bitter aftertaste in Montreal.

Despite those warnings I knew we could succeed, and I accepted the challenge because of three simple assumptions:

—The United States of America is the greatest country in the world and every one of us knows how lucky we are to live here.

—If enough Americans believe in an idea or project, anything is possible.

—Patriotism is alive and well and all the people needed was a rallying point to give them reason to stand up and cheer for their country, their communities, themselves, and share their great spirit with the peoples of the world.

Made in America is the story of how we defied the doomsayers and pulled together the disparate public and private sectors to stage a wildly successful Olympics witnessed by half the world and create a $215 million legacy for the youth of this nation. It is a story that changed my life and, I like to think, made our country proud.

This book is a thanks to the seventy-two thousand staff and volunteers and a salute to the forty million people who stood along the roads of America to watch the Olympic flame on its journey from New York to Los Angeles.

—Peter V. Ueberroth

Los Angeles, California
July, 1985

CONTENTS

CONTENTS

MADE IN AMERICA

THE FINAL SCENE

I WAS LATHERING my face and Ginny was sitting on the edge of the bathtub in her robe, sipping a cup of coffee as she does almost every morning. This is the time we discuss the business of the day to come and the small crises going on in the lives of our four children. But today we were silent. We were exhausted. I could see the strain in both our faces.

It was August 12, 1984, the sixteenth and last morning of the Olympic Games, and I was worried. We had been lucky to avoid a terrorist attack till now, and I prayed silently that our good fortune would continue.

I looked in the mirror at Ginny and sensed the same thoughts going through her mind. Five years of devotion to the Games would end in the evening, and we were looking forward to the moment when our family could resume its normal life-style.

I knew we weren't the only ones who were worn out. I had seen signs of fatigue during the past few days in our volunteer army, those who had been working so hard to make the Games a success. Everybody was wired tight. Tempers were starting to flare, and there were reports that some law enforcement officers were getting edgy. Our organization's seams were strained and starting to split. I hoped the fabric of the Games would hold through the day's end.

Ginny finally broke the silence.

"I'd like to sit with the children and our friends tonight."

We had spent almost the entire opening ceremonies closed off in the president's box high atop the Los Angeles Memorial Coliseum and hadn't really felt the drama of the event. In many respects, the closing would be much more emotional and Ginny wanted to be with our family and friends. We had a row reserved in the stands, but most likely I'd have to spend the entire time in the box.

"Save me a seat," I said. "Maybe I'll get lucky and get to spend a few minutes with you."

We had been living at the Biltmore Hotel in downtown Los Angeles for the past month, and at precisely 8:45 A.M. on August 12 I joined International Olympic Committee President Juan Antonio Samaranch and IOC Director Monique Berlioux in Samaranch's suite. This was Samaranch's first Olympics as IOC president and he was ebullient. I was cautious.

The first order of business was to inform Samaranch and Berlioux about the arrangements the Los Angeles Olympic Organizing Committee had made to accommodate all the athletes who wanted to march in the closing ceremonies. Unlike the opening, where all athletes march, the Olympic Charter allows only six from each national Olympic committee at the closing. In the past, many athletes had immediately returned home after competing and now the IOC was worried that television would show the world an empty field. For the first time in Olympic history, most competitors had made plans to attend the final event. While this was the highest form of flattery to Los Angeles, the volunteers, and the people of the United States, it also created a problem: We feared the athletes would storm the field and disrupt the ceremony if they weren't allowed to participate.

David Wolper was in charge. His opening ceremonies, which were brilliant and had received rave reviews from all over the world, had extended a warm and emotional welcome to the athletes and visitors and set an upbeat, festive tone for the Games. The closing was to be a party for the athletes.

Samaranch, Berlioux, and I then discussed the volatile situation involving Sikh demonstrators. During the field hockey competition the Sikhs, members of a powerful Indian religious sect widespread in southern California, demonstrated against the Indian team. On several other occasions, protesters had carried placards and flags to the competitions, causing insult swapping and some pushing and shoving. In each case, security quelled the crowds before anybody got hurt.

I was angered by reports that Ashwini Kumar, who was a member of the IOC Executive Board and chairman of its security commission, had played a role in escalating one such incident following the field hockey match between Pakistan and India.

Kumar had complained bitterly to Samaranch about chaos at East Los Angeles College, the site of field hockey. But our investigation uncovered Kumar's role as provocateur and I suggested that Samaranch tell Kumar to cool his heels.

The next meeting I had was at the Marina Center, a former helicopter-assembly plant near the Los Angeles International Airport in Culver City, which served as LAOOC headquarters for a year. I hopped into a helicopter on top of the Biltmore for the eight-minute ride to the office. Before taking off, the pilot, Joe Allen, a Vietnam veteran, flashed me a big grin, and as he always did, repeated Bette Davis's famous line, "Fasten your seatbelts. It's going to be a bumpy night."

Every morning Harry Usher, general manager of the Games, presided over the operations meeting. This was our last one and it was hard to believe we were actually discussing tearing down what had taken so long to build. In most cases, we'd be out of the facilities and have them restored within a week.

Ed Keen, our vice-president of architecture and construction, brought a note of cheer to this tired group by relating the highlight of Wolper's midnight rehearsal the night before.

In a deep southern drawl he said, "It looked good until

they brought in this helicopter carrying this big, aluminum, ringlike contraption with blinking lights attached to it. The minute it came into the Coliseum, the damned thing folded in half like a flying taco."

My sense of humor was long gone, and I didn't laugh with the others. The "Flying Taco," a spaceship, was Wolper's icing on the cake. I had always thought the plan to land the flying saucer in the Coliseum was too risky. But David is a showman and he had confidence it would work. When you delegate authority and put somebody in charge of a project, you've got to go forward, especially when you have the best. Wolper *was* the best, the ultimate volunteer. He had produced *Roots, The Thorn Birds,* the official film of the 1972 Olympic Games at Munich, and hundreds of films and documentaries. He had won forty Emmys and two Academy Awards. So we went forward.

Later that morning, a California Highway Patrol helicopter crashed on the Harbor Freeway just a mile from the Coliseum. Fortunately no one was seriously hurt, but I dreaded it was a prelude of things to come.

There was still much to be cautious about. We had to make it through the last two competitions—the equestrian individual jumping and the men's marathon—and get all the athletes to the stadium in time for a closing ceremony that would be watched by half the world. We also had to manage traffic congestion, stage a fireworks show without destroying south central Los Angeles, and, for one last time, avoid a major security incident.

By the time our driver, Wayne Ichiyasu, delivered Ginny and me to the Coliseum at 4 P.M., two hours before the start of the show, the helicopter debris had been cleared away and all lanes were flowing freely. I had made it a point to arrive early to check last-minute details with Wolper and to work on my speech.

"The kids are all set for tonight," Ginny said. We had just arrived in the president's box.

I nodded. Sensing my nervousness she went about her business of greeting guests.

From the president's box I could see people entering the Coliseum. The sixty-year-old stadium had never looked better, even after eight days of track-and-field competition. The flame at the western end burned brilliantly in the bright afternoon sunshine. The leaders of the marathon, who were then edging closer to the finish line inside the Coliseum, were being shown on two giant scoreboards on either side of the flame.

A sporting event would play a major role in the closing ceremony for the first time in Olympic history. Usher and I had pushed for this, because the marathon was a symbol of the Olympic struggle and we thought it fitting for the runners to enter the stadium and finish the twenty-six-mile, 385-yard race in front of a hundred thousand cheering fans.

Meanwhile the VIPs—Olympic family members, elected officials, and sponsors—began trooping in, and I began making my protocol rounds. My anxiety increased as the box filled. A lot could still go wrong. People congratulated me right and left, but I told them it wasn't over yet. "Only a few hours to go," I said to no one in particular.

Ginny returned from the other end of the box. She patted my arm reassuringly and said, "It'll go by quickly." She kissed me for luck and I watched as she walked downstairs to the stands to join the kids.

The stadium was filled to capacity by the time the first marathon runner, Carlos Lopes of Portugal, entered it. The crowd stood up and cheered throughout his final lap, and it also roared for John Treacy of Ireland and Charles Spedding of Great Britain, who finished second and third, respectively. As Treacy crossed the finish line, I glanced at Lord Killanin, Honorary Life President of the IOC and who, as president in 1979, had awarded the Games to Los Angeles. He was beaming from ear to ear.

After the medals were awarded for the marathon, Killanin and Fritz Widmer, secretary-general of the International Equestrian Federation, passed out the last awards of the Games to the winners of the individual horse-jumping competition. Then came the parade of national flags and the entrance of the athletes, who weren't exactly orderly. Instead of marching they ran, breaking ranks and cavorting all over the field. They were so happy. I couldn't help but smile, even though they were wreaking havoc with Wolper's schedule, putting us thirty minutes behind.

Just as the traditional exchange of the Olympic flag between Los Angeles and Seoul, Korea, the next city to host the Games, started, Jay Moorhead, the director of our Washington, D.C., office and LAOOC liaison to the White House, came by. Bad news was written all over his face, and he was in no mood to play poker. I could see he had been dealt a lousy hand and was about to ask me to play it.

"The White House says no," he told me.

I shook my head. I couldn't understand it. Samaranch had asked President Reagan for a statement to include in his farewell speech. To Samaranch, this was a supreme gesture of goodwill. He was offering Reagan, the president of the United States, a wonderful opportunity to deliver a message of friendship. Where could you find a bigger or better audience?

"It can't be true," I said to Jay. "Reagan never misses an opportunity to call to congratulate the winner of every hundred-mile race and every college bowl game. He's already signed baseballs for every member of the U.S. baseball team."

"We're getting through to Mike Deaver's assistant in Santa Barbara, but they just don't want to say anything."

"Keep trying."

We had learned early on never to assume or expect anything where government was concerned. Now I had to explain to Samaranch that Reagan had declined his offer.

As I started down the aisle toward Samaranch, I was stopped by Ed Best, our security director. Some drunken athletes had arrived late for the ceremony and had picked a fight with a few guards who barred their entrance to the stadium. I asked Ed to find out which countries they were from and to fix it. He went off to get the job done.

Two steps farther on, one of David Wolper's assistants told me the ceremonies were way behind schedule. The international television networks, he said, were threatening to go off the air before the ceremony was over unless we sped things up. I took that all in and continued on. It wasn't time to panic—yet.

I bumped into Usher, who had just returned from participating in the flag ceremony on the field. He was ecstatic.

"It was the high point of the Games for me," he said.

Images of Usher in action over the last five years flashed through my mind: Usher at staff meetings; Usher hammering out agreement after agreement; Usher's pride over the look of the Games; Usher engaged in hot legal debate with his top aides, Carol Daniels and Jane Ellison; and Usher wearily slipping into a chair in my office late at night to discuss the latest problems.

"I hoped it would be," I told him. "You deserved it."

Pandemonium continued on the field. The athletes were racing back and forth, waving banners and flags. The Australians were using their flag to toss a female teammate into the air. The crowd was responding to their exuberance, and I was getting edgy. I could only hope the athletes wouldn't get entirely out of hand.

By the time I reached Samaranch I wasn't sure which problem to share with him first. He was talking with Mayor Tom Bradley and other local officials. After the appropriate greetings, it was time for us to leave the group and go down to the field to officially close the Games.

"Let's go," Samaranch said. "I'm ready." Samaranch, a diminutive, fastidious man and career diplomat, is always more than ready. He was Spain's ambassador to the Soviet Union for several years before becoming IOC president and he probably had two speeches prepared: one if the Games were a success, and the other if they failed. I knew he had his memorized, and I felt guilty that I hadn't spent any time preparing my own remarks. I had never found the time.

Riding down in the elevator I told him that President Reagan hadn't sent the message we were expecting. Samaranch looked chagrined and bewildered. He didn't say a word, but I'm sure he couldn't imagine why a politician would refuse the opportunity.

We got out of the elevator and walked through the tunnel

leading to the field, which was jammed with staff and stage-hands. The steps leading to the field were slippery from the early evening mist. I made a mental note to have them wiped off so the breakdancers scheduled for later in the show wouldn't fall. As I stepped onto the field, I spotted Ginny and the kids sitting with all our friends in the stands. I hoped they couldn't see how nervous I was.

When I heard my name announced I walked to the microphone set on the huge, round stage in the middle of the field. The lights were so bright I couldn't really see. But I could hear, and it sounded like thunder. At first I didn't know what it was. It took a couple of seconds to sort out the sights and sounds and to realize the crowd was on its feet, cheering for me. I choked up. I had to suppress an incredible urge to tell the world how much Ginny and my children, Vicki, Heidi, Keri, and Joe, meant to me and how their love and support had enabled me to get through this long project. After a few more seconds I raised my arms and asked the crowd for time out by forming a *T* with my hands.

This was a special moment. After almost five years, the people of L.A. were thanking me and, more important, everybody involved with the Games for a job well done. I knew the ceremony was running late, so I began my remarks as soon as the thunder diminished. There was so much to say, so many people to thank, yet so little time. I concentrated on thanking the athletes—the real heroes and heroines of the Games. I ended my speech with the following message:

"Our hope for the future is that all the athletes who have competed here will maintain their new friendships and go forth as ambassadors of peace and goodwill.

"If somehow we have brought the world just a little bit closer together, then we have, indeed, staged a successful Olympic Games. And, in a small way, perhaps we have secured a better future for all the children of the world."

It was a relief when Samaranch took the microphone. After he presented me the Olympic Order in Gold—the highest award in the Olympic Movement—he declared the Games of the XXIIIrd Olympiad closed, and he thanked the people of southern California, particularly the volunteers.

Still somewhat dazed by the reaction of the audience, I managed to point out the slippery steps to a stage manager as I walked off the field and asked him to dry them off before somebody got hurt.

Back up in the president's box where there were still decisions to be made, I watched the Coliseum grow dark. Two incredibly bright spotlights highlighted the Olympic flag as it was lowered and carried from the stadium. Actor Richard Basehart delivered Pindar's dramatic words, which he had written for the ancient Games:

> "Creatures of a day . . .
> What is someone?
> What is no one?
> Man is merely a shadow's dream . . .
> But when God-given glory comes, upon him in victory . . .
> A bright light shines upon us and our life is sweet . . .
> When the end comes, the loss of flame brings darkness . . .
> But his glory is bright forever."

With that, the Olympic flame was extinguished and the party began.

Ed Best wasn't ready to party just yet. He'd discovered that the fuss was still going on and it involved members of the U.S. team. I asked William Simon and Colonel F. Don Miller to help the police quiet them down. They left the box to take care of the problem. Simon and Miller, president and executive director of the U.S. Olympic Committee, had enjoyed a tremendous two weeks and were as anxious as I to keep a minor incident from growing into a major one.

Down the hall, I checked the security control booth and was told everything was going well, which was a welcome relief.

A couple of doors farther down, I barged in on David Wolper who was still somewhat frazzled over the program delays.

"Are we still on schedule?" I asked, knowing he was in no mood for joking.

He looked at me like I'd lost my mind. "Are you kidding? At the rate we're going, these Games may never end."

Wolper had it under control. He was catching up bit by bit. Finally, I addressed my main concern.

"Will the helicopter and spaceship work?" I asked.

David feigned a wince. He specializes in wincing. I think it's his way of recognizing the humor of a tough situation. He was able to diffuse the tension with a simple gesture. It was for his benefit as well as mine.

"It's my headache, Peter," he said. "Go enjoy the rest of the show with your family." I left and took my seat next to Ginny.

The spaceship worked, a half-hour fireworks display saluting previous Olympic host cities lit the night, and Lionel Richie dazzled the crowd. When the balloons dropped from the sky and the giant screens at the end of the stadium lit up with "See you in Seoul, Korea," the ceremony had officially ended. But not for me.

The celebrators wouldn't leave the field, and a large number jumped on the stage. I tensed. Hundreds of people had been working under the stage throughout the day and there were at least forty under it now. There would be serious injuries if it collapsed.

Fortunately, our security people and the ceremonies staff were on top of the situation. They got the announcer to ask the athletes to move off the stage and toward the exit. There was some last-minute dancing around the field and the competitors, never realizing the potential danger they created, left the stadium to continue their partying elsewhere.

As the last ones left the field I hugged Ginny and the children. We stood with our arms around each other and wept in happiness and relief. It was over.

GOING PUBLIC

I HAD A good job. I was chairman of the board of my own company, called my own shots, lived comfortably, and wasn't really looking for a change when Norm Roberts of Korn Ferry, International, walked into my office one afternoon in the fall of 1978.

Roberts sat down, looked me in the eye, and said, "How would you like to be a candidate for the presidency of the Los Angeles Olympic Organizing Committee?"

I leaned back in my chair and laughed. "Are you from *Candid Camera*?"

"No, I'm serious. You should consider it."

I had thought that Roberts only wanted to talk about how my travel company and his executive search firm could work together in cities across the country. He was really throwing me a curve ball.

My business, First Travel Corporation, was then the largest travel enterprise in North America next to American Express. I had built the company from scratch and was proud of its rapid growth. Our headquarters were in an old factory in Van Nuys that we had purchased, and which Ginny and our friend Bonnie Smith had renovated. It had won the 1978 Los Angeles Beautiful Award as one of the most admired additions to the community. It was a pleasant and relaxing place to be, only three miles from our home, and it had tennis courts, fountains, and gardens. As a matter of fact, I had played tennis that afternoon and was still wearing my tennis clothes.

Roberts explained how Korn Ferry was reviewing more than two hundred applications for the LAOOC presidency and developing a profile of the executive who would run the Games.

"It'll take somebody who loves sports," said Roberts. "Somebody who can start up, build up, and run a large corporation."

I just sat and listened. Like millions of other southern Californians, I'd followed the saga of how Los Angeles had bid for the 1984 Games, gotten them, and how the people of Los Angeles—myself included—had then voted against any taxpayer funds going toward the staging of them.

"It'll also take a person with a good fix on global issues and commerce," he continued. "Personally, I think you're tailor-made for the job."

"I'm flattered you thought of me, but I'm not interested," I told him.

"Think about it," he said.

I told him I would. My instincts told me the job was trouble, if not impossible. I knew some of the inside story about the problems the early organizers were having because several months earlier I had played golf with John Argue, a prominent Los Angeles lawyer and president of the Southern California Committee for the Olympic Games, or SCCOG. (The Olympic world reduces almost all names to alphabet soup. The Los Angeles Olympic Organizing Committee, naturally, became the LAOOC, or LAY-OC, as it was pronounced by people around the world.) Argue had negotiated with both the U.S. Olympic Committee (USOC) and the International Olympic Committee (IOC) to get the Games. It would be the second time around for L.A.; the first was in 1932. The only other cities to host the Games twice were London, in 1908 and 1948, and Paris, in 1900 and 1924.

Argue had help from powerful associates. Among the

original organizers were Los Angeles Mayor Tom Bradley; David Wolper; Justin Dart, a southern California industrialist; Howard Allen, president of Southern California Edison; William Robertson, executive secretary-treasurer of the L.A. County Federation of Labor; Rodney Rood, vice-president of ARCO; and attorney Paul Ziffren. But it was Argue's drive that got the bid, and it was his ability to work with the mayor that kept it after the voters rejected public funding of the Games.

Supporting the Olympic Games was a family tradition for Argue and he was following in his father's footsteps as president of SCCOG. Established in 1939, SCCOG evolved from the civic pride generated by the 1932 Olympics. The Argues were part of it then and pursued it until John, a second-generation Argue, closed the deal. In my opinion, he never received enough credit for his efforts.

During the course of our golf match, Argue told me of his great joy in winning the bid in October 1978, and then the bitter disappointment over the passage only a month later of a city charter amendment prohibiting the use of public funds for the Games. He had had to go back to the IOC and restructure L.A.'s bid and negotiate a rule that allowed a private group to stage the Games.

Customarily, the IOC awards the Games after reviewing numerous bid recommendations from various national Olympic committees, but in 1978 it was in a spot: Los Angeles was the only city interested in hosting the 1984 Games. (Teheran, Iran, submitted a halfhearted bid but eventually withdrew.) The tragic slayings of Israeli athletes in Munich at the 1972 Games and the financial debacle at Montreal four years later had discouraged potential suitors. The IOC had no choice but to accept L.A.'s conditions.

Being privately financed, these Games would be different. Argue knew that Los Angeles organizers would take a great risk and would face monumental obstacles in funding and securing the Games. What's more, it was obvious that the people of Los Angeles were opposed to hosting the Games and could be expected to keep a vigilant eye on the fiscal integrity of the organizers to make sure public funds were not used. Their tight-fisted attitude stemmed from an over-whelmingly popular 1978 California referendum—Proposition 13—that limited statewide property tax increases to 1 percent.

Even I was one of the vast majority who voted for Proposition 13 and later against taxpayer money being used to underwrite the Games. I believed then—as I do now—that there are many important programs much more deserving of government support than a sports event, even one as special as the Olympic Games. Also, as a concerned resident, I didn't want my tax dollars wasted in Los Angeles in the same way as was done in Montreal.

I didn't speak to Roberts during the next few months. Meanwhile, several prominent names were mentioned as being the leading candidates for the presidency of the organizing committee. Among them were former Secretary of State Alexander Haig, National Football League Commissioner Pete Rozelle, sports announcer Curt Gowdy, and Chrysler chairman Lee Iacocca. I hadn't given much thought to Roberts's suggestion, even though he'd said the profile was a perfect description of me: a southern Californian between the ages of forty and fifty-five who had start-up business experience, an interest in sports, financial independence, and was familiar with international affairs.

I knew my profile lacked one vital element—name recognition. It was inconceivable to me that an unknown businessman from the San Fernando Valley could gain the support necessary to get the job done. Furthermore, most people can't even pronounce "Ueberroth," let alone spell it.

Nonetheless, my curiosity had been piqued. I read every news item on the emerging organizing committee, and somehow Argue had heard about my meeting with Roberts and was encouraging me to reconsider.

About that time I had lunch with Dick Ferry, one of the principals of the search firm. He strongly urged me to meet with a panel of local leaders who were making the final selection. Ferry thought I had a long-shot's chance. I wondered why they were pushing me.

Ginny and I discussed it that night.

"It might be fun" was Ginny's assessment.

"Sounds to me like a disaster waiting to happen," I replied.

"What have you got to lose by meeting the people involved?" she asked.

Ginny was right. There wasn't much harm in pursuing it. I called Ferry and agreed to meet the LAOOC search-panel members one on one. By this time, SCCOG had become the LAOOC and it had twenty-two board members, eight of whom were interviewing the candidates and would make a recommendation to the full board.

Since this selection potentially could change my life in a major way, I decided to examine it on my own terms. I would have to interview the panel members as they were interviewing me.

My first meeting was with Justin Dart, who at that time was one of the most powerful leaders in southern California and an intimidating presence. The interview took place in his office. For every question he asked, I asked three. After about twenty minutes, he picked up his phone. "Just a minute," he said to me.

I thought he might be calling somebody to show me the door. Instead, he placed a call to Dick Ferry and said, "I found a man to run the Olympic Games. Don't interview anybody else. Don't send anyone else to see me."

I was shocked. To this day I don't know why he did it. He was a tough curmudgeon and about the most patriotic person I had ever met. Dart and his wife, Jane, became good friends of ours and Justin, a helpful adviser. I was saddened by his death just before the Games opened in 1984 and I often thought how proud he would've been had he lived long enough to see the outcome.

Mayor Tom Bradley was next. He was polite, courteous, and friendly. But I knew from the beginning I wasn't his choice. He was backing Ed Steidle, a formidable businessman from downtown Los Angeles who, as chairman of the board of the May Company, had just been honored as the Urban League Man of the Year. He was well liked by big business,

labor, the political establishment, and the minority community.

Next, I met with the Federation of Labor's top official in
L.A., Bill Robertson, a mainstay in the southern California
political spectrum. He kept me waiting more than an hour
and before the perfunctory meeting was over, I knew he was
one individual who would never want me to be involved. Ours
was bad chemistry, and it never completely changed throughout the course of our Olympic relationship.

I then met with two more downtown business types,
Howard Allen of Southern California Edison, and Rod Rood
of the Atlantic Richfield Company. Both were committed to
Steidle. After the interviews, however, I thought they had
second thoughts.

I had already met David Wolper and it hadn't been a
friendly encounter. Six years earlier, Wolper had sought fresh
money for the International Volleyball Association, and he
held a meeting for potential investors at his house. At that
time, professional leagues were springing up like wildflowers.
There were the World Football League, the American Basketball Association, the World Hockey Association, and the
International Track and Field Association. Following the 1972
Olympics, Wolper and several of his show business colleagues
fell in love with volleyball and formed the IVA.

For some reason, good, sound businessmen seem to
waive all their business principles when they get involved with
sports. I wasn't about to do that. I went to Wolper's meeting
hoping to walk away with a volleyball franchise in San Jose,
which if managed properly would be a good investment. San
Jose was a good market. Besides, having grown up there, I
had a special fondness for the community.

Wolper and I clashed at every turn. He had a big-bucks
Hollywood attitude. He was prepared to spend a lot of
money. I wasn't. If the league was to survive, I believed it
would have to be low budget and well managed. I told Wolper
he was barking up the wrong tree and predicted his league
would fail. Wolper didn't appreciate some upstart coming into
his home and telling him how to run his business. I left at
about the same time Wolper was getting ready to throw me
out. (As it turned out, the league folded.)

Now, six years later, I entered Wolper's office with some trepidation. Wolper was an Olympic fanatic and had produced *Visions of Eight,* the highly acclaimed official film of the Munich Olympics. A man of extremely firm ideas and opinions, he is without question one of the most creative individuals I've ever met. He can develop one hundred brilliant ideas for any given situation on a moment's notice. Nonetheless, he is a good listener and capable of reversing his opinions when faced with a good argument. Although he didn't commit himself, I believed I had his support.

After a pleasant meeting with Yvonne Braithwaite Burke, former U.S. congresswoman from Los Angeles whom I knew would support the mayor's choice, I arranged for the final interview. It was to be with Paul Ziffren and it turned out to be the most important one.

Ziffren cut an imposing figure—tall and lean with a shock of white hair and big, thick horn-rimmed glasses. He was deeply involved with the Democratic National Committee, having served as a member of its executive committee from 1953 to 1960. Over the years, he'd been friends with presidents and senators and had been one of his party's major fundraisers. He was a wise power broker. Going in, I knew Ziffren would back Steidle. Ziffren, even in those early days, recognized the political football the Olympics would become and felt strongly that the leader chosen should be a political animal. That left me out. While my business savvy showed, it didn't compensate for political inexperience. But the meeting did plant seeds of understanding between us, and I left feeling that he was someone I wanted to know better.

The interview process was over. I had met interesting people and had begun to get a feel for civic involvement and the politics associated with it. The Olympic Games would present a complex and difficult challenge for the city, its people, and especially the person who ran it. The idea of doing something so dramatically different stimulated me. But realistically, I sensed I wasn't what they had in mind.

At a dinner party several weeks later, I got a sample of the anger that the Olympic controversy was generating in California. Over cocktails in front of the fireplace at the home of

John and Susan Shumway, I heated up a room already
warmed by the fire by asking John's brother, Forrest, what he
thought about the Olympic Games coming to Los Angeles.
Forrest, an astute businessman with the Signal Companies
and a friend whom I respected, cut loose with a ten-minute
tirade.

"It's the worst thing that's ever happened to this city," he
said for openers. He hoped the Games wouldn't stay and, if
they did, predicted they certainly would wind up in bankruptcy. He was sure that under no circumstances would the
people ever support the Games. They were an imposition on
their lives and a danger to the community. And he went on
from there.

A few days later, Dick Ferry called me out of the blue.
He told me I was one of two final candidates. Months had
elapsed and while name recognition was important, I no
longer felt it was absolutely necessary. The job intrigued me.
I knew I could do it better than anyone else.

Ken Reich, a reporter from the *Los Angeles Times* who
had covered the Los Angeles bid from the outset, made an
appointment to see me. He knew more than I about the selection process and from his inside information gave me an overview on the status of the search. He had polled all twenty-two
voting members of the newly created executive committee
and discovered that only one candidate had enough commitments to be elected. He told me I might get three votes. Only
Dart's was firm.

On Friday morning, March 23, as Ginny, Keri, and Joe
were preparing to go skiing in Vail over spring break, the papers reported that the LAOOC Executive Committee would
select a chairman and president on the following Monday. We
were amused.

"If I thought you'd win, I'd stay," Ginny said.

I told her it wasn't necessary. I was staying home with
our two older daughters, Vicki and Heidi, and we had a big
week planned.

That Monday I was in my office when my secretary,
Sherry Cockle, told me Paul Ziffren was on the line.

"Pete, I want to be the first to tell you that you were

elected president of the Los Angeles Olympic Organizing Committee and I have been elected chairman," Ziffren said.

I was stunned. How did it happen? It turned out that Dart and Wolper were so supportive of my candidacy that they actively campaigned and convinced enough board members to vote for me. I had won by one vote over Steidle.

Ziffren wanted to meet immediately, so I agreed to see him at his office that afternoon.

I called Ginny with the news.

"Are you kidding?" she asked.

I laughed. "Who would kid about something like this?"

I wasn't sure what I had done or was about to do, but during the course of the phone call I realized I was committed. Then Vicki called. Then Heidi. Both were thrilled and we made plans to celebrate over dinner.

In retrospect, I had begun to realize during the interview process that I couldn't accomplish much more at First Travel. I already had the best people possible to run each of our three subsidiary companies. Each was secure in his job, each was left to his own devices, and in each case the person was excelling.

My brother, John, ran Ask Mr. Foster's Travel Services, which was growing faster than we could track it; Wally Smith ran our flourishing hotel company; Don Hough was in charge of the original company, TCI, and was having a record year. They didn't need me anymore. I was the one who needed something different and more challenging. At that time, I thought I could have the best of both worlds and stay on as company chairman while organizing the Olympics.

With that in mind, Ziffren and I met. We shook hands on a simple agreement: I would run the Games with full authority for all personnel and expenditures as the chief executive officer and he, as chairman of the board, would conduct the board meetings and serve as a buffer, keeping the politicians and interest groups at bay and out of the day-to-day operations. It seemed like an easy and fair division of labor. Paul got the tougher end of the deal, however. To this day I believe he's the only person alive who could have done it.

After that meeting, I got together with Hank Reiger and Rene Henry, the two volunteers handling the committee's public relations. They had scheduled a 10 A.M. news conference for the next day and began preparing me.

As I'd never participated in one before, they drilled me for hours on every conceivable aspect of public interest in the Games. They outlined questions and answers on financing, security, revenue raising, site selection, transportation, and my own personal business background. They impressed upon me the importance of being up front with the media and getting off on the right foot. I realized that even while most southern Californians were extremely wary about hosting the Games, some were very supportive. There were strong people willing to give their time freely and help the Games move forward. Reiger and Henry were two such individuals. They had been volunteering their time for two years and I was grateful for their professional expertise.

The briefing lasted well into the night. I lost all track of time and it was late when I realized I'd missed a date with the girls. An apology didn't do the trick. They sounded less thrilled about the Olympics than they had earlier in the day. I hoped it wasn't a sign of things to come.

The news conference was held at the Los Angeles Press Club, a dingy, dilapidated building located in Hollywood off the Hollywood Freeway. As Reiger had predicted, media interest was great. Reporters were surprised that an unknown had been selected. They knew nothing about me and ransacking newspaper morgues hadn't helped either. In seventeen years, the *Los Angeles Times* had made only one brief reference to me or my company.

I hadn't anticipated being asked if my travel business constituted a potential conflict of interest. I promised to leave First Travel out of the Olympics. I realized then that there'd be a great deal of public scrutiny of the Games down the line. I'd have to anticipate questions and be on my toes to deal with that successfully. It's the unexpected that makes the most news.

I returned to my office late in the day and began making

phone calls to assure managers of our offices around the country that I would remain as chairman of the board and the company's growth would continue.

At the end of the day I got my first taste of Olympic planning. A beaten-up cardboard box arrived by messenger from city hall. There was no note attached, only a crayon scrawl on the side that read: "All the records of the Los Angeles Olympic Games."

FAST FORWARD

MY FAMILY ALWAYS comes first; I never take it for granted. I've tried hard to be aware of my children's moods, particularly when things are happening quickly. But I'd never stopped to evaluate the impact the Games might have on them until I accepted the LAOOC presidency. Ginny and I knew there would be changes, but we were most surprised by the reaction of our ten-year-old son, Joe. I'm especially sensitive to him because he's the youngest.

Joe was moping around the house one afternoon, so I suggested a game of basketball. After a few games, I asked him what was bothering him. He was reluctant to say anything at first, but finally asked, "What's going to happen to me?"

I wasn't sure what he meant, so I probed deeper.

"Are you really going to sell the company? What am I supposed to do?"

Unbeknownst to me he'd already made the assumption that First Travel was his destiny. I was touched. I welcomed this opportunity because it gave me a chance to discuss his future.

"You'll do better than I have," I told him. "And you'll do it on your own. What could be more fun than that?"

I explained how it was often painful for a son to take

over his father's business. How it could stifle creativity and limit choices. I didn't want him to feel locked in.

This conversation reminded me of ones I used to have with my father.

I was born on September 2, 1937, in Evanston, Illinois, to Victor and Laura Ueberroth; my sister, Jill, was then six years old.

The Depression was ending and my father worked as a salesman at Sears, Roebuck until he broke a leg trying to teach Jill how to ice skate. Employee benefits were not great in those days: If you were absent for any length of time for any reason, you were replaced. That's what happened to my father.

We moved around a lot after that, keeping up with my father, who became a traveling salesman of aluminum products for various companies. He'd work an area, tap out the market, and move on. He was good at it, but the constant relocating was difficult on my mother. She was ill with cancer and I have memories of her lying on the couch while neighbors took care of us children.

We were living in Madison, Wisconsin, when she died of leukemia in 1941. I was four years old. All I remember is that Jill and I were sent to our mother's relatives for a few days and were brought back to attend something called a funeral. I remember little about my mother except a most vivid memory of her as a beautiful woman.

The times that followed were especially difficult for Jill, who filled in for Mom. The fact that she was able to do so was a tribute to the way Mother had raised us.

A year later my father met and married Nancy Green, and we then moved to Davenport, Iowa, where Dad continued selling aluminum products. That summer Jill and I visited one of my father's two brothers, Harry, in California. He was a successful movie actor whose stage name was Allan Curtis and he was married to the beautiful Hungarian actress Illona Massey.

It was a fun summer. My uncle taught us how to fish and swim and drove us around town in his sports car, which was a big deal for a couple of kids from the Midwest. They must have enjoyed having us, because when the summer was over my uncle asked to keep us permanently. My father had missed us, though, and, as tough as things were, wanted us back.

Nancy worked as an accountant and kept house and together they worked toward their goal of settling in the West. But first my dad was transferred to Upper Darby, Pennsylvania, where my brother, John, was born. I was six years old.

We moved to California in stages. In 1943, Jill and I were sent ahead to spend the summer with Nancy's parents in Laguna Beach. Then we were reunited with the rest of the family up north in Burlingame, because Dad had gotten a job selling radio advertising in nearby San Francisco. For the first time in my life, we settled down.

My father always kept stacks of encyclopedias and newspapers next to the dinner table, and each night he'd select a volume or a section of the paper and quiz us on different subjects. Those quizzes inevitably led to heated family discussions in which we learned to articulate various points of view. On some occasions Dad would be the debater, on others the moderator. For someone with less than a high school education, his knowledge about a variety of subjects seemed endless.

Dad never took an interest in sports, which became my main focus during my teens. He saw me compete only once at a high school, B-team basketball game to which Jill had to drag him. I was a freshman and the team's fourth guard but she knew I'd get to play because one of the other guards had gotten hurt. Then, during warm-ups, another guard sprained an ankle, which meant I'd play the entire game. It was one of those lucky days. On one play, I threw a bad pass to the center—it was too high—and it went into the basket. I scored 12 points. Afterward my father said, "I knew you'd do okay." I was proud. Coming from him, a tough taskmaster, this was high praise, indeed.

My father was an internationalist and insisted that we pay attention to what was happening in the world. I can remember his excitement when the United Nations first met in San Francisco. He explained how it was the successor to the League of Nations and how he believed it was an important step toward world peace. Although a registered Republican, he was impressed by plain-talking politicians, regardless of party, and was supportive of Harry Truman.

He never flew, but that didn't diminish his fascination for the aviation industry. He and I used to park on the Bayshore Highway near our house and talk while we watched the Pan Am Clipper seaplanes land on the water. Over and over, he'd explain how aviation would supplant other forms of domestic and international travel. It was from those discussions that many years later I would take a cue.

He never pushed grades or the need to go to college. He would always say, "You have to decide what you want to learn." He'd leave it to us to pursue our own course. "You ought to put yourself in a place that causes transactions to happen," he used to say, "because that's what makes business vital. To be on the selling end, on the implementing side, causes action. If you are on the action side, you have independence."

I realized the merit of his philosophy years later while holding down a summer job as a traveling seed salesman for the Ferry-Morse Company. I was between my sophomore and junior years in college. Early one morning en route to San Jose from Reno to join a girlfriend and another couple, I came around a bend at too high a speed, swerved, and sailed over an embankment, rolling a station wagon that belonged to the company. Fortunately, I wasn't hurt and managed to escape by the back door just before the car exploded. Badly shaken, I hitchhiked to Clear Lake Oaks—population twelve—and contacted the company, which sent someone to get me. After a doctor checked me out, I went to corporate headquarters. I was certain my pink slip awaited me, and deservedly so. I'd been three hundred miles out of my territory and had destroyed a company car and a load of samples with it, all while taking the day off to spend with the latest love of my life.

Imagine my surprise when the supervisor handed me the

keys to a new company car and told me to be careful. He suggested that in the future I stay in my territory and to ask when I needed a day off. As one of the company's top twenty salesman, I had made a lot of things happen, and the company didn't want to lose me. I'm convinced that had I been involved in any other phase of the business, I would have been fired.

My first job was delivering newspapers. By the time I was fourteen years old, I was the supervisor of ten delivery boys, including my brother, John, for the *Burlingame Shopping News*. Nepotism ended there. He had three hundred papers to deliver, which wasn't easy for him. He was small and had to walk his route every day instead of riding his bicycle like the others. Sometimes he complained that other kids ditched their papers down the sewer, but I wouldn't let him do that. He had an obligation and he had to live up to it.

I was offered a job at a local children's home, Twelveacres, when I was fifteen. It was a great chance to be independent. I had my own cabin; there were wonderful sports facilities; and, on top of it all, I got paid. I liked kids and my goal then was to become a coach. I'd go home on weekends, but I always made sure I was out of the house before Nancy made me mow the lawn or trim the trees for nothing. Besides, I could make money caddying at the local golf course. I was turning into a workaholic at an early age. It was also when I discovered that I liked being in charge.

I worked at Twelveacres throughout high school and I vividly remember my graduation when twenty-eight Twelveacres kids stood in the stands and cheered as I walked across the field to receive my diploma. It made me feel warm all over, as though a whole second family were there.

It was also at graduation when my high school swim coach introduced me to Ed Rudloff, the San Jose State water polo coach, and said: "Pete here is a good swimmer, he has a strong arm, and likes body contact. He should be a good water polo player." Although I had never seen a water polo game, the introduction paid off when I attended San Jose State the next year.

It was fall 1955, and I had no idea how I would support myself at San Jose State. One day in the gym Rudloff asked me what I was up to. I told him I hadn't been able to get any classes. He took my class schedule out of my hands, made some notes, and rearranged it. "If you'll come out for freshman water polo, I'll see that you get your classes," he told me. I told him I'd see him at practice. Not only did he get me classes, he arranged for a grant-in-aid scholarship that partially paid my way through four years of school.

I fell in love with water polo. I became captain of the freshman team and a year later joined Rudloff on the Olympic Club water polo team. The Olympic Club was a San Francisco men's club that drew the best college players from the area. Our team was the best in the country and, as the best, entered the U.S. Olympic trials for the 1956 Games. Just trying out for the team was a great honor for me. I didn't make it—wasn't even close—but from then on I began following the Olympics.

Over the next two years I became better at water polo. I led the league in scoring each year and would have tried out for the Olympic team again in 1960 had other things not begun to happen in my life, the most important of which was meeting Virginia Mae Nicolaus, the daughter of a Long Beach baker. Toward the end of my junior year, Bruce Waldie, a Delta Upsilon fraternity brother, fixed us up on a blind date. My funds were tight and she agreed, when I insisted, that we go Dutch treat our first few dates.

That summer, 1958, between my junior and senior years, I went to Hawaii with Dick Sargent, a college friend and later a business associate, and two other friends. We flew on a DC-4 and each of us carried a sleeping bag and a good wool suit. On the sixteen-hour flight, Dick talked to one of the stewardesses and learned a key piece of information. The locals would beat us to a bloody pulp if we tried to sleep on the beach. With that in mind, we split into two groups when we arrived and hitchhiked into Waikiki. One of the fellows who drove us into town offered to put us up. We accepted and spent our first night on the floor of his apartment; we didn't want to test the locals.

The next day we rented a one-bedroom termite palace and I found a job with Great Lakes Airlines, the carrier that had flown us to Hawaii. The other guys took the summer off. We spent all our spare time surfing and playing volleyball at the Outrigger Canoe Club. In fact, we snuck into the club so many times they thought we were members.

It was idyllic for four college men out for a good time. Remember, this wasn't the Hawaii of the matching mumus. Hawaii wasn't even a state yet. It was raw and beautiful. When I wasn't working, I was surfing, and it didn't take long to learn you didn't mess with the local surfers. They didn't like the *pelau coast haole bugga*. In other words, they beat up anybody from the mainland who was crowding their surfing waters. Sargent and I picked up on this very quickly, once we saw a few servicemen get clobbered. We befriended Rabbit Kae Kai, then recognized as the king of the surfers, who allowed us onto his territory to surf.

When Sargent and I weren't surfing, we looked for other challenges, one being sailing because it didn't look difficult. Surfing wasn't and we'd already mastered the medium-sized waves.

For our first sail Sargent and I borrowed a catamaran on the Ala Wai Canal with every intention of sailing it out into the Pacific. Since we didn't have any money, we told the owner we were in the market for a sailboat. He showed us the catamaran and offered us a trial run. It took an hour just to get the sail up, and that was the *easy* part. In the canal we lost all control. The boom swung every which way, and somehow we managed to crack the mast. As we started drifting out of the canal and into real trouble, I dived overboard, grabbed the bowline, and used every ounce of strength I had to tow the boat back to its slip while Dick steered. We tried to slink out of the harbor area since we'd all but destroyed the boat. But the owner caught sight of us.

"Hey, fellas, how'd you like her?" he called out.

Dick deferred to me. "It's a nice boat," I yelled back, "but a little too small for us."

We beat a hasty retreat, and that was the extent of my sailing. For Dick's part, he fell in love with the sport and became an expert sailor.

I was in love, too. During my senior year, Ginny and I became inseparable. The first time I brought Ginny home my family was hooked on her. Particularly my dad. "If you don't marry Ginny," he told me, "don't bring anyone else around." By Christmas she was a regular at the Ueberroth Sunday family dinners.

The airline contacts I made that summer in Hawaii paid off later on. I managed to swing a job during the school year for an association of nonscheduled airlines, which represented such noteworthy carriers as Portland Rose, Standard Pink Cloud, United States Overseas Airways, Currey Air Transport, Miami International Airlines, and Blatz. I returned to Hawaii to work over the Thanksgiving holiday and stretched a one-week trip into two. That Christmas the association paid me $5,000 to represent its interests at the Monterey Airport.

My job was to arrange air transport for stranded GIs from nearby Fort Ord. Compared to the polished efficiency of the major airlines, mine was a hand-to-mouth operation. While their employees worked out of plush office space, I set up card tables in the middle of the terminal. I brought in pretty co-eds from school to serve as hostesses and got a bunch of my caddy friends to handle the baggage. I even convinced a local diner to shut down its normal operation and make box lunches for the passengers at a one-dollar profit per box. We loaded up thirty airplanes of all sizes, shapes, and colors with seventy to eighty servicemen each and flew them all over the country. To illustrate how small some of these airlines were, the owner of Portland Rose Airways, a one-plane operation, was a butcher.

But the butcher had an easier time than another independent owner, Kirk Kerkorian. One of Kerkorian's L.A. Air Service planes blew an engine, and even though we had managed to replace it within twenty-four-hours, most of his passengers had already departed on other airplanes. The few left were going to varied destinations across the country. Rather than let them down, I arranged for the plane to land at three major cities and informed the passengers they'd have to drop off at the point closest to their destinations and make other arrangements for their final leg. Two years later, Kerkorian hired me to run the Hawaiian end of his company.

I graduated from San Jose State in 1959 with a degree in business. First, I tried finding work locally to be close to Ginny, who was in her junior year. About thirty corporations recruited on campus for San Jose State graduates and I tried to interview with as many as possible. All but one turned me down and I didn't take the rejections very well. The one offer came from Personal Products, but my pride at that time prevented me from accepting a job where I would have to explain I was making a living selling feminine hygiene products. So I decided to try Hawaii, where I believed the rapidly growing islands held employment opportunities.

Long-distance relationships weren't for me. Ginny's father, Nick Nicolaus, didn't like spending a fortune on my collect calls to his daughter. By August I had made up my mind, and I sent Ginny an engagement ring that had belonged to my mother. I attached a note that said: "Will you marry me?" The next month we were married in Long Beach, and a day later we left for Honolulu. We had $500 between us.

Ginny and I started married life in a square little box across from the Ala Wai Canal where Dick and I had wrecked the catamaran in 1958. The apartment was so small you had to stand outside the door to photograph somebody inside.

Before joining Kerkorian, I sold copying machines for 3M—Minnesota, Mining & Manufacturing—and then worked Great Lakes' travel desk at the Biltmore Hotel in Honolulu. Meanwhile, to make ends meet, Ginny sold lingerie at Sears in the evenings after attending the University of Hawaii during the day.

Sargent had also returned to Hawaii and the two of us learned a lot about dealing with people while working the counter for Great Lakes. As young businessmen on the move we took ourselves seriously and worked hard. Yet we always found time to laugh.

We still chuckle about one New Yorker who left home on a Saturday and arrived in Honolulu the following Wednesday. He appeared at our ticket desk that Wednesday, his bags in his hands, and his clothes rumpled.

"I want the first flight out of here," he said.

Dick and I looked at each other. We knew he'd just arrived.

"But according to your ticket, you don't leave until Saturday," I told him.

"I know. But I have to be back at work on Monday or else I'll get fired."

From New York he'd taken a detour through Pittsburgh because of mechanical problems, broke down in Cleveland, then went through Chicago, Denver, Oakland, and L.A. He didn't reach Hawaii until the fifth day of his vacation. Because of that, all he could afford was twelve hours in paradise.

As manager of Kerkorian's L.A. Air Service, which he later renamed TransInternational Airlines at my suggestion, I sold commercial flights from the mainland to Hawaii. With the exception of Dick Sargent, I hired only Hawaiians, who took great pride in their community, and before long we captured most of the business between the mainland and the islands. I was learning the importance of having people on my side who were familiar with the territory.

When Kerkorian decided to beef up operations on the West Coast, he asked me to return to California to run the commercial operation at his Los Angeles headquarters. After three happy years in Hawaii, Ginny and I moved to Encino, California, where we remained for the next twenty-two years.

Working at Kerkorian's side was fascinating because he taught me the value of taking business risks. He was a quiet, thoughtful man with a street fighter's savvy and had been a former professional fighter who had an uncanny ability to size up and analyze people instantly. He always maintained direct eye contact, which never wavered in the toughest of negotiations. His is one of the great success stories of our time. A product of a poor Armenian background, without even a secondary school education, he managed to acquire Western Airlines and MGM, among other holdings, and became one of the wealthiest men in the country.

For the most part Kerkorian and I got along very well,
but occasionally our mutual stubbornness got in the way. I
vividly remember one argument we had. Ginny and I had
gone to Las Vegas with Kerkorian and his wife, and we had
the run of the place, a yacht on Lake Mead with a speedboat
to water ski, massages at the Desert Inn, and free dinner
shows. You name it. One night a friend of Kerkorian's signed
a $6,000 marker at the crap table and lost it on one roll of the
dice. Later that night, we argued over giving termination pay
to some of our employees whom we had to let go because of
the Civil Aeronautics Board's ruling that prohibited nonscheduled airlines from selling passenger tickets on a regular
basis. I wanted to increase it by $6,000.

"Your friend lost that much on one roll of the dice," I
said.

Kerkorian became furious. "Who the hell do you think
you are? What you do in business and what you do in your
personal life are two different things," he said.

I didn't agree with him then but later I learned he was
right.

Not long after the CAB ruling, which increased my suspicions about government intervention in business, we shut
down our commercial operation. Kerkorian, however, continued to run charters for the military. After some debate, I sold
him the 3 percent interest I had acquired in the company,
according to an agreed-upon formula, but got very little for it.
I believed for a twenty-four-year-old I had considerable business experience—enough to venture out on my own.

I started Travel Consultants Inc. over the phone from our
tiny San Fernando Valley apartment. Once I established an
opening wedge in the marketplace and began pursuing repre-
sentation of small international air carriers and steamship
lines seeking U.S. business, I opened an office in a cubbyhole
in Hollywood. After spending a year sailing around Tahiti,
South America, and the Caribbean, Dick Sargent rejoined me
and we began booking business for such carriers as Alaska
Airlines, Garuda Indonesia Airways, South Pacific Airlines,
Hawaiian Airlines, and Ethiopian Airlines.

My business philosophy has always been that you don't spend more than you have. Those early days were lean. I was pulling in $100 a week and Dick drew $50. Being married, I explained, I had to draw double.

Even though the business grew rapidly, we had problems, specifically at the Seattle World's Fair, which we viewed as an opportunity for ferrying the many southern Californians who wanted to visit it. We advertised heavily in the *Los Angeles Times* and distributed leaflets at all the local travel agencies. We offered three- and four-day visits to the fair, including roundtrip airfare, hotel rooms, airport transfers, and entrance passes for only $126—the same rate United and Western were charging for the roundtrip flight alone. We had leased a DC-6 from some fly-by-night company out of Miami and were doing well until the Seattle hotels pulled the rug out from under us. One Thursday night I got a telephone call informing me that the hotels were charging double for the group about to check out and would charge the same for the group about to check in. The hotels, having built up their expectations, were doing poor business, which, I later learned, is usually the case at big events. There was nothing we could do but pay the rate—we couldn't leave the people stranded—and scramble to cover our losses. Within a week we pulled out completely. We refunded everybody's money and paid all our bills, except for the huge advertising and telephone costs. It took awhile, but eventually we paid off those debts too.

Years later I remembered the false hopes and inflated expectations of the Seattle hotel industry when we began our official Olympic hotel program for the games. I wasn't about to get burned again and having learned the hard way, guaranteed our hotels 100 percent occupancy in return for stable rates.

Needless to say, I was unnerved by the Seattle losses for a while—about $100,000—but fortunately before long TCI, which was coming into its own, bailed us out. Our overseas research started to pay dividends and renewed contacts began taking me all over the world. TCI soon expanded into a small office in San Francisco, then into offices around the country.

Kerkorian continued to be an adviser and friend. In 1963

he told me he'd been counseled to take his company public and asked me if I would be interested in investing in it. I not only invested in some shares, I also followed his lead and took my company public a couple of years later.

This gave Ginny and me some financial stability and eventually allowed us to purchase a one-and-a-half acre, five-bedroom house in Encino. By 1969, we had three daughters. Vicki, named after my father, was born in 1962; Heidi, three years later; and Keri in 1967. Shortly after we moved into the Encino house, our son, Joe, was born. Ginny continued her quest for a bachelor's degree and graduated from California State University at Northridge—the first in her family to graduate from college—and then taught elementary school part time for a few years.

Our lives were built around the family, and almost always my evenings and weekends were reserved for Ginny and the kids. Saturday was Ginny's rest day. The girls and I shopped for the week in the mornings and rode bicycles in the afternoon. Sometimes I took them fishing in Malibu. On Sundays we usually rode our bikes to the local pancake house for brunch and then went to the park for an art exhibition, dog show, or whatever else was happening there.

Meanwhile, I began using company stock and funds to buy small travel agencies around the country. When Ask Mr. Foster's Travel Services, an eighty-year-old travel business, went on the market in 1972, I snapped it up.

My philosophy about hiring employees had proved itself. Since I had been lucky and had enjoyed numerous opportunities at a young age, I had no compunctions about bucking conventional hiring practices. If a person had talent, the ability to grow, and loyalty—the three characteristics I've always looked for in employees—that person had a chance with me, regardless of sex, race, creed, age, or education. It's good business to make room for those other companies pass up.

By the mid-1970s, the business—now called First Travel Corporation—had 1,500 employees in two hundred offices around the world and was grossing more than $300 million a year. We'd also expanded into hotels and operated ten of them.

The business offered my family great freedom. We took vacations together, and I'd take one of the children with me on business trips. Vicki once went with me to Oregon, where I spoke publicly for the first time and she got a big kick out of being introduced to the audience.

In the summer of 1976, most of which I spent commuting to Chicago while negotiating in bankruptcy court to buy Bon Voyage Travel, Ginny moved the family to our summer home in Laguna Beach.

Little did I know then that Ginny was struggling, that she'd been seeing doctors because of a breast tumor. She broke the news to me one Friday evening, entered the hospital the following Sunday, and had surgery the next day. It turned out to be more than just an overnight stay and I had to tell the three youngest children. Vicki, the oldest, was a foreign exchange student in London.

I'm usually good at containing my emotions, but I couldn't then. It was tough explaining to the kids that their mother had a malignant tumor, that it had been taken care of, and that she would be fine. I cried.

I choked up again a week later when Vicki returned. She hadn't had an especially fun summer in London—she was lonely—and was delighted to be home. She chatted gaily all the way to the beach while I listened quietly and answered her questions in monosyllables. At the beach I pulled over to the side of the road and told her what had happened. She was shaken.

"You're the oldest," I said. "I need your help. This is the toughest thing we've ever had to face and we have to do everything we can for your mom. I don't know what we'd do without her. I couldn't even shave in the morning if she wasn't there."

I'm an individual who reacts to problems. Illness gives me a feeling of ineptitude and helplessness and makes me realize how insignificant a person can be. It took me awhile to regain my footing. I turned over my business responsibilities to Dick Sargent and devoted the rest of the summer to Ginny's recovery—which was fast. Life returned to normal. Business and our family bloomed once more.

CHAPTER FOUR

STARTING FROM SCRATCH

I DIDN'T GET much done the first day on the job. Dick Sargent had located a small office in a Century City highrise and we were excited as we met for breakfast. Starting out on a new adventure together was like old times.

Sargent had prepared a checklist covering all the details. I asked the questions; he did the checking.

"Phones in?"

Sargent nodded.

"Desks?"

Sargent nodded again.

"Chairs?"

"Yes," said Sargent looking up from his list.

"Is the lease signed?"

"Of course."

"Did you call Sherry?"

He nodded.

"Will she bring the files over?"

"Pete," he said, his exasperation showing, "everything is covered and under control."

We were ready to roll. On the way to the office, where Sherry Cockle, my secretary for the past twelve years, would join us, we continued checking. Dick was right—everything *was* under control. We were champing at the bit to get started by the time we reached our office.

"Dick, give me the key," I said.

Handing it over he said in typical Dick fashion, "After all this volunteer work, the least you could do is carry me over the threshold."

I ignored him because the phones were ringing and I wanted to answer them. It was important people knew we were on the job.

But answering the calls had to wait—the key didn't work. I tried it again and again, and then Sargent tried it.

"It worked yesterday when I checked the phones," he said.

The lock had been changed. Soon Sherry arrived, loaded down with files and office supplies. So she stacked the files against the wall and stayed behind while Sargent and I tracked down the building agent.

He told us the building's owner had reneged on our lease and had ordered the lock changed. The agent was apologetic; I was irate. We even offered to pay the first year's rent in advance, but the answer was still no.

This was a strong, clear signal that organizing the Olympic Games wasn't going to be easy. The media had constantly reminded Angelenos that Montreal taxpayers were still paying for the 1976 Olympics and would continue to pay until the year 2000. A plurality in Los Angeles didn't want anything to do with the 1984 Games, a sentiment obviously shared by Alcoa, the landlord.

Two days later another leasing agent introduced us to Walter Elcock, president of Piedmont Insurance Company, who was moving his corporate headquarters to North Carolina. Elcock offered to share some of his already-vacant Century City office space. We accepted, and in the end took over his entire lease. Long after he had retired from Piedmont and right before the Games, Sherry reminisced about Elcock. Glad to have the opportunity to repay his kindness, albeit five years later, I invited him and his wife to the Games as guests of the LAOOC.

Once we had an office, the next order of business was to open a checking account, which I did with $100 of my own money. What we really needed was operating capital, so I put the word out that the television rights were up for bid and demanded that each interested party ante up a refundable $750,000 deposit. Five companies—the three networks; Tandem Communications, an independent television network production company; and Getty Oil's cable television network, ESPN—quickly came to the table, each bearing a check. We deposited the money in an interest-bearing account and put the interest—about $1,000 a day—to good use for operating expenses.

Another important order of business was international relations. I took my first trip abroad after three months on the job. I had two planned stops: Lausanne, Switzerland, to meet International Olympic Committee Director Monique Berlioux for the first time and to visit Château de Vidy, IOC headquarters; and Moscow, to be a guest of Soviet sports leaders at the Spartakiade—the USSR's national sports festival—and to observe how they were preparing for the 1980 Olympic Games.

I boarded an Air France jet on July 28, 1979—exactly five years before the opening ceremonies of the Los Angeles Games. Prepared to work nonstop, I traveled alone. As soon as the plane took off, Ueberroth's rules for traveling went into effect: I took off my shoes and changed into an old, beat-up navy blue sweat suit. Being a veteran traveler, I believe in comfort on long trips.

I studied volumes of Olympic paperwork during that flight, so I was well prepped on the history and politics of the Movement.

Baron Pierre de Coubertin founded the International Olympic Committee in 1894 and organized the first modern Olympic Games in Athens two years later. Since that time the Games have been held every four years with the exceptions of 1916, 1940, and 1944, when the Games were canceled because of war. Coubertin was a French idealist who envisioned the rebirth of the ancient Games as a means to developing well-rounded individuals. He devoted his life to the Olympic

Movement and served as IOC president from 1896 to 1916 and again from 1919 to 1925. He summarized the Olympic credo when he said, "The important thing in the Olympic Games is not to win but to take part, the important thing in life is not the triumph but the struggle. The essential thing is not to have conquered but to have fought well."

The IOC owns the Olympic Games lock, stock, barrel, and logo. The Olympic Charter specifies that the Games are to be awarded to a city government with the full support of its nation, but that provision had been waived since Los Angeles was the only city to bid.

The IOC also determines which countries can compete in its Games. To become eligible, a nation must form a national Olympic committee, which in turn must be recognized by at least five international sports federations. In virtually every country of the world but the United States, where professional sports dominate public interest and the press, amateur sports play the most important roles. It is common in all other countries for high-level government officials to preside over national Olympic committees, which, again, is not true in America.

International sports federations represent every imaginable athletic event—and a few most people have never heard of. They range from archery to Ping-Pong and from roller skating to orienteering (a cross-country race in which participants navigate the course using maps and compasses). Each federation elects a president and secretary-general and sets its own rules and schedule of events. For example, the International Amateur Athletic Federation (IAAF) is the track-and-field federation, and the most powerful one. You need IAAF sanctioning for every track meet, official, and competitor—without it, a meet doesn't have a prayer of attracting world-class athletes. Every world record is carefully scrutinized before the federation approves it.

By reviewing the IOC directory you can see which countries take amateur sports and the Olympics seriously. Most Communist countries have concentrated on amateur sports at the highest levels because they recognize the great influence sports have on worldwide public opinion. As a result, the

Eastern Europeans dominate such major sports as gymnastics, cycling, and swimming.

The IOC currently has a fluctuating membership of ninety-two. Every country that has held the Olympic Games is entitled to two members. Ireland, although it has never hosted the Games, also has two members. Today, IOC members represent all walks of life. There are sheiks, princes, businessmen and women, doctors, lawyers, and athletes, who reflect various cultures. In theory, an IOC member doesn't represent his country but is the IOC's designee from his part of the world. The member is supposed to act in the best interests of the Games and the movement. At least that's how the baron perceived it.

A car and driver were waiting for me at the airport and I was whisked to Château de Vidy, which sits on the shore of Lake Geneva, surrounded by a beautiful park. Inside, there are sixty uniformed staff members who always seem to be bustling around, giving it a beehive atmosphere.

Before leaving Los Angeles, I had been tipped off as to what to expect from Berlioux, who is the most powerful woman in sports. She is also a stickler for detail and I was warned she would demonstrate her superiority by subtly testing my knowledge of the Olympic Movement and the Olympic Charter.

Berlioux has an interesting background. She joined the French Resistance as a freedom fighter during the Nazi occupation in World War II. After the war, Berlioux pursued her dream of swimming in the Olympic Games, which she did at the 1948 Games in London. When she retired from competition, she became a sports-information attaché in the French Sports Ministry during Charles de Gaulle's presidency. In 1967, she joined the International Olympic Committee as its press-information director and quickly rose through the ranks. Within four years, the then IOC president, Avery Brundage, made her IOC director.

Berlioux's influence peaked from 1972 through 1980, while Lord Killanin was IOC president. Since Killanin presided over the Olympic Movement from his home in Ireland,

Berlioux virtually ran the organization and handled the day-to-day workload from the IOC headquarters.

Berlioux greeted me upon arrival and then gave me a short tour of the grounds. Afterward, we continued our conversation in her second-floor office, where we traded news clips and discussed general preparations for the Games and my upcoming visit to the Spartakiade.

The only pressing piece of business was getting her approval on the LAOOC's basic agreement about sponsors. Berlioux had sought to review each contract, but this just wasn't practical. I explained that the international corporations with which we were dealing insisted on total confidentiality. They had every right to that and they considered such a review an intrusion. Ultimately, she agreed and we went on to other matters, developing a relationship that remained strong for the next five years.

Berlioux also briefed me on my next stop—Moscow.

As the Aeroflot jet lifted off from Geneva, I thought about the Soviet Union and a trip I had made there ten years earlier.

In a joint operation with Alaska Airlines, I had organized the inaugural flight across the Bering Sea and the Pacific Ocean, from Anchorage to Siberia. This high-risk venture stemmed from an idea that Bob Giersdorf, vice-president of Alaska Airlines, and I had while visiting Big and Little Diomede, two small islands in the Bering Strait. Although only about two miles apart, they are separated by the International Date Line. So Little Diomede is in U.S. territory, and Big Diomede in the USSR. But no Iron Curtain separates the two. The islands are joined by ice when the sea freezes during winter, allowing people to travel freely from one island to the other. Life, though harsh and difficult in this part of the world, is unencumbered by interference from the two super powers.

I took the idea of traveling into Soviet territory from the east a few steps farther—to the Soviet mainland. Travel between Alaska and Siberia was new to the tourist business and I intended to be there first with my company. Crossing new territory is always risky, and in this case it was also expensive. Both Intourist, the Soviet tourist bureau, and the charter wanted their money in advance.

Our first trip, for which we charged $1,000 per person, was a three-week tour of the Soviet Union, beginning at Khabarovsk in the southeast and concluding at Leningrad in the northwest. We invited American journalists and aviation VIPs to go along with the tourists. We also had a Soviet navigator on board, plus the Soviet equivalent to Secor Brown, then the chairman of the U.S. Civil Aeronautics Board. As we approached Siberia from the northeast—over the Kamchatka Peninsula—two Soviet MiGs appeared.

One member of the camera crew from *60 Minutes,* which was accompanying us, told me about our MiG escort. I went to the cockpit to investigate.

I saw this project headed for disaster when I heard clipped voices saying over the radio, *"Nyet, nyet."* I had invested a small fortune in this venture and the last thing I wanted to do was turn back. It was frightening, and when our Russian navigator tried to show the MiG pilots our permit through the window it became absurd. I glanced around the cramped cockpit, noted the tense faces, and knew the situation was serious. Clearer heads prevailed and we followed the pilot's advice. He turned to me and said, "The nearest alternate airport is Tokyo. It's a long way, but we've got to land there and sort this out."

Although Japanese officials allowed us to land in Tokyo, they feared an international incident and didn't want anything to do with us. After cooling our heels on the ground for several hours, Secor Brown intervened on our behalf. Fluent in Japanese, he pushed the right buttons and cleared the bureaucratic blunder that had caused the detour. Within the hour we were en route to Khabarovsk, where a thousand people and the mayor turned out to greet us.

The tour was a success and during the next few years I traveled extensively throughout the Soviet Union. As I visited the different regions of the country, I made it a point to absorb as much as possible about the people and their culture. I spent the most time along the southern border. Besides Moscow, Kiev, Leningrad, and Khabarovsk, I've been to Irkutsk, Novosibirsk, Alma-Ata, Tashkent, Samarkand, Yerevan, and Tbilisi, among others, and I'm sure I've been to more places in the Soviet Union than most Russians.

Now, as president of the LAOOC, I was back in the USSR to see the preparations for the Spartakiade and the 1980 Games. I had rejected the offer of the Soviet sports leaders to pay my expenses. By paying my own way I was telling them, and the IOC, that the LAOOC wouldn't spend millions on the perquisites and excessive frills that are usually lavished on the Olympic family. Also, by traveling alone, I felt I'd be less obtrusive and better able to learn what an international sporting event was all about.

I was astounded by the massive operations for the Spartakiade. The way the Soviets managed twenty-three stadiums in action at the same time—the competitions, security, transportation, interpreting, food services and hospitality, plus all the other ancillary services—gave me a realistic look into the future. If it is possible to be simultaneously frightened and challenged, I was.

I saw firsthand a nation's total commitment to the event: from the mobilization of the military for the construction of facilities and roads, to the dedication and willingness of the people. The workers' knowledge of Olympic history and sports surprised me—the Games were obviously the greatest thing to hit Moscow in a long time—and they were taking great personal pride in their contributions.

At the velodrome, which was still under construction and would become a beautiful, multimillion-dollar, state-of-the-art Olympic facility, the workers knew more about cycling than anyone else I'd ever talked to. I was moved by the way they referred to "their velodrome." I met a group of workers, one of whom gave me a hard hat and said, "Here is a memory of Moscow and the world's greatest velodrome." I still have it.

I also learned that it was impossible to compare one Olympic Games to another. Each host city has its own character, culture, and way of doing business. Host cities are no better or worse, just different. Nonetheless, I also knew it would be impossible to avoid comparisons. The Soviet and U.S. political systems, being so polarized, provided a natural news hook for journalists. Comparing the Moscow to the forthcoming L.A. Games would be a propaganda game the LAOOC couldn't win.

I was bothered by the beating the Moscow organizers took from the international sports federations. They wanted extra officials, more tickets, better accommodations, special arrangements for certain athletes—all at the organizers' expense. It worried me even more that the Soviets capitulated on every point. Of course they had the bankroll of the government at their disposal. But capitulation didn't set well with me. I knew I'd have to draw the line on satisfying the federations without giving away the store. I decided then and there that the LAOOC's top priority would be the athletes' welfare and I wouldn't permit the petty demands of federation officials to derail us. It was clear that their first priority was themselves, not the athletes. But I had to find a middle ground because I needed their cooperation to make the Games work.

I spent a wonderful evening during Spartakiade with Vitaly Smirnov and Ignaty Novikov, who were top leaders of the world of Soviet sports. Smirnov was a member of the IOC Executive Board and Novikov was my counterpart for the Moscow Games. Novikov looked like he came directly out of central casting, right down to his rubber-soled shoes and shiny suit. Smirnov, on the other hand, was well dressed, and he was also a political pro who had survived many changes in Soviet sport leadership. Smirnov spoke fluent English; Novikov didn't.

Around a table covered with bottles of soda water, mineral water, and soft drinks, we amiably discussed general sports issues. They were gracious hosts and I left Moscow laden with information—and anxiety. I couldn't get to Los Angeles fast enough. It was time to step up the pace.

During a layover in London, I called Sherry Cockle and asked her to have the staff assembled on my return.

All ten LAOOC staff members were in the conference room the next day when I arrived. Most had just come aboard, so I knew they'd be unprepared for what I had in mind—and they were.

"Dick, you've been with the committee the longest. Who was the first president of the IOC?" I asked Dick Sargent.

"Baron de Coubertin," he replied.

"Wrong. Joel, who are the three vice-presidents of the IOC?" Joel Rubenstein had been a marketing expert with Mattel Toy Company.

"Smirnov, Samaranch, and Kiyokawa."

"Good," I said. "Conrad, what's F-I-S-A stand for?"

"It's like MasterCharge," our comptroller, Conrad Freund, answered.

Everyone laughed but me. "This may seem mundane to you," I told them, "but we have to live with these people and organizations for the next five years. Five years may seem like a long time, but it isn't. If we're lucky, it'll barely be enough for us to complete what has to be done, what we have to create. The wheels are turning and we have to get control of them now. I want everyone to study the IOC Charter and directory and know everything in it so we can work effectively with the Olympic family."

I told them that the first IOC president was a Greek, Demetrius Vikelas, and FISA is the French acronym for the International Rowing Federation. I told them about my experiences in Moscow and when the staff left the meeting, they went with a sense of urgency.

Everyone had a good fix on the complexities involved and the magnitude of the task that lay ahead: to cut through all boundaries—geographical, political, religious, and cultural—and create bridges that would join all the participants of the Games for sixteen brief days.

Every organizing committee produces a detailed final report and I had read several cover to cover. The one from Montreal on the 1976 Olympics was interesting, and it didn't take long to figure out how they had gotten themselves into financial straits. The Munich report covered the details of the tragic slayings of the eleven Israeli athletes and left a lasting impression on me. Security planning, I realized, would be our primary concern.

Each Olympics had labels. Mexico City's were heat, altitude, and air quality; Munich's was security; and Montreal's was finances. In fact, another financial label was developing at Lake Placid, the site of the 1980 Winter Olympic Games. Despite $100 million in government aid, the organizers there were facing huge cost overruns. Reports that New York taxpayers were up in arms over government funding wouldn't help our battle with the tightfisted L.A. taxpayers. Also, the continuing investigations into Montreal's finances would place additional pressure on us to get money in the bank.

This was going to be serious business. We were already in hock to the U.S. Olympic Committee to the tune of $300,000, and we owed another $50,000 to the Southern California Committee for the work these organizations had done in getting the Games for Los Angeles. We went to work.

Traditionally, there have been three sources of Olympic funding: government funding (the largest), lotteries, and donations. Montreal had cost more than $1 billion in government funds, and the Soviets had already spent more than $5 billion in government money and their Games were still several months away. Canada had raised another $250 million through lotteries and the Soviets were expecting to raise twice that much.

Local government funding was out because of the city charter amendment prohibiting public funding of the Olympic Games. A few Olympic board members had discussed the possibility of requesting federal funds to build facilities, but that was remote. Lotteries were illegal in California, and, by our own choice, donations were out of the question. Considering the general ill will that already existed, it would've been insensitive and ill advised to compete against churches, synagogues, hospitals, YMCAs, Girl Scouts, and all the other worthy organizations that rely on charity for survival. Also, the U.S. Olympic Committee depends almost entirely on donations and we didn't want to compete for the same dollars.

This meant we had to depend totally on our entrepreneurial skills, and I sensed the time was right for private-sector initiative to play a leading role. I had already begun to experiment on ways this could be done by asking some accountant friends to determine how to best use the sources of available revenue. There were three principal sources: television rights sales, commercial sponsorships, and ticket sales. Somehow these revenue sources would have to produce at least 90 percent of all the funds required to run the Games. To produce an Olympic Games of the highest quality, we estimated our operations would cost between $450 and $500 million. The prognosis of collecting that much money looked grim, considering that all previous organizing committees had failed to reap as much as $75 million from those sources. I saw myself as Don Quixote tilting at windmills. But it was the only way open to us. We had to begin somewhere.

Corporations had begun making preliminary contacts as soon as we opened shop, and many were sponsors of the Lake Placid Games. Joel Rubenstein went to Lake Placid to study the sponsorship program there and to begin laying the groundwork for our own program. He reported that the organizers had more than three hundred commercial sponsors, but the result of all this was lifetime supplies of Chap Stick and yogurt—and less than $10 million in cash. That just wouldn't work for us. So we set our sights on raising $200 million. Doubling, tripling, or quadrupling Lake Placid's sponsorship revenue might have been realistic. But marketing experts will tell you that a 2,000 percent increase was not.

Rubenstein then came up with a wonderful idea: to limit sponsorships to thirty to avoid clutter and duplication, and to select only major advertisers as sponsors, one per category. This would increase the value of each sponsorship and create a more valuable marketing tool. If we could persuade sponsors to promote goodwill and public support during the last year prior to the Games, it would save us from using capital for advertising.

I decided to set a $4 million floor for each potential sponsor. Establishing a floor, or minimum, is a negotiating concept that has always worked for me. You can be as arbitrary as you like and at the same time you see who dares to walk across the line. This separates the serious businessmen from the phonies who want to take part in something just for the sake of it, and from those looking for a cheap opportunity. It also forces bidders to think in terms of the numbers you want to deal with. In the end, if the winning bid is somewhere near your floor, the bidder feels he accomplished something—on his terms.

Since Coca-Cola and Pepsi-Cola were first in line, it made sense to begin there. Our exclusivity program ensured that the winning bidder would be the only official soft drink at the Games, the only one sold at Olympic stadiums, and the only one allowed to use the Olympic rings and other Olympic logos and themes. When we opened the bidding process, we also invited 7-Up, Dr Pepper, Royal Crown Cola and a few smaller companies to participate, but the real contest would be between Coke and Pepsi.

I met privately with representatives of each in the Century Plaza Hotel coffee shop, which had become our unofficial negotiating headquarters. It was located on the lower level of the hotel and had a breezy, relaxed ambience that was unusual for a busy hotel. Lacking a conference room, this was a good substitute, and most of the people we were doing business with stayed at the hotel.

Another of my business philosophies came into play: Always deal directly with the top executive. I was seeking total corporate commitment—not just a fee, not just advertising promotion for four years—and that usually comes directly from the chairman of each company. I also believed that at some point I'd need these corporate execs to call on the president of the United States to seek his support of the Olympic Games.

I didn't have much luck with the chairman of Coca-Cola. He wouldn't return my calls. I talked briefly with Don Kendall, Pepsi's chairman, whom I had met seven years earlier. I wasn't sure Kendall even remembered me, but he was interested in the Olympics and sent one of his key executives to conduct preliminary discussions before making an offer.

In the meantime, Ziffren had set up various citizen advisory commissions, including one on licensing and merchandising that was chaired by Card Walker, who was president of the Disney Corporation. Commission members were well meaning but there was no constructive role available for them at that time.

I discussed this with Ginny one night over a quiet dinner.

"Paul has pulled together an impressive group of people for each of the advisory commissions," I told her. "He sees them as a volunteer base for the Games. But I'm not even convinced a volunteer concept will work."

"Why not?" she asked.

"Our demands will be too great, and I can't see people spending a month on the Games."

"I disagree," she said. "Paul's right." Ginny had been involved with several volunteer organizations over the years and was a firm believer. "Once volunteers get behind a project, they'll stick with it to the end—they'll be the best employees of all," she added.

Even though the chairman of Coke was unavailable, the company sent John Cooper to pursue its interests. Coke enjoyed a twenty-five-year history of Olympic participation. It had sponsored Olympic Games, and it also sponsored the Olympic teams of more than thirty countries. It was imperative that I get Coke's attention and get it moving in our direction.

I liked Cooper immediately, but nothing I said registered until I mentioned Kendall. I found out later that it was the brief mention of Kendall's name that got the wheels spinning at Coke's headquarters in Atlanta. A few days later the president of Coke arrived. Don Keough is not your typical corporate president. He's a very up-front guy, willing to take risks, and approaches business from a marketing and merchandising point of view. Now that the two main players had joined me at the table, I gave them a week to submit bids.

Meanwhile, I came to the conclusion that the advisory commission had vastly underestimated the value of a soft drink sponsor and was counting on $1 million at the most. I saw no need to build expectations among our own group, so I didn't reveal the $4 million floor to anybody other than those with a need to know.

Pepsi submitted its written proposal by mail and followed up with a telegram; Cooper and other Coke executives delivered their bid in person.

The entire bidding process was a high-stakes poker game

and I didn't know what to expect. As the representative from Coca-Cola handed me their offer, I steeled myself not to register any emotion. I quickly read my way through the legalese, anxious to get to the bottom line. Eight figures—$12.6 million! All those zeros—boy, did I love those zeros! They leaped off the page, but I did my level best to keep my excitement in check.

This was perfect. This was *real* money. We could build on it. The sum would shock the sporting world, but it confirmed my belief that we could achieve $200 million in sponsorships alone. More important, it was the first tangible proof we could stage a financially responsible Games.

Coke was it.

Lawyers for both sides immediately began dickering over the contractual details. Coke's counsel was tough. This was more money than the company had ever committed to a single sports promotion. Henry Steinman of Latham & Watkins represented the committee. Besides being a skillful attorney, Henry epitomizes what I like best in a lawyer—he's a deal maker, not a deal breaker. Some lawyers always manage to find problem areas that they delight in so they can create endless hours of discussion over minutia, always to no avail. They are deal breakers. A deal maker is a lawyer who finds difficult areas, gets them on the table, brings the parties together, and closes a deal that doesn't result in litigation down the line.

Even with Steinman working hard for us, the deal was floundering when Keough arrived for a final meeting. He came with a couple of his aides. One had a bottle of champagne and gave it to Keough.

"I'd like to drink this bottle of champagne and I'd like to have dinner with you tonight, Pete," Keough said.

I didn't feel like celebrating just yet. I wanted to conclude the deal.

"Let's get the deal done first," I said.

Keough handed the bottle of champagne back to his aide and grabbed a blank piece of paper.

"Let's take this piece of paper," he said, "and let's both sign it at the bottom." Keough signed his name and passed the paper to me. "You sign it and let's give it to the attorneys and tell them to make a final agreement. I feel comfortable that we can be good partners. Let's take the risk."

I didn't hesitate. I signed it and gave the paper back to him. Talk about innovators. That was a novel approach and a good one. I was ready to celebrate.

Hours later, long after the champagne, I remembered that according to LAOOC by-laws I lacked the authority to make a decision on financial matters exceeding $50,000 without approval from our board.

The LAOOC's original board of directors consisted of sixty-two prominent business and civic leaders and a handful of Olympians. There were numerous small factions I had to deal with and everybody, it seemed, wanted to run the Games his way. The presidency was designed to have very limited powers. Important decisions, including those involving capital in excess of $50,000, were supposed to be made by the board. The deal with Coke was the first precedent-setting agreement. I suspected there would be many more.

In the process of creating my independent power base I was also violating another rule, this time my own, which is to inform your people of an important development before they learn it elsewhere. I purposely did not inform the members of our board about the Coca-Cola deal because I had to eliminate their approval powers in order to survive. It had to be done with a single stroke or the board would hamstring me on every decision. I did, however, tell Ziffren, with whom a good working relationship was absolutely necessary. He understood it was impossible to run the committee by concensus, so I always kept him advised of what was going on.

Somehow, Ken Reich of the *Los Angeles Times* got the story of the Coke sponsorship. As I expected, the board reacted badly when they saw the headlines the next day. I wasn't disappointed, however. I had wanted the board to feel left out and I had succeeded. One of my objectives was to let all the parties know that this was going to be my style from here on out. It also notified the world that the LAOOC was in business and that we wouldn't sell sponsorships cheaply.

I learned long ago that if you're going to be in charge, then take charge. Authority is 20 percent given—which was about all the board had given me to date—and 80 percent taken. When you're in charge, you assume complete and total authority, and your decisions reduce everything else to mere record keeping and back-up functions.

Tangential to this principle is identifying and hiring the best people possible, because those people will make the pyramid stronger. Our small group was functioning well together, and I was determined to keep it that way.

The news of the Coca-Cola deal kicked off our television negotiations. I'd been holding weekly meetings with David Wolper during the summer of 1979 and we analyzed how best to control the negotiations. He'd done all the preliminary research and had immediate access to and great rapport with the network chiefs. Our past differences long forgotten, we became a team—one that lasted through the Games and continues to this day. Wolper's expertise in television is unequaled. But while he was giving us plenty of advice on television production, we were vulnerable on the advertising and income sides. Joel Rubenstein used some of his advertising contacts, and so did I, to conduct marketing studies.

The results surprised us. Our worst-case scenario of potential ad revenues amounted to $300 million. Once again the advisory commission grossly underestimated the value of our product, figuring we'd get only $100 million for the TV rights.

Wolper and I also factored into our negotiations a provision requiring the winning bidder to be host broadcaster and provide facilities for all visiting broadcasters from around the world. This included technical equipment, broadcast booths at each event, camera positions, and an international broadcast center to work in. It would cost the winner an additional $75 million and would remove a massive management headache from the organizing committee.

We decided to ask for more than $200 million for television rights—not including host broadcasting arrangements. Furthermore, a large portion would have to be paid up front.

The TV negotiations took place in the screening room of Wolper's large, Mediterranean-style house, which is tucked away in the Bel Air hills north of UCLA. Roone Arledge and

Fred Pierce, who headed the negotiating team for ABC, were joined by Arledge's assistant John Martin and by two of their technical experts, Marvin Bader and Jules Barnathan. They made an impressive team. Arledge's Olympic experience was and still is far ahead of the field, but experience was not the bottom line. Money was. The other bidders—CBS, NBC, and ESPN—were also lusting after the rights, as was Tandem's Jerry Perenchio.

I established the "caucus rule" for the negotiations. Anytime anyone on either negotiating side said "caucus," each group would separate to review its position. This prevented negotiations from going in the wrong direction.

I can remember calling out "caucus" dozens of times and then moving our group downstairs to debate our position or that of the other party. We caucused often to discuss ABC's proposals to leave certain items open-ended; I wanted to nail down every fine point, leaving no room for later arguments. For example, ABC wanted to negotiate the host broadcasting at a later time. From our viewpoint it had to be part of the total package, and we held firm. One area that remained open-ended was a provision for a potential boycott. There was no way we could accurately determine the financial effect of a boycott, so we agreed to factor in a formula based on the final ratings and the nonparticipation of teams.

Meanwhile, I was headed for a battle with the LAOOC board. I wanted a floor of $200 million for the TV rights, and I also wanted substantial money in advance. With large amounts of up-front money coming in from the television and sponsor deals, the committee could operate through 1982 on interest income alone. But some of the so-called experts on the advisory committee weren't so farsighted. They said a $200 million floor was embarrassing and threatened to walk out if I persisted. Once again, it was time for everyone to know who was in charge. Wolper and I prevailed; the rest is history. ABC agreed to pay $225 million and to serve as host broadcaster. This meant the deal was worth $300 million.

Only one hitch remained: The International Olympic Committee, our partner and, in effect, co-negotiator, retained the right to review and approve all matters associated with the Olympic Games. This veto power is exercised mainly by IOC Director Monique Berlioux. Her blessing is the Olympic seal of approval. We had to wait for her to come to Los Angeles and bestow it.

The checklist for her impending visit was encyclopedic. We had to make sure that a swimming pool was available, that Evian water was supplied, that there were exquisite flower arrangements, that the room service met her French tastes, that restaurant arrangements were made at the finest eateries, that appointments were not scheduled either early in the morning or late at night, and that her traveling staff received equally impeccable treatment.

Rubenstein's eye for detail made him perfect for this job. With such a small staff at the time, we had to double up on responsibilities. So Rubenstein handled arrangements for visiting dignitaries in addition to his marketing job.

Berlioux knows the Olympics better than any human being alive and she protects its traditions and integrity as a mother would a child. I'd already discovered that Berlioux, although a fine administrator, had a unique ability to find fault with many things. She never failed to dot an "i" or cross a "t" in our dealings. If she was on your side, you had clear sailing. If she sensed any Olympic Charter violations or potential damage to the movement, there was no more formidable foe. In this instance she was very supportive, because the IOC was entitled to one third of the rights fee, or $33 million. This was far more cash than it had ever had before—enough to support its operations for a long time. Even though she was ambivalent about ABC, she understood they knew how to cover the Games and the dollar signs assuaged any feelings of ill will she had.

I wasn't particularly worried because David McKenzie, the IOC member from Australia, had slipped me a copy of the IOC's financial report. It proved that the IOC had a very minimal net worth.

We held a news conference, with Berlioux present, at the Century Plaza on September 26, 1979, and announced the largest television rights deal in history. After the news conference I sent a congratulatory note to each member of the LAOOC staff. The note read, "You are a part of helping us make history today." Since most of the staff was working without, or with very little, compensation at that point, I added a bonus check.

Several weeks later at an IOC Executive Board meeting in Nagoya, Japan, Lord Killanin and the Executive Board gave their formal approval, and along with the ABC executives we signed the contract. I had brought a $25 million check to give to the IOC, the balance of the $33 million to be paid later.

The first IOC meeting was Thursday morning. I purposely prolonged the discussion and didn't turn the check over to IOC counsel Daniel Mortereaux until Friday. He had to rush to the airport to catch a plane to India and was unable to deposit it. I patted myself on the back for having saved $9,000, one day's interest on that sum. Little did I know—or the IOC—that Mortereaux would carry the check around with him for the next twenty days. This financial carelessness gave me insight into why the IOC was having a cash-flow problem.

Another interesting development occurred at the Nagoya meeting that would have far-reaching implications nearly five years later at the Los Angeles Games. The IOC entertained its first serious talks about recognizing the People's Republic of China as a member of the Olympic family.

One mistake the committee made then was calling the Games "Spartan." This was done to impress upon the public that the LAOOC wasn't going to tolerate the wild spending that had typified previous Games. Besides, the LAOOC didn't have funds for frills. But I underestimated how this word would be interpreted internationally. "Spartan" was grist for the media mill. This one adjective led to various news stories critical of the LAOOC's capitalistic and stingy approach toward organizing the Games, and it never died, even though we tried to put it to rest.

The press's reaction gave me my first indication of the international difficulties of the job. What makes sense locally doesn't always make sense half the world away—in Lausanne at the IOC headquarters.

The IOC Charter is the bible of the Olympic Movement. It covers every facet of how the Games are organized. One provision was already giving me a headache. The charter specifically states that an organizing committee can be seen but not heard from until its quadrennial begins. This meant we weren't supposed to make news until the Moscow Games were over. Our premature announcements of the Coca-Cola and ABC deals had brought a swift hand slap and a plethora of angry Telexes from Berlioux, telling us in no uncertain terms that we were out of line.

Before we totally burned the bridge behind us on this type of issue, we disclosed the $10 million deal with Anheuser-Busch, our third official sponsor. In deference to Berlioux, we then held silent on the rest of the sponsor announcements, although we continued making deals.

By late 1979 we were more sophisticated. We had created a shopping list of our needs and tried to match them with corporate sponsors and suppliers. Sometimes we had to stretch our imagination. In looking for a sponsor to build a velodrome we decided to approach the Southland Corporation, because its 7-Eleven stores have a bike-in clientele. In California you can't pass a 7-Eleven without seeing a rack full of bicycles.

I pitched Jere and John Thompson one day over lunch at a restaurant in Century City where our offices were still located. I knew the Thompsons through our association with the Young Presidents' Organization, an international group of corporate executives under the age of fifty.

"Do you know what a velodrome is?" I asked them. Neither knew. I explained that it was a facility for cycling competition and that an international-class track didn't exist in the United States. Building an even stronger case I added that cycling was a fast-paced, fast-growing sport which was immensely popular in Europe and would surely catch on in the United States. Finally I appealed to their self-interest, and during the two-hundred-yard walk from the restaurant to our office we made a deal. Southland became so involved in the program that they also built a velodrome at the USOC's training center in Colorado Springs, plus the Olympic track at California State College, Dominguez Hills. Today, Southland is synonymous in the United States with the sport of cycling.

We completed our sponsorship program within the next two years, as thirty international corporations, all of which were leaders in their fields, joined us as partners in staging the Games. The categories most difficult to fill were cars and film.

Considering that the Games were to be held in Los Angeles, and given the decline facing the domestic auto industry, it would have been unconscionable to have had a foreign automaker. Yet we almost did. It appeared we'd have no choice. At Lake Placid, every group with wheels—federations, national governing bodies, the organizing committee, different Olympic committees, and what seemed like individual athletes—had a different official car sponsor. The American automakers believed they had been ripped off, and with good reason.

Datsun and Toyota essentially offered us blank checks; Mercedes indicated interest, too; but Detroit wanted nothing to do with us. We were rejected more than once by Ford, General Motors, and Chrysler.

Then Rubenstein got a call from a representative of Competitive Edge, a public relations firm for an association of American-car dealers in the southwest. Rubenstein's request for seven hundred American-made cars didn't faze the rep but I was skeptical—until I met the employer, Lee Galles. "It's your choice," I told him. "Do you want Toyota or Datsun to benefit from this country's Olympic Games, or are you willing to take a chance?" He introduced me to Lloyd Reuss, general manager of the Buick division of GM, who committed Buick as a sponsor of the Games.

Dan Greenwood had joined the LAOOC in the sponsorship area and, with Rubenstein, headed the film negotiations. On that front, everyone assumed Kodak would step forward with a big check, and the local Kodak people assured us hundreds of times that Kodak's sponsorship was a *fait accompli*. It had been a sponsor of the Games before and it had also sponsored the U.S. team. Kodak dominated the field, and it was this strength that ruined any chance of making a deal. Kodak was smug. Kodak's lead lawyer played games with us, believing we had no other choice. He persisted in offering only half of our $4 million floor. Kodak underestimated us.

Meanwhile, Dentsu, Inc., a Japanese advertising agency, brought in Fuji Film. We asked Dentsu to put Fuji on ice. Finally we told Kodak to fish or cut bait. Kodak missed its deadline, and we gave Fuji seventy-two hours to sign. Fuji came in for $7 million and agreed to process, without charge, all news photographers' film at the Games—something Kodak had never even contemplated.

We then heard from Kodak again. "I thought we had a deal," their lawyer said. So did we was our reply. Heads rolled at Kodak. The lawyer tried to sue us after he lost his job—the suit is still pending.

Later on, in order to recover a semblance of Olympic association, Kodak became a sponsor of the U.S. track and field team and mounted a full-scale campaign to stop any momentum Fuji had gained in the U.S. film market. Because of Fuji's aggressive sponsorship, it made strong inroads into the U.S. and other markets.

I've always thought that for a partnership to be sound equal benefits had to accrue to all parties. This proved to be the case for all sponsors of the Games, although it wasn't always smooth sailing. Some resented the ground rules we set. After asking heavy financial commitments, which no doubt caused eyes to roll in some corporate boardrooms, we controlled marketing campaigns, strictly enforced their use of Olympic identity, and insisted on directing their involvement in youth and community programs. Time and again we went back to them and asked for more. They always gave. We had them. They knew it.

The dignity of our sponsorship program was really a tribute to corporate courage. Thirty stepped forward to meet the trying demands of a risky venture and they never wavered or lost faith in our cause. By identifying themselves with an event as far-reaching and wholesome as the Olympic Games, they recognized the intrinsic value of the positive image within their grasp. Once they grabbed hold, there was no way they could ever let go.

CHAPTER FIVE

GOVERNMENT BLUES

OUR FINANCIAL SITUATION was looking good but our public credibility kept coming apart at the seams. We'd inherited a host of local political problems that just wouldn't go away and Mayor Tom Bradley persisted in making them worse by seeking a federal handout.

Bradley and I had first discussed federal funding two weeks after I became LAOOC president. We met in his office, which had two chairs separated by a long, comfortable couch. He sat in one chair and I in the other. Bradley had two overriding concerns that I would learn were constant: his political future and the welfare of the city. In this conference he focused on the prospective move of the Raiders football team from Oakland to Los Angeles and how the refurbishment of the Coliseum would expedite that. Bradley was direct and to the point: He wanted the Raiders because the people of Los Angeles wanted them.

Bradley said he was about to request federal funding and his plan earmarked $60 million for revamping the Coliseum. I asked him to reconsider. He said, no, he knew best. Since the Lake Placid organizers had received $60 million from the government, he said, Los Angeles should get at least that much. Proposition 13 had just swept California and I feared that

Bradley's plan, coupled with the City charter amendment on the Games, would lead to another tax revolt. I didn't like his decision, but I had no choice but to support the mayor—there had to be harmony among community leaders.

As Bradley promised me, on May 21, 1979, he announced a plan to ask Congress for $141 million for the Games. In addition to the Coliseum recommendation, Bradley planned a massive sports complex in the Sepulveda basin where Olympic archery, cycling, rowing, and canoeing could be held. Public outcry was swift and furious.

A few days later the *New York Times* reported that the Games had already touched off charges of "official deception and cost overruns." Baxter Ward, a former television anchorman and a Los Angeles County supervisor, demanded the contract to hold the Games in Los Angeles be revoked. Editorials in newspapers throughout southern California echoed Ward's cry. City Controller Ira Reiner announced the formation of a group dedicated to a ballot initiative prohibiting government funding of any kind. It was bedlam. I left the mayor to his own devices while I charted a more realistic financial course.

That summer, after returning from the Spartakiade in Moscow, we tried to neutralize the damage. First, we announced that one half of all tickets would go to southern Californians. Second, we presented our financial plan to the public. We hoped that the former would generate a foundation of public support, which we sorely needed, and that the latter would build confidence in our efforts and abilities.

The financial plan clearly stated that the Games would operate at a surplus, a *real* surplus, not a deficit—with or without federal aid. With the blessing of two accounting firms, Arthur Young & Co., and Peat, Marwick & Mitchell, which we put at risk along with ourselves, we announced we'd spend roughly $350 million and net a surplus of $20 million.

We made a conscious decision to underestimate projected revenues as this was our only protection against unknown cost factors and an unstable international political environment. I had learned from studying Olympic Games' final reports that certain common features existed. For example, there had never been a complete sellout in Olympic history. Also, the closer the organizers got to the Games, the more their negotiating leverage diminished. The only problem-solving option left to an organizing committee on the eve of the Games, or during them, was to throw money at it and hope it disappeared. We wanted to cut as many early deals as possible, particularly those involving labor.

First we had to reconcile the lingering issue of federal funding. There was a time and place for dealing with the federal government and I knew exactly what we needed: coordination on security, assistance in streamlining the immigration procedures for the athletes and Olympic family members for the Games, and a commemorative coin program. What we didn't want or need was a handout for facilities.

However, Mayor Bradley was still determined to get government funds and ignored discouraging signals from the White House and doggedly tried to arrange a meeting with President Jimmy Carter. Local politicians were creating a lynch mob atmosphere, and the LAOOC was trapped in the middle, trying to support the mayor yet keep its pledge at the same time.

At one meeting of the Sherman Oaks Homeowners' group, many of my neighbors, who are fairly well-to-do professionals, subjected Ginny, the kids, and me to hate and ridicule. They jeered and got nasty, and nothing I said could convince them I wasn't going to bankrupt the city, put pavement over grass, build facilities in their parks, attract gambling interests, and turn the community into a cross between Gomorrah and a police state.

Ira Reiner was the most vocal critic of government spending and made the most news with the media. At a rally at Birmingham High School in the San Fernando Valley, where two of my daughters attended, Reiner held a "No Olympic Tax" revival meeting. He delivered the usual rhetoric, predicting the Olympics would devastate Los Angeles. During the program his aides distributed pamphlets that contained the addresses of Mayor Bradley and me. He told the people to contact us. The mayor got lucky—his address was listed as City Hall; but they used my home address, just ten blocks away.

Less than one hour after that rally our dogs—a playful Weimaraner and the world's friendliest Doberman pinscher— were poisoned by strychnine-laced meat, which was tossed over a five-foot brick wall by an unknown assailant. Ginny was home alone with the kids, and to this day, they have vivid memories of the dogs foaming at the mouth. Neither dog fully recovered. I remain convinced the two incidents were related, despite the absence of proof. For the first time, fear entered our lives.

Bradley finally nailed down a meeting with President Carter on December 3, 1979. Though I felt whipsawed, it was still a thrill to meet with the president. Our delegation consisted of Bradley, City Councilman John Ferraro (who had played an active role in the bid process), and Deputy Mayor Ray Remy.

We each had a role in the pleas made to Carter and two staff members, Stu Eisenstadt and Jack Watson. The mayor led off with reasons why the funding was needed and how important it was to L.A. I used a comparison: If Lake Placid, a town of only three thousand or so taxpayers, had already been allotted more than $60 million for the Winter Games, then Los Angeles, with its millions of taxpayers, deserved much more.

Bradley, a staunch Carter supporter, was confident entering the meeting. After twenty minutes Carter turned to Bradley and said, "Tom, there's no way I can support giving Los Angeles one cent—not one penny—considering the financial condition the country is in. Other communities are building brand-new stadiums using state or public-sector bonds." One example he gave was Seattle, which had recently built the Kingdome. In short, the answer was no.

Bradley didn't want to take no for an answer. He continued to push. The whole process was counterproductive, so much so that the thought of federal spending would never be exorcised from the public consciousness. (A poll conducted four years later, just before the Games started, showed that more than half of those surveyed in southern California still believed government funds were used to stage the Games.)

It became clear a month later that Carter didn't understand how the rest of the world felt about the Olympics. Two weeks after the Soviet Union invaded Afghanistan in late December 1979, Carter threatened a U.S. boycott of the 1980 Games unless the USSR withdrew its troops.

Joel Rubenstein called me at home and told me about the boycott. My first impression was that our country must be very weak if this was our best retaliatory shot. Threatening not to send a few hundred athletes to a sporting event was not much of an international ploy. I also believed Carter was bluffing.

The public, however, caught boycott fever. I circled our wagons. Would all our sponsors defect? Would all the international television negotiations come to a halt? What operational shifts would we have to make? Would the IOC yank the Games?

The word "boycott" hadn't meant anything to me until Carter's announcement. But it wasn't new to the Olympics. Boycotts dated back to the first modern Olympiad in Athens in 1896, when Great Britain refused at the last moment to send its team because it viewed the Olympics as a fly-by-night operation. After that almost all the early Games were politicized, but disruptive politicization didn't begin until 1956. There were two boycotts of the Games that year in Melbourne: Egypt, Iraq, and Lebanon withdrew in protest over the Israeli-led takeover of the Suez Canal; and Holland and Spain boycotted because of the USSR's invasion of Hungary. The Melbourne Games were also the site of the famous bloody water polo match between the Soviet Union and Hungary in which the Hungarian team, which had defected en masse, took out its resentment on the Soviet team.

As far as the world would know, the first major boycott took place in 1976 at Montreal. Literally on the eve of the Games, the black African nations, joined by Iraq and Guyana, walked out of the village. The Africans had demanded that the IOC expel the New Zealand Olympic team because that nation's rugby team had played in South Africa. It was a ridiculous demand and the IOC refused on the grounds that rugby was not an Olympic sport and had no control over the travel of rugby teams.

I remember poignant film footage of black athletes leaving the Montreal village in tears and being consoled by colleagues from other nations. Years of training for the Olympics were wasted. Meanwhile, rugby tours to and from South Africa continue to this day and the boycott did absolutely nothing to stop South Africa's apartheid policies, which were the obvious objections of the boycotting nations. As we'd see time and again, the only ones hurt by boycotts are the athletes.

Why Carter thought the Soviets would alter their foreign policy because we threatened to ruin their track meet was beyond me. Though politically naïve, I didn't have to be a genius to understand his motives. The hostages had just been taken in Iran, negotiations for their release were stalled, and Carter was perceived as a weakling by the international press. Additionally, members of his own party had taken to the hustings to challenge him for the presidential nomination. With the primary season just beginning, Carter desperately needed a bold public relations stroke to put his image back on the track.

Carter's tactic worked. It was popular with the public and the media, and he milked the issue by setting a deadline for the Soviets to pull out their troops.

However, the feedback I got was extremely negative. Carter had insulted the IOC by refusing to attend the opening of the Winter Games in Lake Placid; he sent Vice President Mondale in his place. Lord Killanin, Berlioux, and the other representatives of federations were angered by the slight. The boycott reinforced widespread anti-American sentiment within the Olympic Movement and provoked a worldwide call for the removal of the Games from Los Angeles. I remember getting off an airplane at O'Hare Airport in Chicago and seeing a banner headline on the *Chicago Tribune* that read: SOVIETS SAY: L.A. TO LOSE THE GAMES.

In the meantime, the LAOOC staff had grown to twenty-two and I arranged for all of them to attend Lake Placid in shifts to get a glimpse of the Olympic world in all its glory. We were treated like pariahs. The Olympic family barely acknowledged our presence. In fact, we weren't even accredited at any of the IOC meetings as observers. Outside the meetings, we were berated for the proposed boycott and the commercialization of both the Los Angeles and Lake Placid Games.

During all this time—a month and a half from the time Carter made his first announcement—no one from his administration ever contacted me or anyone else at the LAOOC, either to enlist our aid or to give us a courtesy briefing. In Lake Placid, I introduced myself to Lloyd Cutler, counsel to Carter, whom Carter had appointed his boycott coordinator. Cutler was also in charge of developing plans for alternate games for the one hundred nations the Carter administration was certain wouldn't attend the Olympic Games.

I told Cutler the alternate games would fail because they required the sanction of the international federations. Without those sanctions, there was no way the national Olympic committees would send athletes to the event. He assured me he had the cooperation of most heads of state and that the United Nations' vote against Soviet aggression in Afghanistan was about as unanimous as you could get. "Nobody's going to Moscow," Cutler boldly said. I didn't know who was doing his research—and I never found out—but it was clear he and his associates didn't know a thing about international amateur sports.

I was really torn between supporting my government or supporting the athletes who were caught in the middle and would suffer the most. I supported the athletes.

The LAOOC's board of directors held a vigorous debate over the issue. One group advised against voting at all, pointing out it was none of the board's business and a stand would surely alienate either the Carter administration or the IOC, depending on the outcome of the vote. Others on the board hoped for some type of federal funding and believed that by supporting Carter we would win favorable notice from him. In the end the board voted to support the administration. David

Wolper cast the only dissenting vote. If I'd had a vote on the board, I would have voted with him.

I offered my assistance in making the best of a bad situation when Wolper and I were invited to the White House for a meeting in the War Room that April. Lloyd Cutler, National Security Advisor Zbigniew Breszinski, CIA Director Admiral Stansfield Turner, and Secretary of State Cyrus Vance, among others, attended the meeting. I felt I was there as an Olympic presence. They had hoped that Wolper, with his vast Olympic and television experience, would help them organize the alternate games, an idea Wolper supported because of his concern for the welfare of the American athletes.

Cutler was obviously in charge. He's a very intelligent, astute lawyer, and an excellent public servant who served Carter well. However, I don't think he was ever entirely comfortable with his Olympic role.

The only issue I raised was the futility of past boycotts—that the black boycott of the Montreal Games had done nothing to stop apartheid in South Africa. They ignored my comments. The real purpose of the meeting was clear—to decide how best to show the American people Carter's great strength in confronting the Soviets. At one point I asked which nations were sympathetic to Carter's proposal and would attend the alternate games. Cutler and Breszinski listed France, England, Italy, the Federal Republic of Germany, Austria, and almost every other European country. Cutler said Australia and New Zealand were guaranteed and that embassies from around the world had reported that most countries in Africa and Asia would support the United States as well.

As the meeting was wrapping up, a list of all the countries the State Department had cabled asking for support was distributed. South Africa stood out like a beacon. Damn it, I thought, Carter, Cutler, and the rest of them didn't have a clue. South Africa hadn't participated in an Olympic Games since 1960 when the IOC banned it from the Olympic Movement because of its racist policies. The slightest hint of contact with South Africa on this issue would jeopardize everything the president was trying to do, and the gesture would offend almost every nation.

Wolper subsequently accompanied Cutler to Geneva to drum up support for the alternate games. Wolper told me later that he'd had the misfortune to run into Berlioux, who vented her fury for the boycott and everyone involved with it. No decisions were made in Geneva. Just a lot of smoke. Next Wolper went to London to solicit the support of the British Olympic Association president, Sir Denis Follows, who told him, "Screw off. We're not going to any alternate games." In fact, Follows would tell his government to do the same, and he sent a team to Moscow. So much for Cutler's assurances of support.

The furor over the boycott and the attempts to organize alternate games prevented the LAOOC from making progress. There was considerable skepticism about the Los Angeles Games, and we desperately needed positive reinforcement from the IOC.

I arranged a special meeting with Killanin and Berlioux to get it. The international federations were meeting in Lausanne later that April, so we convened at a hotel in Geneva about a hundred miles away over a late-night dinner.

The three of us were dead tired—me from flying nonstop from Los Angeles, and Killanin and Berlioux from nonstop meetings with sport federation officials. While Killanin understood the need to press on with planning the L.A. Games, as the signatory to the agreement awarding the Games to L.A. and at the same time as president of the Olympics the U.S. was doing its best to destroy, he had mixed feelings.

"I sympathize with you, Peter," Killanin said. "It's difficult to deal with those people."

By "those" Killanin was referring to President Carter and his staff. He recounted his visit to the White House on October 20, 1978, to formally award the 1984 Games to Los Angeles. This was a big deal and Killanin, Berlioux, and the Los Angeles contingent had expected Carter to make a brief appearance. Although in the next room, Carter didn't even bother to drop in and say hello.

Killanin, the epitome of integrity, didn't let that stand in the way of his relationship with the LAOOC. He acted in the best interests of the Olympic Movement and dictated a simple agreement that Berlioux copied in longhand on graph paper, which she pulled from her briefcase. It assured the world that the 1984 Games would remain in Los Angeles.

The statement said:

> Mr.Peter Uberroth, President of the LAOOC, met Lord Killanin, President of the IOC, on his way to Lausanne for IOC meetings. The President of the IOC stated that the Olympic Games are the property of the IOC which designates who will be in charge of staging them. He confirmed that there was no question of moving the Games from Los Angeles with which an agreement was made in 1978.
>
> The IOC is very pleased with the LAOOC and the way their administration is conducted.
>
> Within the next two days the situation regarding the Games of the 22nd Olympiad will be discussed.

Killanin and I signed the agreement and dated it April 19, 1980.

With the time difference between Switzerland and Los Angeles on my side, I called Ken Reich of the *L.A. Times* and read him the text. His front-page story the next day allayed the concerns of our employees, sponsors, board of directors, and everybody else associated with our efforts.

The United States Olympic Committee had a difficult choice to make. According to the Olympic Charter, all national Olympic committees are obligated to respond to their invitations six weeks prior to the start of the Games. The USOC house of delegates met on May 24, 1980, to vote on its participation in the Games. Carter sent Mondale. I sent Harry Usher.

Usher is the brightest and most effective lawyer I've ever known. We'd met through our wives several years earlier at a charity tennis tournament and soon after developed a business relationship as well as a strong friendship. Bright, articulate, and aggressive, not to mention a wonderful sense of humor, he became the counsel to my travel company.

Usher was raised in Rutherford, New Jersey, under very modest circumstances. An honor student in high school, he had decided to become a lawyer because of an incident as a teenager. A traffic court judge, before whom young Usher appeared to fight a minor moving violation, had insulted his integrity, saying he was just another juvenile delinquent destined for the junk heap. Usher swore he'd prove the judge wrong.

Sports also played an important role in his life. Excellent in baseball and football, Usher attended Brown University on an athletic scholarship. In his senior year, he played quarterback for the varsity football team and graduated first in his class. He then attended Stanford University Law School on scholarship and was editor of the Law Review.

Everything Usher has ever touched has turned to gold, so I wasn't exactly going out on a limb when I put him in charge of selling First Travel, and later asked him to run the day-to-day operations of the LAOOC as executive vice-president and general manager. He'd only been with the committee a few months when I sent him to Colorado Springs for the USOC meeting.

Usher told me the Carter administration had pulled out all the stops to get the USOC to support the boycott. Privately, it had threatened USOC leaders with loss of future federal support. Usher reported he'd heard the government, which owns the property where the USOC maintains its training center and headquarters in Colorado Springs, had threatened to renegotiate the USOC's sweetheart lease if it didn't go along with the boycott. The administration was also considering withdrawing its support of legislation that would allow taxpayers to donate $1 to the USOC by checking a box on tax returns. The USOC had no choice, and over strong protest by numerous athletes during the course of the meeting, voted to support the boycott.

"By the time William Simon and Walter Mondale finished with ruffles and flourishes, motherhood and apple pie,"

Usher said upon his return, "it was all over but the shouting—and the tears of the U.S. athletes."

A small LAOOC delegation went to Moscow in July to deliver our first official report to the IOC prior to the opening of the 1980 Games. We knew we'd be treated as outcasts—we were getting used to it—and we planned to leave before the opening ceremony. I thought it best to fly directly to Finland, rest there a day, and then head on to Moscow. The delegation consisted of Usher, Rubenstein, Sargent, John Argue, and two newcomers, Dr. Anthony F. Daly, our medical director, and Charlotte Hyde, my dear friend and an executive with my travel company. She is a gracious Frenchwoman who married a British officer after World War II. She became a close friend and confidante of Monique Berlioux.

Our flight from Helsinki was loaded with Olympic family members and Finnish fans. Several Soviet protocol chiefs were at the airport to greet our arrival. One directed sixty of us to a hospitality suite where all but the LAOOC delegation were efficiently processed on an individual basis and escorted into town. We waited for more than three hours before our hosts informed us that our documents were in order and took us to the hotel. When we unpacked we discovered our luggage had been thoroughly searched. It was then that we understood the true nature of the delay.

The failure of the Carter boycott was evident: Most of our staunchest allies were present in Moscow. The British team was there and so were the Australians, French, Italians, Swiss, and Belgians, as well as the competing African and Asian nations. Even Puerto Rico, a U.S. territory that competes separately under IOC rules, had come in full force. I was sure that German Reickehoff, president of the Puerto Rican NOC, must have had Communist tendencies because of his vociferous stance against the boycott. I changed my mind four years later when Rieckehoff's opposition to the Soviet boycott was even stronger.

Even though we were being ignored by most of the Olympic family, we hung tough together and managed a few laughs, mostly over the services—or lack thereof—at the

Moscow Hotel. Rubenstein, the fashion plate of the delegation, on one occasion sent some shirts and a suit to the hotel laundry. The service was efficient—the laundry was returned before the day was out. Rubenstein had no complaint there. However, he didn't appreciate the fact that the suit had been washed, ironed, and folded just like the shirts and packaged along with them. Outraged, Rubenstein stormed into the hall and berated the floor maid in English, a language she of course didn't understand. But she understood the gestures, as did a pair of machine-gun-bearing soldiers positioned about fifty feet down the hall. Sargent, who was with Rubenstein and was enjoying the show, exercised good sense and yanked him back into the room before the soldiers took matters into their own hands.

Late that night we sat around playing poker for kopeks. As we played into the early hours of the morning, we discussed the presentations we were to make to the full IOC session the next morning. Daly had prepared a paper proposing the addition of a women's marathon to the Games program. We expected stiff resistance to that for two reasons: first, because of the myths surrounding women's long-distance running; and second, because of the Eastern bloc's dearth of long-distance female talent.

The IOC informed us the next morning that only six of our seven-member delegation were allowed into the session. Daly, there for a special presentation apart from the LAOOC's official report, sat outside after delivering the proposal, unable to participate in the discussions. We learned a great deal about Olympic timing and the roundabout way the IOC reaches decisions. Despite our campaign, the IOC tried its best to reject a women's marathon. Some of its members claimed, as we had predicted, that a woman's body was not capable of running such long distances. The IOC was behind the times, you might say. Daly's exhaustive research reported quite the contrary. A heated argument ensued on the floor of the session and, finally, when the IOC suggested the motion be tabled until its next session, we gladly agreed. The IOC members then questioned us on our preparations.

The first salvo was fired by Sir Reginald Alexander of

Kenya, who succeeded in making points with our Soviet hosts. Alexander's status was a curious one. He was elected a lifetime member of the IOC in 1960, and as a former employee of Standard Oil in Kenya had survived the collapse there of British colonial rule. Thus, he was a white man representing a black nation.

He concluded by pointing directly at me and saying, "You, Mr. Ueberroth, represent the ugly face of capitalism." He must have enjoyed the image because he repeated it. "You represent the ugly face of capitalism and its attempt to take over the Olympic Movement and commercialize the Olympic Games."

Both Killanin and Berlioux were supportive. The Soviets were strangely quiet. In the end we had one surprising ally— Dr. Arpad Csanadi of Hungary. As the technical director for sports, he was widely respected in the IOC. Csanadi said, "These past two hours we have heard the most excellent report given by any organizing committee in my sixteen years as a member of the IOC."

Before and after the session, our little group split up into smaller units to observe various facets of Soviet preparations for the Games. The Soviets were very cooperative and clearly proud of what they'd accomplished. Like many organizing committees before them, workers were still applying finishing touches right up to the last minute.

This was the case at the Olympic Village where I witnessed a welcoming ceremony for a special guest. The administrators had rolled out the red carpet for Yasser Arafat, leader of the Palestinian Liberation Organization, who was being pandered to by the organizing committee and government officials as well as visiting dignitaries. Journalists hovered over him, pressing him for pearls of wisdom.

Arafat looked like he was having the time of his life. He was waving his arms and holding up his fingers in the victory sign. He announced it wouldn't be long before the PLO fielded a team in the Olympics. It sickened me. I was disgusted by the short memories of Olympic officials. It had only been eight years since a faction of the PLO—Black Sep-

tember—had murdered eleven Israeli athletes at the Munich
Games. I swore that there would be no PLO team at the 1984
Olympic Games.

The Carter administration's vendetta toward the Olympic
Games never subsided; it just got pettier. Traditionally at the
closing ceremony, the organizers signal the beginning of the
next Olympic quadrennial by lowering the flag of the host
country and raising that of the next country to host the
Games. It's a custom required by the Olympic Charter, not a
political statement. Nonetheless, the Carter administration refused to allow the U.S. flag to fly over Lenin Stadium.
Enough damage had been done and enough people hurt for
my taste. Before going to Moscow, I had asked Cutler many
times to reconsider, but each time he adamantly refused, saying that the American flag would remain home with the athletes.

The flag question reached crisis proportions a week before the Games began in Moscow, and it even overshadowed
the election of His Excellency Juan Antonio Samaranch as the
new president of the IOC. But Berlioux saved the day. She
asked if I could arrange to have the L.A. city flag fly at the
closing ceremony. I didn't even know the city had a flag.

I called Mayor Bradley, waking him from a sound sleep
at 2 A.M. California time, and asked if he would try to get the
city council to approve use of L.A.'s flag at Moscow. It took
him about twenty seconds to get his bearings. "I'm the approval," he said. "I'll give it to you and you get it to Moscow."

We had briefly considered remaining in Moscow to learn
more from the Soviet experience of hosting the Games, but I
was inclined not to for a couple reasons. One, I just wanted to
get the hell out. Getting the political cold shoulder made me
uncomfortable. Two, if the U.S. athletes weren't there, we
shouldn't be there either.

I made the final decision to leave, however, the instant
I saw Russian photographers snapping pictures of V. V.
Kuznetsov sharing a champagne toast with an IOC member. I
was farther down the reception line at a formal gathering, in

the magnificent Hall of Heroes deep within the Kremlin, that top Politburo members were having for the Olympic family the night before the opening ceremony. The Soviet propaganda machine was going full blast. I could envison a wire photo of me and Kuznetsov toasting the Moscow Games going around the world, which would have been an insult to the athletes and government of my country. I wasn't going to be part of it. As our hosts moved in my direction, followed by the bountiful champagne tray and a cadre of photographers, I composed myself.

As Kuznetsov and his entourage stopped in front of me, an interpreter by his side, Kuznetsov greeted me with a broad smile and a glass of champagne. I smiled back. A waiter then offered me champagne. I noticed photographers positioning themselves. I grasped my hands behind my back and said, "No, thank you."

The Soviet laughed, thinking I was joking. "Please, Mr. Ueberroth, let's drink a toast to our mutual Olympic successes."

"No, thank you," I said again.

My host became embarrassed and tried to persuade me to at least hold up a glass in friendship. Once more I demurred. Ruffled, he moved on. The LAOOC delegation returned to Los Angeles the next day.

The first day back, a Monday, I called David Simon, our government relations director, into my office. "David," I said, "your job is to get the flag to Moscow in time for the closing ceremony." The ceremony was Sunday.

Simon got the flag from the mayor's office. That was the easy part. Having just come from Moscow, we knew it was an armed camp and getting anything into the country was going to be difficult. I decided against Simon accompanying the flag because I wanted to avoid LAOOC visibility at all costs. Simon had arranged with Lufthansa Airlines to transport the flag through a network of its airline personnel. At each of two stops, Lufthansa advised us of its progress. On Wednesday, the day the flag was scheduled to arrive, we heard nothing. I got edgy when we still hadn't received confirmation the following morning.

"David, what's happening?" I asked.

Simon was nervous, too. "We've done everything we could, Peter. It's in Lufthansa's hands, and they assured us it would arrive in time."

"If we don't get word by seven A.M. tomorrow you're taking a flag to Moscow."

Simon procured a backup flag, obtained the necessary paperwork, kissed his wife good-bye early that morning, and was just about to catch a ride to the airport when a Telex came saying the flag had been delivered. David unpacked; I breathed a sigh of relief.

Throughout the week, I avidly followed news reports of the Games and watched the late-night television broadcast of the competitions. Americans got short shrift in terms of Olympic coverage, but there was no question that Moscow had operated and staged a magnificent Games, one they deserved to be proud of.

During the two weeks of the Moscow Games, the U.S. Swim Federation held a meet at Mission Viejo, California, that was designed to showcase American swimmers and compare their times to those posted in Moscow. I went to the competition to support the athletes and to meet Ronald Reagan, the Republican presidential nominee, who was there to present medals. As arranged, I left my family in the stands and went to a glass-enclosed room located behind the swim stadium. Reagan and Nancy were surrounded by well-wishers who were being ushered out by his aides. When everybody else had moved on, I was told to go in.

The start to that brief meeting must have looked like an outtake from a Marx brothers movie. I said good evening and offered my hand to the governor just as Nancy offered hers to me. I turned to shake her hand, which was the polite thing to do, and noticed then that Reagan had offered his. Nancy jerked her hand back. I jerked mine back. I then went to shake hands with Reagan just as he had begun to pull his back. Nancy smiled broadly and said, "Gentlemen, if you will stop all this we can start over." We all had a good laugh and got the handshaking out of the way.

I launched into a five-minute talk on the importance of

the Games to our country. The boycott, I told him, was pure folly and made us look foolish in the eyes of the world. I explained how we were organizing the Games through the private sector, which I felt would be of interest to him as private-sector initiative was one of the themes of his campaign. He listened quietly to the briefing. His face never registered any emotion. I finished. They thanked me. Disappointed at his apparent lack of interest, I turned and left.

In the stands, Ginny asked me how it went.

"Ginny, he didn't even pay attention," I told her. "I don't think he understood a word I said. It's too bad because what we're doing is exactly what he champions."

Reagan was introduced to the crowd for the medal presentations, which were being televised nationally. After beginning with a humorous anecdote about his brief swimming career in college, he launched into a concise, three-minute presentation that summed up everything I had just told him. He delivered the idea as though it were his own, which was fine with me. I don't ever remember having been more impressed by a person's ability to absorb and articulate thoughts more accurately and swiftly.

Visiting Moscow had opened my eyes to the enormity and complexity of staging an Olympic Games. What previously had been a kaleidoscope of images had crystallized into a reality from which we were able to set objectives and priorities.

Having seen Moscow decked out for the Games and the way its people were behind the event made me realize how vastly we had underestimated our staffing needs. We had counted on thirty thousand staff and volunteers to do the job. That estimate was revised to seventy thousand—the largest volunteer force ever assembled in peacetime. To manage that force, a leadership base of talented, spirited, sports-minded individuals who would put business and personal lives on hold and join us for a short time was desperately needed. All we had to offer were long hours, low pay, and guaranteed unemployment.

Although we'd already begun solidifying our funding, we

had to accelerate our sponsorship, supplier, and licensing programs and get moving on the largest ticket-marketing program in history and launch a commemorative coin program.

But government cast a shadow over all our operations. Everything we touched, everywhere we went, we were confronted by layers upon layers of government and bureaucrats. We had to get going. We didn't have the kind of time that government required to get things done.

The boycott had also heaped more responsibilities on us. It forced us to establish our own foreign policy and repair the international damage that the L.A. Games had suffered. At the same time we had to work with our government to make sure it respected and upheld the Olympic Charter.

From a sheer functional standpoint we had to locate and lease suitable facilities and arrange for all necessary construction to be completed at least a year before the start of the Games. We needed solutions to traffic congestion. We had to find housing for the Olympic family and journalists. We had to arrange the Olympic arts festival to complement the Games.

Most important, to secure the Games we would need the cooperation and goodwill of city, county, and state governments, and a federal overlay of thirty different agencies. It would be a totally new experience for most of them, because for a short period of time they would have to form a partnership with the private sector and take direction from us.

On August 4, 1980, the morning following the end of the Moscow Games, a photograph of the L.A. city flag flying over Lenin Stadium stared back at me from page one of the *Los Angeles Times*. A lump formed in my throat. It was our turn. Our quadrennial had begun. Four years didn't seem like such a long time anymore.

THE WORLD'S GREATEST PLAYGROUND

IT WAS NOW time for the LAOOC to transform an area two hundred miles long by fifty miles wide into a giant Olympic playground. Most people called it Los Angeles; I called it a nightmare.

This task also required us to manage twenty-seven stadiums and facilities located in three states, nine counties, and twenty-nine cities—including satellite soccer sites in Palo Alto, Boston, and Annapolis—and would be tougher than staging ten Super Bowls a day for sixteen straight days. We would build permanent facilities for swimming and diving at the University of Southern California; for cycling at California State College, Dominguez Hills; for shooting at Prado Recreational Area in San Bernardino County; and a temporary facility for rowing and canoeing at Lake Casitas in Ventura County. We also had to refurbish or modify at least a dozen existing stadiums and arenas to bring each up to Olympic specifications. To accommodate cycling road racing and the marathons, we'd arrange for a freeway to be closed for part of one day and for city streets to be blocked along the twenty-six-mile marathon course.

I had already visited the Olympic sites in Moscow, Melbourne, Montreal, Munich, and Mexico City and in each case was stunned by the nature of the legacies left behind. So many facilities lay dormant, monuments to waste and the shortsighted internal politics of the Olympic Movement. Historically, international sports federations bludgeon organizers into constructing costly facilities that are later written off as Olympic-related expenses and explained to the public as long-term civic improvements. Invariably, the IOC sides with the international federations at the expense of the host city. In the end, after the Olympic torch is extinguished, the so-called improvements become albatrosses for the taxpayer.

Montreal is the most vivid example. As of 1985, its Olympic stadium, which was built for the 1976 Games, was still without a roof and its $86.5 million, indoor, state-of-the-art velodrome has remained empty for all but a few nights over the last nine years. Though wonderful for the Olympics, the velodrome is simply too expensive to maintain and lease.

After Moscow, I had sensed that organizing the Olympic Games was like a train picking up steam. We had eased out of the station and were now rolling in open country. Dick Sargent, Harry Usher, Katy Wright, and I began meeting three times a week. Sargent updated us on the status of the venue searches. ("Venue" is the Olympic term for a competition site. To those of us in the LAOOC, the Coliseum, for example, was no longer a stadium; it was a venue.) His job was to identify, locate, and begin the preliminary negotiations so Usher could button up the contracts. Wright, who had just returned from attending Olympic Academy seminars in Greece, was our sports researcher. Her job was to identify training sites and equipment.

I announced at a meeting in early September 1980 that all the venues had to be wrapped up by October 1, 1981, the day we were to deliver our next official report to the IOC at its congress in Baden-Baden. A congress brings together all members of the Olympic family: the IOC, the international federations, and the national Olympic committees. It's a global forum for the exchange of ideas—and subterfuges. Congresses are few and far between, and this one, only the eleventh in the IOC's eighty-seven-year history, would be especially important because the IOC would examine us closely, more so than usual because of the Carter boycott.

"Baden-Baden is our world debut," I told the small group. "I want results to give them. Numbers. We need all twenty-three venues locked up so that the Olympic family will leave that congress knowing we are physically ready to stage our Games."

So far it hadn't been easy. L.A.'s original bid outlined the existing facilities available and the construction needed. We were fortunate that John Argue, the architect of the bid, had the foresight to allow some leeway in the proposal's language. That gave us the freedom to honor the intent of the bid but also to circumvent it.

Sargent's first stop was Long Beach, twenty-four miles south of L.A., to line up the Long Beach Marina for yachting. That was an easy one. Sargent, an expert sailor, knew all the players and we signed on March 24, 1980. At that time he also tried to nail down the Los Angeles Sports Arena, downtown and adjacent to the Coliseum, for basketball. This had been specified in the original bid for the Games. Feeling no sense of urgency, however, the Coliseum commission, operator of the Coliseum and the Sports Arena, waffled and refused to get down to brass tacks.

This frustrated Sargent, who came to me in mid-April and asked, "How do we get a message to the city that we're in the venue business now?"

"If the city won't work with us, work around it," I told him. "We'll hold these Games in communities that want us. We ought to go back to the IOC and have them award the Games to Long Beach."

In business, if a competitor goes in one direction, you go in the other. During the early 1960s, when I was still struggling to make First Travel successful, I was threatened by a rival travel company that offered a wide range of fringe benefits to tour groups. I had already lost some business and feared losing a great deal more. But I couldn't afford to match his frills—complimentary hotel room for one night, champagne, luggage tags, and everything else. I retaliated by launching a no-frills, service-oriented campaign that struck at the core of the travel business. The campaign was a success and it blew the rival out of the water.

I twisted this little bit of business philosophy and told Sargent to try the Forum, where the bid had placed boxing. The Forum is located in Inglewood, an incorporated city near Los Angeles International Airport. Sargent smiled at the thought. He knew that Jerry Buss, the owner and operator of the Forum and its principal tenants, the Lakers (basketball) and the Kings (ice hockey), would give his eyeteeth to host the basketball competition.

I thought if we took basketball to the Forum it would seem like déjà-vu to the Coliseum commission. Almost thirteen years earlier, the Coliseum commission had tried to bully Jack Kent Cooke the same way they were bullying us. Cooke was an aggressive Canadian entrepreneur who owned the Lakers and leased the Sports Arena for Laker home games.

During embittered negotiations over a new lease, Cooke had walked out. He said he would build his own arena, and he did. Since opening its doors in December 1967, the Forum, one of the finest multifunctional, indoor facilities in the country, has attracted practically every major indoor event and concert in southern California. It made Cooke another fortune, thanks in part to the generosity of Inglewood officials who wanted a world-class indoor facility. While the Forum flourished, the Sports Arena became a white elephant. I told Sargent if we moved basketball it would send a clear signal to the city that we weren't going to stand still for its nonsense. It would also give us an opportunity to set a precedent for all future venue agreements.

Buss gave us a sweetheart deal: 50 percent of all food and beverage concessions, 100 percent of souvenirs, a $5,000 credit against labor costs, plus 10 percent of the gate, which is standard for sports lease deals. In return, Buss got all the parking revenues and tickets for some of his season ticket holders.

Buss, a self-made millionaire, already had a reputation for being a playboy when he bought the Forum, Lakers, and Kings from Cooke in 1979. He liked to titillate sports writers by showing off a scrapbook of his girlfriends. Fully aware of the publicity the Games attracted, he felt compelled to keep his association with the LAOOC in the background. This surprised me, and when I asked him about it, he said: "I have an image of somebody who drinks too much and spends more than his share of time with beautiful women. I don't think that's the kind of image you want associated with young athletes and Olympic hopefuls." I admired his attitude, *and* his support of the Games.

A month and a half after signing the deal with Buss, two LAOOC board members, who also served on the Coliseum commission, came hat in hand to Sargent, begging that the Sports Arena be included in the Games. We were happy to oblige and offered them boxing. After Sargent explained how they could sell more seats because boxing required less space, they accepted and left—embarrassed but happy.

Sargent's excellent rapport with Long Beach officials continued to pay off. He negotiated contracts for archery at El Dorado Park and for volleyball and fencing at the Long Beach Arena and Convention Center.

One year before Baden-Baden, though, there was still much to do. We came to terms with the Coliseum commission on November 19, 1980, to use the Coliseum for the opening and closing ceremonies and for track and field. The Coliseum would be the main stadium for the Games, just as it had been in 1932. This contract, however, was the most difficult, and disagreements over terms continued virtually up until the morning of the opening ceremonies. Some commission members didn't know the word "integrity."

The Atlantic Richfield Company then stepped forward as a corporate sponsor. It agreed to match us dollar for dollar in the $10 million refurbishment of the Coliseum, which also meant financing the installation of a world-class track at the Coliseum and nine more training tracks in southern California.

Problems began as soon as we started work. Many of the restrooms didn't function and those that did had toilets that flushed into the concession stands. The electrical system was hopelessly outmoded, and it couldn't carry the power required for the Games. The stadium had been neglected and it looked it.

In 1979 the owner of the Los Angeles Rams, Carroll Rosenbloom, had moved his team to Anaheim. The commission had played its only-game-in-town hand and lost once again, as it had with Jack Kent Cooke. All Rosenbloom had wanted were improvements to the facility. When Anaheim offered Rosenbloom a lucrative land deal to move there, he called the commission's bluff and moved south. Now the Coliseum desperately needed a new tenant and if it was going to attract another football team, improvements would have to be made. The LAOOC, the commission figured, was the tooth fairy.

In fairness to the commission, part of the reason it's such a mess is its ridiculous management structure. It is governed by three parents—the state, county, and city—but it's treated like an orphan. The governor of California appoints three representatives, a combination of supporters and legislators; the county board of supervisors names three of its own membership; and the mayor assigns a mixture of three supporters and city council members. In short, the commission has a little bit of everything and a lot of nothing. Adding to the madness—from an LAOOC point of view—two or three LAOOC board members served on the commission at the same time. It's a setup for corruption when you consider that each member is usually allotted tickets for each event: college and professional football, track-and-field competitions, and motocross at the Coliseum; boxing, basketball, and rock concerts at the sports arena. Commission members drove that point home by making tickets a bargaining chip in our negotiations.

Basic points in our contract gave us the use of the Coliseum from June 25 to August 15, 1984, for 10 percent of the gross ticket receipts for the opening and closing ceremonies and the track-and-field competition. We also got 50 percent of food and beverage sales and all but 10 percent of novelty revenues. On each day there was no Olympic activity, we were to pay a $5,000 lease fee.

Although we were unhappy with the physical condition of

the Coliseum, we'd assumed that haggling with the commission was behind us. We began construction but soon learned the commission had given our rights away to Al Davis, the managing partner of the Oakland Raiders football team.

We knew Davis well. We'd given Davis office space and our support when it seemed he was going to move his team to Los Angeles. At that time we had cordially reached a preliminary understanding regarding the luxury boxes he wanted constructed at the Coliseum.

That projected move fell through, however, as did our preliminary deal. Now we had control of all seating. The commission knew this and so did Davis. Nonetheless, the commission, in its desire to have a professional football team, waived ethics and gave Davis the luxury boxes for all events, including the 1984 Olympics. This waiver was worth millions of dollars.

Feeling generous, the commission even cut itself in for 25 percent of the Olympic box revenues. Davis had the rest. I envisioned World War III breaking out when Raider ticket holders tried to crash our stadiums and take the seats belonging to Olympic ticket holders.

We began lengthy negotiations with Davis and the commission and much of it wound up in the press.

We weren't the only ones up in arms. The Coliseum's other regular tenants, the University of Southern California and the University of California, Los Angeles, were too. UCLA, which had played football there for years, was so angry it moved to the Rose Bowl. We considered doing the same. Usher even had schematics prepared showing how the Rose Bowl could be used for track and field. As the spring of 1983 approached, the heat was on to settle. We couldn't wait much longer to announce our ticket program. Finally, on March 2, 1983, after weeks of intensive talks, the LAOOC agreed to pay Davis $3 million in rental fees for all but 8 of the 174 luxury boxes he intended to build. The Coliseum commission reduced its percentage of the gate from 10 to 8 percent. But the whole deal hinged on Davis, who had to commit to construction by April 18, 1983, or postpone his plans until after the Games.

Great amounts of time and energy were wasted, and to this day, the Raiders' luxury boxes exist only on paper.

But back in December 1980, when the original Coliseum deal still seemed firm, we felt good about the progress we'd made lining up facilities. We were anxious to show IOC President Samaranch and Executive Director Berlioux what we had accomplished. Samaranch, on his first visit to Los Angeles, and Berlioux, who was returning for the first time since signing the ABC television deal the year before, were eager to examine our plans to make sure that the IOC's needs hadn't been ignored.

Our twenty-two-member staff worked around the clock preparing for the visit. David Simon, who handled LAOOC protocol in addition to government relations, made full use of his government connections and had the airport wired—from Customs officials to baggage handlers—for Samaranch's arrival the evening of December 6. Berlioux arrived separately. All Samaranch had to do was point to his luggage; Simon took care of everything else.

Before settling in for the night and bidding Simon farewell, Samaranch opened a suitcase and out popped a lot of women's lingerie and dirty clothes. Samaranch and Simon were both embarrassed. "Obviously," Samaranch said dryly, turning to Simon, "this is not my luggage." The bag Samaranch had identified at the airport was identical to his own.

It was past midnight and Simon made a futile call to the airport. He suspected the luggage room was closed and it was. An airlines employee told him nobody had reported a missing bag. Samaranch had only the suit he was wearing, and he had meetings scheduled all the next day and was concerned he wouldn't get his bag back for several days, if ever. Simon assured Samaranch he'd do everything he could. He took the mistaken suitcase and left the chagrined IOC president to cope with jet lag.

Simon lugged the suitcase to the LAOOC's Century City office and searched it for the owner's identification. At 1:30 A.M. he discovered a card belonging to a man living in Portland, Oregon. Simon got the man's telephone number from information and called. The businessman, a salesman, had given luggage as gifts to at least twenty-five people in southern California and had only a few names and telephone numbers handy. Simon kept phoning. He got lucky two hours later and connected with the woman who had Samaranch's luggage.

Samaranch was grateful he had a clean suit the next morning and I was proud of Simon's resourcefulness. Though it was a minor incident in the overall scheme of things, I believe it gave Samaranch and Berlioux an example of our dedication and they respected us more because of it. That helped set a positive tone for their six-day visit, which included presentations at city hall—where Samaranch received a key to the city from Bradley—and resolutions from the Los Angeles County Board of Supervisors, dinners with LAOOC board members and staff, and tours of the facilities.

Bradley still persisted in dangling prospective federal funding before the IOC executives. He even outlined plans for a subsidized rowing and canoeing channel in the Sepulveda Basin of the San Fernando Valley on the northern side of the Santa Monica Mountains.

Samaranch and Berlioux publicly praised the LAOOC and endorsed our concept of private financing. This was reported in the *Los Angeles Times* while they were still in town. We were elated when we put them on the airplane and hopeful they would deliver the same message overseas, where we were still being severely criticized.

The next morning, however, there was another *Los Angeles Times* article, but this one was devastating. It reported that Samaranch and Berlioux were dissatisfied with our efforts. According to the reporter's source, Samaranch and Berlioux believed that Usher and I were too secretive, that government should take a greater role in organizing the Games, and that the LAOOC should make plans to provide special benefits to visiting officials and journalists.

I was incensed. I attributed the substance of the article more to editorializing than to a reflection of the true feelings of Samaranch, who was fully aware of the restrictions we faced in organizing the Games. Ziffren, Usher, and I wasted many hours speculating on the source's identity before deciding it really didn't matter. The damage was done.

One of the most important parts of the venue hunt was making certain that each met the strict criteria of the international federations involved. The original bid for the Games had trapped us in some instances by making promises to various federations that we couldn't afford to keep. If we had followed its exact specifications, the built-in lease options and construction costs would have cost us more than $100 million over our budget projections.

The venues for rowing and canoeing were a good example of this. Our search for a venue led to conflicts with the federation, city officials, and the public. In an effort to please Tom Keller, who at the time of the bid was one of the most powerful men in the Olympic Movement, the Southern California Committee for the Olympic Games had promised to build a rowing and canoeing venue for the competition. Long, narrow rowing channels had been built for every Olympics since 1964. Keller was a triple threat. Not only was he president of both the General Assembly of International Sport Federations (the governing body for all Olympic sports) and the International Rowing Federation, but he was also president of Swiss Timing, which had negotiated contracts to score competitions at our Olympic Games and at previous Games. Because of Keller, I was not surprised that rowing and canoeing channels had been built for every Games since 1964.

Keller, a charming and cunning Swiss, was caught in his own web of special-interest groups: He had to please all federations, especially his own. In dealing with the LAOOC, it was important that it appear he was holding fast to demands for a new facility. Mayor Bradley didn't help us. He and the city's Recreation and Parks Department officials pursued a plan that tied a rowing channel to a San Fernando Valley water-reclamation project. This was called the Sepulveda Dam Project, a masquerade that didn't fool the residents. They opposed it vigorously and interpreted it as a another violation of the LAOOC's pledge to refrain from using public funds.

In January, the Coalition to Save the Sepulveda Basin, a group opposing the Games, sent an open letter to Bradley. It appeared in the *Los Angeles Times* on January 12, 1981, and

stated the coalition's desire to shut the Olympic Games out of
the valley.

Such groups represented the antidevelopment attitude
that had carried over from the mid-1970s. Bradley knew them
well because he'd supported their opposition to the construction of a racetrack at the same site. Now the coalition
reminded him of his previous support and pressured him to
remain consistent.

The letter said, "Just as you had the power and influence
to call off the Hollywood Park racetrack deal [for the basin],
. . . you have the influence now to stop this assault on our
express interests. You were elected by all of us; no one council member was.

"We demand that you speak for us now and put an end to
the proposal to bring an Olympic facility to the basin that the
people don't want, don't need and can't afford. We demand
that you keep your promise. We demand no Olympics in the
Valley, no rowing course in our park land in the Sepulveda
Basin."

This attack didn't surprise me. Our earlier attempts to
place archery and cycling in the valley had been loudly re-
buffed, even though we planned to add major improvements
to the community. We had offered to renovate an old, worn-
down, outdoor velodrome in Encino and reconstruct its track
to international cycling standards. We also intended to restore
baseball fields next to the velodrome and make badly needed
improvements to the park area. But suspicion in the valley
ran high. The residents believed we had ulterior motives and
would destroy their neighborhoods. So we took the cycling
venue to Carson, seventeen miles south of Los Angeles, and
built the first world-class velodrome in the western United
States, at California State College, Dominguez Hills.

Keller visited us often during 1980 and 1981, and he and
Sargent toured every body of water between Seattle and San
Diego. Every time we thought we had convinced Keller we
didn't need a new facility, he would read a news report about
how Los Angeles city officials were pushing for the Sepulveda
Dam Project and would then renew his original demands.

It wasn't until the residents of the valley killed the project once and for all that Keller asked his federation to bless Lake Casitas, a lake about eighty miles north of Los Angeles. Keller was agreeable to this venue because the 1980 World Rowing Championships had been successfully conducted on a natural body of water in New Zealand, and Lake Casitas complied with the federation requirement that competition be held on a body of water not influenced by tides.

One of our bigger headaches had been resolved. On June 29, 1981, we announced Lake Casitas, and Keller and his federation were happy.

Sargent had done a magnificent job. Mostly through his efforts, the LAOOC had already lined up venues for eighteen of the twenty-one sports, including archery, athletics (track and field), basketball, boxing, canoeing, cycling, equestrian, fencing, football (soccer), gymnastics, team handball, judo, rowing, swimming and diving, volleyball, weightlifting, wrestling, and yachting.

We had even leased Dodger Stadium as the venue for baseball, which was one of two demonstration sports added to the 1984 Olympic program by the IOC. The other was tennis. We never gave up trying to gain medal status for baseball, but that never happened.

Venues for field hockey, modern pentathlon, and water polo were easily resolved, though not in time for Baden-Baden.

Shooting wasn't just a headache; it was a migraine. Our problems became severe when we learned the Orange County developers of the Coal Canyon site, fifty miles south of Los Angeles, had lost their financing and couldn't complete construction in time for the Games. We dropped Coal Canyon and left no stone unturned looking for a new site, which had to accommodate trap and skeet shooting as well as have pistol and rifle ranges. Nobody wanted it. Many citizens wondered why it was included in the Olympic program at all. We looked at police academies, military bases, open fields, private ranges. No luck.

At one point I sent Sargent and a busload of International Shooting Federation officials to inspect a Boy Scouts camp out in the wilds of San Bernardino County. They had to trek over two miles of undeveloped terrain and through a driving rain to get there, only to find the site located in a blind canyon, the configuration of which would cause ricochets and possible injuries.

We even considered a parking lot at Caesars Palace in Las Vegas. That drew condemnation from the entire Olympic world, especially from the Eastern bloc. It wasn't until June 21, 1983, that we reached an agreement with San Bernardino County to build a site fifty miles east of Los Angeles at the Prado Recreation Area.

Meanwhile, the International Soccer Federation (FIFA), one of the richest and most powerful sports federations, pushed us to the limit in locating suitable preliminary-round soccer fields. To our horror, we discovered that few of the seemingly countless football stadiums and fields throughout southern California and the country were large enough to meet FIFA's specifications, one of which was a grass playing field. It took years of bickering and great patience on our part before we got FIFA officials to accept four sites in different regions of the country for those preliminary competitions. Besides the Rose Bowl in Pasadena, our other soccer sites were at three of the most prestigious universities in the country— Harvard, the U.S. Naval Academy, and Stanford.

As the deadline for the Baden-Baden meeting approached, the significance of it grew. I had our entire staff, which by then had reached sixty, brainstorm and prepare our second official report to the IOC. I knew we had to dazzle them. Sargent and Rubenstein went to Baden-Baden two weeks early to case the city, the congress preparations, and the overall atmosphere. As the illegitimate children of the movement, we had been booked into a truly inferior hotel. Sargent and Rubenstein moved us out of town to a good hotel in the Black Forest, far from the meeting site and the rest of the Olympic family.

They returned in time to report before our delegation left that the Sarajevo Organizing Committee, along with the Moscow Organizing Committee and delegations bidding to host the 1988 Olympic Games and Winter Olympic Games, had been preparing lavish exhibits and receptions at the old Baden-Baden train station, which had been converted into a convention hall.

I was glad to hear that. I had already decided we would not have an exhibit at the train station. In keeping with one of my favorite themes, made famous by old-time baseball player Wee Willie Keeler—"Hit 'em where they ain't"—I had Rubenstein arrange for office space directly across from the IOC hotel in downtown Baden-Baden.

When Rubenstein returned to Baden-Baden with the rest of our ten-person delegation several days later, he established a bona fide office. Our message to the IOC was clear: The LAOOC represented substance not style. We weren't going to be the whipping people for the Carter boycott.

Delegates to the congress couldn't leave the meeting without seeing the LAOOC flag flying proudly from a balcony across the street. The word spread quickly that I was conducting one-on-one meetings with Olympic officials and taking note of individual requests. We also gave each visitor a basket of California fruit. But what really appealed to their self-interest was our accreditation system. We had staffers taking photos and laminating so-called LAOOC badges. This so attracted delegates, who enjoy being badged and tagged, that they began lining up at our office door at 8 A.M. every morning. In the following years, delegates who had attended Baden-Baden would occasionally appear at LAOOC offices in Los Angeles and proudly present their Baden-Baden badge in expectation of some sort of special treatment.

Through face-to-face encounters I met just about every national Olympic committee and international federation president and secretary-general. I nodded my head a lot, listened to some outrageous requests, learned a little, but made no commitments. I succeeded, however, in making each visitor feel more comfortable with the LAOOC. That and our report, which was enhanced by a slickly produced slide presentation, inspired confidence.

Of all the people I met in Baden-Baden the most impressive was His Royal Highness Prince Philip, Duke of Edinburgh, whose role in the Olympic Movement is president of the International Equestrian Federation, known for its elitism and snobbery. Other than Prince Philip, those who run it are among the most demanding of all federation officials and they often trade on Prince Philip's name.

I returned to our hotel one afternoon and found its staff buzzing with news that Prince Philip had called and left a message for me to return his call. First I perused a worn copy of the U.S. State Department protocol manual to see how one should properly speak to royalty. I learned to address him as Your Royal Highness and not to ask questions about the Royal Family. I returned his call, and we had a delightful lunch at his hotel the next day. We discussed sports and the Olympics, and he made it clear that those were his priorities and that he would support us. He kept his word. He added the common touch to a sport rife with pretensions.

At Baden-Baden we asserted ourselves and were successful in reaching out to the Olympic family and solidifying personal relationships. It also reconfirmed what we had learned at Moscow and other international sports gatherings: All policy and operational decisions are made behind the scenes. Unless you worm your way into the inner circle, you are powerless to affect them. Public meetings such as Baden-Baden are merely forums for show and tell and lavish social gatherings.

This was obvious as we watched the bid selection for the 1988 Games and saw how leverage is brought to bear on the organizing committee. Before Baden-Baden, it had been assumed that Nagoya, Japan, would get the 1988 Games. The IOC had quietly let it be known it was time the Olympics were returned to that part of the world. Seoul was a serious contender but was clearly the underdog because of its unstable political climate. Each bid city hosted costly receptions showcasing the best of its country's culture and cuisine. At the train station, the bid cities' exhibits were impeccable, and they lobbied IOC members hard for their vote. Each bid city gave away shopping bags filled with trinkets and brochures. Seoul also gave away, quietly, two first-class roundtrip tickets to each IOC member. The tickets were easily redeemed for cash; many were.

Shortly before the vote for the 1988 Olympic site, citizens of Nagoya who didn't want to host the Games for fear they would destroy their beautiful city, staged a well-orchestrated anti-Olympic demonstration outside the hotel where the IOC was meeting. Following that demonstration, Masaji Kiokawa, Japan's IOC member and an IOC Executive Board member, criticized Seoul in a vitriolic outburst that alienated many IOC members from the Arab-Asian bloc.

The demonstration, Kiokawa's bad manners, and the newfound strength of the Arab-Asian bloc all seemed to contribute to the IOC's reversing its field and awarding the Games to Seoul. But the free tickets had already turned the trick.

POSSE COMITATUS

TWENTY YEARS OF business experience had given me some idea of how to finance, staff, and manage the Games. But nothing in my background prepared me for assuring the security and physical welfare of twenty thousand athletes and indirectly being accountable for the safety of hundreds of thousands of visitors.

Moscow's example of mobilizing the military was of no use to us. The security plans of Montreal, Munich, or any other Games didn't help either. There were no primers telling us how to do it. We had to start from scratch and go on instinct.

The bottom line was that security could not be guaranteed—no matter what we did. Munich had taught us that.

Terrorism at the 1972 Olympic Games destroyed five years of hard work and damaged the reputation of a nation. It could happen again, at any time, from any direction, in support of any cause.

The Federal Republic of Germany had promoted the 1972 Olympics as the "friendly Games." They had hoped to bury their World War II image through efficiency, hospitality, and great competition. The Olympics were a wonderful opportunity for West Germany to come full circle in terms of

national public relations and demonstrate how it had recovered both physically and emotionally and was a developing
industrial nation to be reckoned with.

For ten days Munich bathed in Olympic glory. Peace
ended on the eleventh day. Eight Palestinian terrorists invaded the Olympic Village, murdered two Israeli athletes,
and took nine more hostage. The Olympics came to a standstill. The terrorists demanded the release of two hundred Is-
raeli-held prisoners and safe passage for themselves out of the
country. After twenty hours of negotiation, German authorities transported the terrorists and hostages to the airport.
There, German sharpshooters attempted to pick off the terrorists as they boarded the aircraft. In the ensuing battle, five
terrorists and all nine Israelis were killed.

Munich's meticulous security planning had been laid to
waste. So had the new image it wanted to bring its country. It
also changed the face of the Olympic Movement forever.

Images of Munich and Howard Cosell's riveting commentary came back to me in October 1981 as I prepared for a
meeting of representatives from the federal, state, and local
agencies involved with securing the Games.

Until then local law enforcement had been critical of the
LAOOC for dragging its feet. The Los Angeles Police Department, Los Angeles Sheriff's Department, and the FBI's
Los Angeles office had formed its own Olympic security committee shortly after Los Angeles was awarded the Games and
they were anxious for our input. They were also eager for us
to begin funding their trips and planning. As soon as Los Angeles was awarded the Games in 1979, they began making
frequent fact-finding missions to various international sporting
events to investigate security arrangements. With this information, they began building the foundation of a security plan
that, in part, was subsequently adapted for the Games.

Money was going to be a problem. There had already
been one episode where the Los Angeles Sheriff's Department had included expense items in its Olympic budget,
knowing the LAOOC was obligated to pay for all Olympic-
related services. I contacted Sheriff Peter Pitchess, who held
the office at the time, and his under-sheriff, Sherman Block,

when this came to my attention. I explained we weren't prepared to start the meter running. They were understanding
and deleted the charges.

From the beginning, I had no shortage of advice from
lawmen. Virtually all of them told me to stall.

Once again I had the perfect man for the job: Dick
Sargent. Nobody is more clever at a holding action than Dick.
His wonderfully engaging personality allows him to get along
with people from all walks of life, and he has a great ability to
absorb information without appearing to do so. Besides, he
was the only one on the early staff who had law enforcement
experience, even if admittedly limited experience. He'd
served on the Catalina Island police force one summer during
college and had been a supply sergeant in the army.

The importance of security really hit home in August
1981. Among the many pieces of junk and hate mail I had
begun receiving was correspondence from a man who at first
offered general advice about the Games; later he made long,
rambling demands for employment and ultimately made
threats of extortion. I arrived early one morning at the UCLA
extension building (where we had just moved from Century
City) to discover that on a routine search UCLA police had
found my pen pal on the floor immediately above my office.
He'd spent the night there, waiting for me.

The officers held him for questioning and psychiatric
evaluation before releasing him; they had no grounds to hold
him. This convinced me that an ounce of prevention was
worth a pound of cure. This was a new and painful experience
for me. The poisoning of our dogs, threatening phone calls
and letters were things I hadn't expected.

It was one thing to explain long hours and time away
from home to Ginny and the kids and another that we'd become targets for unstable people and possibly of organized
terrorist attacks.

That evening I told Ginny we should go ahead and arrange for personal security, a subject we had discussed before
but rejected as an invasion of privacy.

"I never thought we'd be a target," I told Ginny.

She steeled herself for another massive change in our
lives. "Given the alternative," she said, "we have no choice."

Shortly thereafter I hired Wayne Ichiyasu, an officer with the UCLA police department, as my driver and bodyguard. He and his wife, Kathy, moved into the guest house on our property in Encino, where he had an elaborate security system installed. We were covered twenty-four-hours a day.

For two years, beginning in the spring of 1979, Sargent had met regularly with law enforcement representatives. He had monitored their planning, answered questions, and promised them the LAOOC would play a leadership role as soon as it was ready. Otherwise, he promised them nothing. Sargent discovered trouble—interagency bickering and petty territorial jealousies over jurisdictions.

There is no such thing as a national police force in the United States. The Constitution makes a clear distinction between the military and law enforcement with the concept of *posse comitatus,* which specifies that military organizations in the United States are prohibited from acting in law enforcement roles. The result is a complicated system of jurisdictional authority with extensive overlaps among federal, state, and local law enforcement agencies. It begs the question, who's in charge here?

Transporting the athletes from the Olympic villages to training and competition sites throughout southern California was an example of this confusion. Since athletes would be transported through more than forty separate law enforcement jurisdictions during the Games, we needed a system that would work and lessen the prospects of disaster.

I could envision a busload of Turkish athletes—one of the most endangered Olympic delegations—being passed from one police department to another as it traveled thirty-three miles from the village at the University of California, Los Angeles, in Westwood to the Anaheim Convention Center for Olympic wrestling.

Practically speaking, the state police, responsible for the UCLA campus, would begin protecting the Turkish athletes on their journey—but only to the edge of the campus. From there the LAPD would assume responsibility—but only to the San Diego Freeway, a mile away. The California Highway Patrol would take over at the freeway entrance ramp and provide protection along the freeway system. Entrusted with the security of the team, the CHP would have helicopter support provided by either the LAPD or the Los Angeles Sheriff's Department in conjunction with the Federal Aviation Administration. On a good day, the CHP would cover the bus on the entire freeway route and turn over the responsibility to the Anaheim Police Department when the bus rolled off the freeway system. A sudden route change, however, could involve an additional nine local law enforcement agencies.

To make matters more confusing, the agencies were on different wavelengths, literally and figuratively. They needed a compatible communications system just to talk to one another. There was no single person I could go to and ask, "How do I do this?"

Law enforcement needed to be pulled together. There was a lack of unity that had begun to sow seeds of fear within the community and raise questions from overseas about our ability to stage and protect the Games. That's when I decided to call a meeting. When in doubt, I opt for action. Sherry Cockle sent invitations to everybody involved with securing the Games. The conference—which I approached as a board meeting—was set for 10 A.M., October 26, 1981, in the board room of the Sheraton La Reina Hotel near the airport.

The day before, Sargent and David Simon, our government liaisons, briefed the federal contingent as it flew to Los Angeles on board an air force plane. The Reagan administration justified picking up Sargent's and Simon's airfare because they were part of the planeload, but two months later billed each $4.30 for breakfast. The receipts made good souvenirs.

Group dynamics play a vital role in every business meeting. With that in mind, careful attention was paid to seating arrangements to minimize the effect of preexisting animosities. We separated two groups: the FBI and the LAPD.

We had a full house, and all but two law enforcement agencies sent their directors. Those two were represented by their number-two men. There was also a large congregation of reporters, who had learned about the meeting from a local law enforcement leak. It always amazed me how a mere whisper of the word "security" brought reporters out in droves when only a few would come out for our other announcements.

The board room was located on the mezzanine level of the Sheraton. We served coffee and pastries in an anteroom. The meeting room itself had a huge rectangular conference table that comfortably sat all thirty agency chiefs and provided enough space to seat their second and third in commands behind them.

I opened the conference by asking everyone to introduce himself and the agency he represented. Then I took the floor.

"We are undertaking the most visible law enforcement effort in peacetime in our country's history," I told them. "We will only achieve success in this endeavor if we are able to coordinate our planning, communicate continuously and, most important, put jurisdictional differences aside."

I noticed this made a few law enforcement officers uncomfortable. I continued to hit home with the uniqueness of this challenge, how the eyes of the world would be upon us, and how the reputation of our nation would be at stake and to a large degree in the hands of those seated around the table. I didn't want to beat anybody over the head or be overly dramatic, but I had to let them know how important it was to make the Olympic Games secure.

Usher then described the nuts-and-bolts planning process and updated them on the LAOOC's progress on locating venues. When Usher mentioned we would have more than sixty training sites in addition to those for competition, I could hear the cash registers ring like church bells on a Sunday morning. More sites, more protection, more money. It was as simple as that.

To reinforce the magnitude of the Games, we showed a twelve-minute multimedia slide presentation that described the LAOOC's approach to staging the Olympics. We also distributed pamphlets and other written materials, the same ones given to the Olympic family in Baden-Baden. We wanted everyone to operate from the same information base.

At an informal lunch between sessions, the reticence of a few law enforcement chiefs surprised me. I knew the chiefs were turf conscious, but I didn't know that some of them had spent their careers purposely avoiding one another. So I made it a point to greet everyone in the room and even introduced some chiefs to others. This reinforced my belief that the organizing committee would have to be the umbrella for Olympic security.

I laid down a few ground rules in the afternoon. "We're not a bottomless pit for funding," I said. "Under no circumstances will we finance your own learning curves." This went down like the *Hindenburg*. The law enforcement people had visions of riding the Olympic gravy train just like the Coliseum commission. These agencies would bankrupt the Games if allowed to apply their own creative accounting principles. They'd charge us for every meeting, visit, discussion, and breath of fresh air they took on an hourly basis, not to mention runaway charges for exotic security equipment.

I also told them we weren't going to pay for so-called Olympic items needed for their overall law enforcement responsibilities. One of the more outrageous requests had come from the Immigration and Naturalization Service. For years, INS had unsuccessfully lobbied Congress for a new multi-million-dollar inspection station along the Mexican border near San Diego. When the Olympic Games came along, INS tried to pull a fast one. It gave the station an Olympic label and tried to push it through and have it billed as an Olympic expense. Its rationale was that hundreds of thousands of Mexican citizens would attend the Games and enter the country through this station. I told INS that visitors wouldn't be coming by the busload, as Mexico's ticket allotment wouldn't exceed seven thousand, and most purchasers would arrange package deals with airlines and hotels. INS got its station at Otai Mesa, but I was told, only because it was needed and not because of the Olympic Games.

We discussed various ways a planning group could function and ultimately decided on a five-member steering committee to be accountable for securing the Games and for informing the public. In this role, the five members were the only authorized spokespersons for Olympic security. As it evolved the body became known as the Olympic Law Enforcement Coordinating Committee (OLECC). The original

members, besides myself, were LAPD Chief Daryl Gates,
L.A. County Sheriff Pete Pitchess, White House security representative Ed Hickey, and Long Beach Police Chief Charles
Ussery, who represented the independent cities. Later Sherman Block replaced Pitchess and the group expanded to include the FBI's special agent in charge of its L.A. office and a
member of California's Department of General Services.

By appointing spokesmen who represented the federal,
state, and local viewpoints, we hoped to prevent self-styled
security experts from gumming up the works and whipping up
fear among the people of southern California.

One person who impressed me when I opened the discussion to questions and answers was Ed Best, the FBI's special
agent in charge in Los Angeles. He was knowledgeable, ana-
lytical, straightforward, and honest. I knew he wasn't the
most popular person in the room. Some local lawmen, including Gates, mistakenly believed that Best had investigated the
Philadelphia Police Department during a previous assignment
and resented him for it. Actually, police corruption had been
the purview of the Department of Justice and Best had had
nothing to do with it. His reputation at the bureau was superb. He had led investigations into political corruption and
had earned national recognition for his role in the ABSCAM
investigations.

"I think it's important for Hickey to represent the federal
interests from Washington," Best said. "By the same token, it
is equally necessary to have a Los Angeles-based federal
spokesperson because most of the inquiries and most of the
groundwork will come from here."

Best stood out and he became my choice to head security
for the Games. Sargent, who had met with him many times,
gave him high marks. I had met with him twice in the two
weeks before the security meeting. Both were casual meetings. I didn't know it, but Best had already decided to take
early retirement from the FBI and had been investigating private-sector opportunities. He'd decided to leave the FBI at
age fifty, feeling he'd be more marketable then than at fifty-
five, the FBI's mandatory retirement age.

A month after the big security conference, Sargent called together all the agency workhorses, who created the Security Planning Committee to handle daily planning. The SPC, which answered to OLECC, eventually formed eighteen subcommittees to cover all facets of Games security. The subcommittee names illustrate the depth of planning: accreditation, air support, bombs, communications, community relations, crime prevention, criminal justice system, dignitary protection, emergency response, intelligence, international entry, in-transit security, Olympic Village security, rumor center, traffic control, training, transportation, venue/vital point security.

I hoped that the OLECC members would be the clearinghouse for the media's security questions and, through their expertise, knowledge, reasonableness, and leadership, would build a foundation of confidence that discredited the crackpots. I didn't expect one of the more harmful and misleading security stories to emanate from one of our own.

On the way to Rancho Park in West Los Angeles the morning of January 22, 1982, an Olympic report on the car radio caught my attention. Wayne Ichiyasu turned up the sound. It was something about a Soviet plan to disrupt the '84 Games, but the information was sketchy.

At Rancho Park, where we'd arranged an archery exhibition for the press announcement naming the arrow manufacturer Easton Aluminum as an official licensee of the Games, Amy Quinn, our press secretary, met me in the parking lot and told me that a purported Soviet plot to use Soviet Jewish émigrés to disrupt the Games had been included in a forty-two-page LAPD pamphlet on its Olympic planning. L.A. Police Chief Gates had distributed the brochure to a group of newspaper editors and writers the day before. One reporter combed the report and uncovered a section entitled "Soviet Émigré Mafia." This six-paragraph section as reprinted in the *Los Angeles Times* read:

Under the current immigration quota system, Jewish Soviet citizens are being permitted to enter the

United States under a quota allowance recently increased to 50,000 per year. Investigations have disclosed some of these refugees who are not Jewish and were in fact criminals in the Soviet Union . . .

LAPD detectives have identified approximately 20 Soviet émigrés currently in the Los Angeles area who are involved in criminal activity. This activity includes the crimes of murder, theft, fraud, forgery, counterfeiting, extortion, receiving stolen property and various vice activities.

It is readily foreseeable that the crime problem involving Soviets will increase in size and severity as the Soviet emigrant population increases. Additionally, the Soviets apparently believe that the 1984 Olympic Games offer an opportunity to embarrass the United States. The Soviet news agency Tass has already characterized Los Angeles as crime-ridden and smog-beset and has hinted some disaster might befall the Games. It is easy to see how the Soviets might try to make their prediction a reality by planning criminal or terrorist activity that would affect persons involved with the Games.

Predictably, intelligence resources could have considerable impact upon the success of law enforcement's efforts during the Olympic Games. Currently, very limited resources are available to deal with the Soviet émigré threat . . .

The press was out in force. Our small archery exhibition set the stage for the Gates story, which made the national news.

Those few paragraphs turned into three days' worth of news. The next day Gates explained the report was not intended to denigrate members of the Jewish community. He was quoted as saying, "We talked about some posing as Jews." The police commission in turn reprimanded Gates, and the Jewish community called a news conference demanding he prove the allegations or apologize.

I was not amused; neither were the Soviets. I tried to stay

out of it, knowing the Soviets would have a propaganda field day. Any involvement by the organizing committee would only make it worse. As I had previously experienced on the federal-funding issue, public perception once formed never changes. From that moment on, Gates's comments about Soviets planting Jewish émigrés in the United States to disrupt the Games would come back to haunt us.

This wasn't Gates's first ethnic gaffe. His most notorious slip occurred after a black suspect died from a choke hold applied by an LAPD officer. Gates explained during the course of the ensuing investigation that the choke hold was a routine method of police restraint. He didn't leave it at that, but maintained that blacks were more susceptible to injury than whites because of physiological differences.

I hoped that the émigré episode would heighten his sensitivity. It also proved to me it was critical to bring on a strong security director right away.

In the meantime, arrangements had been made for Samaranch and me to confer with President Reagan at the White House on January 28, 1982. Samaranch had pushed for the meeting, seeking assurances from Reagan that the U.S. government would stand by the Olympic Games and the Olympic Charter. Samaranch had been pleased by the October OLECC discussions and felt a Reagan endorsement would soothe the international skepticism surrounding the Games— specifically the issue of security.

The meeting was quick and successful. We left with a letter from Reagan giving the assurances that Samaranch had sought. It was a stronger version of the letter Jimmy Carter had signed when L.A. got the Games. More important, it meant support for the Games had passed from one administration to the next.

Back in Los Angeles, I met with Best again. Before zeroing in on him, I had considered bringing in a big name security type to boost the credibility of the LAOOC. So of those I looked at were Clarence Kelley, former FBI director, retired Air Force General Curtis LeMay, and LAPD Deputy

Police Chief Marvin Iannone. All were good men, but my instincts told me they'd be wrong for the job.

Although Best and I beat around the bush over coffee and eggs, we both knew why we were there. He casually mentioned a very lucrative job offer he'd received from VISA, International, to see if I would walk across the line and better the offer. Knowing that game well, I left it alone.

Within a week, I put Best together with Usher. I interrupted their meeting at one point and instructed Usher to make Best an offer.

"Before you do that," Best said, "I have a question to ask you, Peter. If I take this job, I'm going to be between a rock and a hard place. When all hell breaks loose, I'll have to be in the trenches. Where will you be?"

"Right next to you," I said.

Usher jotted down an offer and handed the slip of paper to Best. He glanced at it and said he'd get back to us. I didn't find out until later that he'd gulped with pleasure when he saw the size of the salary.

Best was in a quandary and I sympathized with him. He wanted to retire from the FBI, make good money, and stay in southern California. Leaving the FBI was not going to be easy. There were three assistant directorships in the bureau, and FBI Director Webster had just offered him the assistant directorship of investigations. Short of being director, it was the best job in the agency and difficult for a career man like Best to turn down.

The Olympic job, on the other hand, was one of the greatest security challenges of the century. Everybody recognized that. However, its prestige would last for only the first twenty-four hours. After that it was a no-win situation. The job held no real authority, meaning the director didn't have the power to muster troops and enforce the law, and it was fraught with political overtones. If something went wrong, after me the director would bear the most blame.

Best bought the once-in-a-lifetime opportunity angle and took the job on April 30, 1982, after clearing the announcement with Webster. We held a press conference and Best was sensational, with one exception.

Afterward, I pulled Best aside. "Ed, you did great but, please, in the future don't refer to the Eastern bloc nations as hostile."

Best hit the ground running. The visibility he brought to the committee immediately generated contacts from members of the worldwide intelligence community—some retired, some still on the streets—who didn't waste any time contacting Best with all sorts of information.

He came into my office a week later carrying a dossier on the Federation for Progress and its membership. As he began reciting the group's history incident by incident I stopped him.

"Stay here," I said. I left to grab Dan Greenwood, our vice-president of corporate relations, and brought him back to the office.

"Dan, are you familiar with this group?" I asked.

He confirmed it was one of several hundred enterprises applying for a piece of the poster action.

"Don't lead them on," I told Dan. "Get a letter out today. Tell them no. Make sure they know there is no hope."

Turning to Best, I said, "Ed, I don't need the history. If you recommend it, that's good enough for me."

I had Best put out word to the staff to be wary of every person and group associated with the federation. The Games were a natural target for the group. At one point, it gained a lot of publicity by airing plans for a massive antinuclear demonstration near the Coliseum the day before opening ceremonies. That one fell through, but demonstrations were always a major concern. Regardless of an IOC Charter regulation expressly forbidding any political demonstrations at Olympic sites, our Constitution guarantees freedom of assembly and we had to abide by it. It was tricky. Law enforcement officers worked closely with different organizations to protect their rights to demonstrate while simultaneously arranging to keep potential protestors off Olympic turf and out of sight of the athletes.

Upon taking office, Best created a security plan that never significantly changed. He divided the Games into three geographical regions and hired three top-level former law enforcement officers to run each. Duane Baker, former police chief of Glendale, California, ran the northern venues; Lou Sporrer, former LAPD assistant chief who barely lost out to Gates as chief, manned the central venues; and former FBI special agent Peter Norregard had the south. Best then devised a comprehensive system of private security, planned for the secure housing and transport of athletes and the Olympic family, and coordinated the activities with each LAOOC department. He established LAOOC authority and served as the committee contact for law enforcement worldwide.

By the fall of 1982, it was time to figure out how to reimburse government bodies for services rendered. This boiled down to making payments on staffing levels, equipment, and expenses. Paying for manpower was particularly unique in that law enforcement in this country is guaranteed by law and not for sale. But somehow we had to set price tags.

Our policy was clear: We would pay only for what was necessary. Law enforcement, however, had its own ideas and had compiled wish lists of sophisticated equipment a mile long—at our expense. Usher and Best rolled up their sleeves. They weren't about to turn Los Angeles into an armed camp. Jurisdiction by jurisdiction, they concluded agreements for security staffing levels.

The toughest deal was with Los Angeles. Usher negotiated with Ira Reiner, who had led the no Olympic tax campaign, LAPD Commander Bill Rathburn, Gates's Olympic liaison, and other city department officials. Reiner had recently been elected city attorney. Rathburn was one of the unsung heroes of the Games. Brutally honest, he kept the negotiations moving and did a helluva job for the city and the LAPD. The negotiators hammered out a contract on October 28, 1982, that protected the City of Los Angeles against any financial liabilities, and Rathburn made sure the LAPD had final authority over staffing levels at the villages and venues in its jurisdiction, a loophole that wouldn't be closed until right before the Games.

The City of Los Angeles had been collecting a one half of 1 percent hotel tax on visitors ever since L.A. was awarded the Games. Those dollars, and those the city would collect from a tax on our tickets, went into the city's Olympic trust fund to be used for Olympic-related expenses, including security. The agreement provided that the city would be paid $19.3 million through the trust fund, $15 million of which was budgeted for the LAPD. If the trust ran dry, we had to make up the difference. We also agreed to provide the LAPD a $2.75 million contingency fund in case of a catastrophe. As in all our other government contracts, we established that our security responsibility was to secure the venues, the villages, and the transit system used to transport athletes and members of the Olympic family.

All through the pre-Games period, curious and in some cases worried national Olympic committees sent delegations to Los Angeles to inspect our arrangements. Most left satisfied. The great majority of delegations had nothing to fear. The Israelis and Turks did, however. Both were targets: The Israelis just for being Israelis, and the Turks because of the large Armenian population in Los Angeles. In January 1982, while on his way to work, the Turkish consul general had been assassinated in his car on Wilshire Boulevard near UCLA, only a few blocks from the LAOOC offices, by Armenian terrorists. Being so close, it brought the message of terrorism home. That incident heightened our concerns about Turkey. Both Israel and Turkey wanted to bring in their own security guards to protect their athletes. We consented, provided they not carry firearms in the villages.

We recognized the importance of intelligence early on and by late 1982 the international intelligence community had begun targeting its networks to potential Olympic threats for analysis and follow-up. In 1981, while still with the FBI, Best attended an international symposium on terrorism at the FBI's training center in Quantico, Virginia, and spoke about the Games. He stressed the need for intelligence and an active role needed by the Central Intelligence Agency. Afterward, in a conversation with a CIA participant, he recommended that the agency make it standard operating procedure to ask one last question in its source debriefings: "Have you uncovered any threats to the 1984 Olympics?"

Information derived from the Olympic intelligence network was shared by all agencies involved and up-to-date, country-by-country threat analyses were harvested on a regular basis. One security survey we received identified fifteen terrorist and violence-prone groups active in the United States. It was a *Who's Who* of nefarious groups and included such organizations as the United Freedom Front, the Revolutionary Fighting Group, Armed Resistance Movement, *Frente Farabundo Marti Para la Liberación Nacional* (FMLN), Young People's Republic, Women Against Imperialism, November 29 Coalition, May 19 Communist Organization, Sam Melville–Jonathan Jackson Brigade, the Jewish Defense League, Black Liberation Army, FALN, various anti-Castro exile groups, and Armenian terrorists.

Newspapers were filled with reports about executive kidnappings and I was grateful for Ichiyasu's presence and attention to the welfare of my family. Through his efforts the FBI and local law enforcement knew the school schedules of each of the children. At this time, all were home and attending local schools except for our oldest, Vicki, who'd just begun her freshman year at the University of Colorado in Boulder.

Ginny and I made a conscious effort to understate the dangers. Although the children were unnerved when the Ichiyasus first moved into our guest house, they quickly adjusted and accepted them as part of the family. Still, Vicki was alarmed when two FBI agents dropped by her sorority house one afternoon to get information on her class schedule. She called in a panic.

"Why are they doing this?" she asked. "Are you in some kind of danger?"

"It's part of the security planning for the Games," I told her. "Everything is fine. Take it in stride."

It was tougher on Heidi, Keri, and Joe. One night while Ginny and I were attending an Olympic dinner, Heidi accidentally tripped the new alarm system. Bells went off all over the house and within minutes uniformed LAPD officers were there in force. The kids were frightened out of their wits and told us about it when we got home.

At the Bel Air Country Club a few weeks later, an intruder came looking for me during a UCLA reception. He told the golf pro's wife he had a meeting with me and asked where I could be found. He was wearing a sweat suit and must have looked out of place. She asked him to stay where he was and searched for me. Meanwhile, he got scared and bolted.

That wasn't the end of him, however. A few days later, he came looking for me in the locker room. Club security was tighter this time because the LAPD had distributed a description of the intruder it had gotten by hypnotizing the golf pro's wife and a club parking attendant. He was arrested for trespassing and later released.

There were hundreds of rumors affecting the security of the Games. Each was investigated but none amounted to an ongoing conspiracy. Two, however, were considered serious enough to raise our blood pressure at the LAOOC. A known Libyan terrorist, supposedly part of a well-trained hit squad, allegedly was en route to the Games when he was identified and detained at the Montreal airport. The second was a rumor that terrorists trained in Mexico were headed in our direction. That washed out.

One other group that threatened the Olympics politically was the USSR. Along with the East Germans, the Soviets were the most meticulous of all Olympic planners. They always arrived with suitcases filled with notebooks and checklists, and with their antennas tuned to propaganda hooks.

A seven-person delegation visited in mid-December 1982, led by former wrestler and Olympian Anatoli Kolesov.

The Russians were a big draw. Every photographer wanted to see, touch, and photograph a Soviet. Every reporter wanted one alone for a few minutes to record the latest diatribe against the Games. They made great copy.

Their first request was one we had heard many times before and would hear many times more over the years. They wanted to visit Disneyland. That was easy to arrange.

When they got down to business, they split into two groups: one to cover the venues and villages and the other to meet with staff for updates on internal planning.

Kolesov and his interpreter met Best in his office. During his briefing, Best noticed that Kolesov had discreetly placed a tape recorder on his desk and it was rolling.

"Mr. Kolesov," Best said, "I don't want to offend you, but I can't allow you to tape this conversation." Always careful, Best had no intention of divulging classified information, but he wasn't about to allow Kolesov such a blatant victory in their sub rosa game of one-upmanship.

Kolesov asked, "Why not?"

Best laughed and said, "It's not appropriate and it's an obstacle to frank discussions."

Kolesov, feigning insult, refused. Best grabbed the recorder, ejected the tape, and returned the empty recorder to Kolesov over his protests. Best then summoned one of his aides and instructed him to erase the tape. Best later told me that it flashed on him he was creating an international incident.

Best said Kolesov complained bitterly for a few minutes before settling down and resuming what turned out to be a good talk.

Kolesov called Best later that day to thank him for having the tape returned. "I have good news and bad news," Kolesov said.

Best was amused at his use of this American colloquialism. "Yes, what might that be?" he replied.

"The good news is your man erased the tape; the bad news is he only erased half of it."

On the local front, the Security Planning Committee, knowing we weren't going to beef up local armories, went directly to the federal government and requested $50 million worth of logistical support equipment. Its inventory included sophisticated communications equipment, up to one hundred helicopters, an Intrusion Detection System for the athlete villages, medical equipment, and construction of a state-of-the-art Olympic security coordinating center. The government consented, based on assurances President Reagan had made earlier in the year to me and Samaranch. The $50 million budget allocation—in various departments but mostly from defense—raised the issue of taxpayer funding once again when the 1984 budget came up for review by the Office of Management and Budget and Congress in March 1983.

While I knew law enforcement needed the equipment and would put it to good use, I had to remain consistent with our pledge to the people of Los Angeles. I issued a very strong statement to the press reiterating the LAOOC policy: "Any government services we request, we will pay for, but we will not pay for any services we do not order." I went on to point out that we couldn't be held accountable for "either continuing services that government agencies perform or are obliged to perform by legislative and constitutional mandate—services and activities for which the organizing committee has no legal jurisdiction, powers, or business conducting."

I decided it was high time to discuss the other side of the balance sheet. We figured the Olympic Games would generate $231 million in federal taxes, $179 million in state and local government revenues, and would create at least sixty-eight thousand job opportunities in southern California. The Games would also leave behind a new world-class swim stadium at the University of Southern California; a new world-class velodrome at California State College, Dominguez Hills; a new administration building at University of California, Los Angeles; nine new world-class training tracks throughout southern California; $1 million worth of improvements to Exposition Park next to the Coliseum, and $10 million in improvements to the Coliseum; a new track and infield at East Los Angeles College; new roads in Ventura County; and new boat-launching ramps and cranes in Long Beach. Journalists rarely reported those things to the public.

To protect the government's investment and allay worries in Washington, Michael Deaver hired retired Army Colonel Charles Beckwith to browse around Los Angeles and check out Olympic security that spring. White House officials had been involved in the broad strokes until then but not the details. They didn't have a comfortable feel for what we were doing and had to cover themselves in the event of a disaster, particularly with a presidential election following on the heels of the Games.

Beckwith was best known for leading the aborted helicopter mission to free the American hostages held in Iran in 1980. I only met him for a few minutes in Best's office. He was quite a character. He was sprawled in a chair, glasses on top of his head. He didn't get up when I walked in and didn't waste any words.

"Mr. Uederrof," he said (I decided not to correct him), "I can tell you're my kind of guy. Are you serious about Olympic security?"

"It's my greatest concern, Colonel," I assured him, "and our largest budget item. We'll do whatever it takes, regardless of cost."

Beckwith met with all the security planners, toured the venues and villages, and inspected law enforcement command centers and facilities. He had seventy-five questions to which he must have received satisfactory responses. He returned to Texas and filed an extensive report to the White House, giving the organizing committee and all Olympic security components high marks. He noted we had strong leadership at all levels. His major concerns were the difficult process of coordinating the FBI and LAPD and the continued smooth flow of intelligence data.

Beckwith's report calmed the nerves of Deaver and other high-level officials. For the final and most important phase, the White House replaced Hickey with Kenneth Hill whom it brought back from a State Department assignment in West Germany to work on the Games and become the federal resources coordinator. The White House felt Hill's security background would be helpful down the stretch.

Right after Beckwith's visit, *Playboy* ran an irresponsible story that could have seriously damaged the Games. Our press policy when it came to security was the less said the better. To outline security planning would've been counterproductive. At the same time, we understood the public's right to know that planning was under way, and we knew that reporters would attempt to uncover as much detail as they could, which was fine.

Playboy, however, went beyond the pale. The writer enlisted the aid of John Miller, a mercenary who, according to

Playboy, had just returned from a job in Angola. Miller took a tour of the venues and described how to terrorize the Games.

At Loyola Marymount University, the site of Olympic weightlifting, Miller told the author, "'Weightlifting is one of their [the Israelis] sports. It could happen here. A cell could take over or rent one of the little private houses on the road in here and use a couple of hand-launched wire-guided missiles. The bus comes by and—zap!—easy escape. L.A. has a lot of roads.'"

Of the Coliseum he said, "'There are 90 ways in here. It'll take an army to vet the spectators. At the Opening Ceremonies, they'll have heads of state, the business and industry sponsors . . .'" When the writer mentioned that it was an election year and that candidates might attend, Miller added, "'and President Reagan. They might try a Sadat-type suicide run, say from the marching athletes . . .'"

Miller even went so far as to suggest ways L.A.'s water supply could be poisoned. This was potent stuff in the hands of crazies. I didn't understand how such a widely read magazine could be so cavalier in its disregard for human life.

Best, meanwhile, continued to monitor the Federation for Progress. Shortly after Olympic tickets went on sale in June 1983, he learned that an alleged member of the Communist Workers' Party had infiltrated the LAOOC's ticket-data center where all the order forms were processed.

The Communist Workers' Party, a part of the Federation for Progress, was a Maoist-oriented group regularly monitored by the FBI. It first came to the FBI's attention on November 3, 1979, when five of its members were killed in a shoot-out with the Ku Klux Klan and the American Nazi Party at a "Death to the Klan" rally in Greensboro, North Carolina. The CWP martyred the five dead, referred to them as the "Greensboro CWP 5," and used the incident as a springboard for future acts of violence.

I was alarmed when Best informed me of the suspected infiltration. If some maladjusted individual wanted to wreak havoc on the Olympic Games, penetrating our ticket system was a good way to do it.

We had secured the data center in a nondescript building in downtown Los Angeles. We had cameras and alarm systems, and an overlay of twenty-four-hour private security. We had the finest computer security system possible and a back-up mainframe at another secured location. Yet we were still vulnerable to being penetrated from the inside by an expert.

The ticket software system was complex in its own right—and rearranging it would undoubtedly result in riots at the venues during the Games. Also, the ticket information on orders was a white-collar-criminal's dream. The computer file contained 330,000 names, addresses, day and night telephone numbers, social security numbers, mothers' maiden names, and credit card or bank account numbers. It was the Yellow Pages of Olympic ticketing and available to anyone with access and the knowledge to use it.

Our main concern in ticketing security until then had been counterfeiting. Ed Smith, vice-president of ticketing, had nightmares that opening ceremonies tickets would be duplicated and two hundred thousand people—twice the amount the Coliseum could accommodate—would show up at the event.

Only Usher, Smith, Best, and I at the LAOOC knew of the suspected infiltration at the data center. We agreed that our internal security staff could take the case no farther and decided to refer it to the FBI. The FBI investigation took two months and confirmed the suspect's membership in the Communist Workers' Party. In a related matter, the FBI discovered that the CWP had taken credit for planting a person in Los Angeles to disrupt the Games. But the investigation found no conclusive evidence that our man was the plant. When questioned by agents he vehemently denied having any involvement in a CWP plot. He was relocated.

With a year to go, Best focused on the LAOOC's critical contribution to securing the Games—forming a force of twelve thousand private security guards. They would be an army without weapons, or as Best called them, the "eyes and ears of law enforcement."

Private security was tricky. It hadn't worked at Lake Placid in 1980. Shortly before those Winter Games, the organizers had demanded that Pinkerton hire local managers instead of using its own well-trained personnel. Given little time to train the locals, Pinkerton had problems. When I was there I often noticed clusters of private guards sitting around arguing over who would take the first break. It didn't inspire confidence and it made me question Best's heavy reliance on private security. At Montreal, the largest user of private security, there were twenty-five hundred private guards. We both knew it would be difficult but he convinced me it was the only way to go.

His theme was to build security around the Games and not the Games around security. He was adamant and often said, "This is an athletic event, not an international security event."

Rafer Johnson (left) and New York Mayor Ed Koch look on as I hand the torch to Gina Hemphill to start the eighty-two-day Olympic torch relay on a rainy Tuesday morning in New York City, May 8, 1984. LAOOC PHOTO BY PAUL SLAUGHTER

My father, Victor Ueberroth. *Center,* the Ueberroths (from left): my father; my sister, Jill; me; and my mother, Laura. *Bottom,* Shortly after this was taken—that's me, seated, far right—I was dropped from the Cub Scouts for failing to wear my scarf. ALL COURTESY OF THE AUTHOR

Right, Ginny and me at a college fraternity party in the spring of 1959. *Below,* our wedding picture: Ginny's parents, Mr. and Mrs. Nick Nicolaus on the left; and my parents, Mr. and Mrs. Victor Ueberroth, on the right. ALL COURTESY OF THE AUTHOR

My sister, Jill, and me on the beach at Laguna Beach, California. COURTESY OF THE AUTHOR

Ginny and me outside our Encino home with our dogs that were poisoned following an anti-Olympics neighborhood rally. COURTESY OF THE AUTHOR

The Ueberroth brothers. COURTESY OF THE AUTHOR

LAOOC Chairman Paul Ziffren and I share a happy moment while signing the city agreement for the reimbursement of the city's expenses. COURTESY OF THE AUTHOR

Los Angeles Mayor Tom Bradley and I get together at an LAOOC social function in 1981. PHOTO BY BARRY LEVINE

LAOOC Equestrian Commissioner Michael Morphy shares a light moment with His Royal Highness Prince Philip. COURTESY OF MICHAEL MORPHY

One of my top Olympic aides, Joel Rubenstein.

At the IOC/NOC meetings in Los Angeles in January 1983, I conferred daily with (from left) LAOOC Executive Vice-president/General Manager Harry L. Usher, IOC Director Monique Berlioux, and IOC President Juan Antonio Samaranch.

Making my remarks on the field of the Los Angeles Memorial Coliseum during the opening ceremonies. COURTESY OF THE LAOOC

Ginny and I meet Pope John II at the Vatican in Rome. COURTESY OF THE
AUTHOR

Demonstrators make a statement outside LAOOC headquarters in Culver City.
COURTESY OF THE LAOOC

IOC Director Monique Berlioux joins me in my office during the early planning stages. LESTER SLOAN

Berlioux and me at a press conference. COURTESY OF THE LAOOC

LAOOC Vice-president Mike O'Hara (third from right) and I (far right) meet with then USSR NOC President Sergei Pavlov (far left) in Moscow in 1982. The other USSR officials are (from left, next to Pavlov) Alexander Cereda, Viktor Khotochkin, two interpreters, and S. Belianov. COURTESY OF THE AUTHOR

During a tour of Disneyland in December 1983, Anatoli Kolesov (right), a member of the USSR NOC delegation, greets Mickey Mouse. COURTESY OF JOEL RUBENSTEIN

USSR NOC President Marat Gramov, who blamed security concerns for the Soviet boycott of the Games, doesn't look too worried as he wraps his arms around Disneyland characters Captain Cook and Peter Pan. COURTESY OF JOEL RUBENSTEIN *Below,* Marat Gramov and I review USSR NOC-LAOOC protocol agreement signed in December 1983. COURTESY OF THE LAOOC

On a visit to East Germany, I signed a protocol agreement with Manfred Ewald (seated, right), the president of the German Democratic Republic NOC. Standing with East German officials are LAOOC Vice-president Mike O'Hara (second from left) and LAOOC judo commissioner Willy Reich (third from left). COURTESY OF THE AUTHOR

Ginny and me with Bibis and Juan Antonio Samaranch. COURTESY OF THE LAOOC

I'm surrounded by members of the Romanian Olympic team outside the athletes' quarters at the University of Southern California village. COURTESY OF THE LAOOC

Nadia Comaneci greets President Ronald Reagan at opening ceremonies as (from left) I, Paul Ziffren, Mrs. Juan Antonio Samaranch, and Nancy Reagan look on. WHITE HOUSE PHOTO BY MICHAEL EVANS

My son, Joe, runs a kilometer of the torch relay in Laguna Beach. *Los Angeles Times* PHOTO BY DON TORMEY

After opening ceremonies I presented David Wolper (second from left), the LAOOC commissioner of opening and closing ceremonies, with the torch that Rafer Johnson used to light the flame at the Coliseum. Behind Wolper are John Argue, a member of the LAOOC Executive Board and the man most responsible for bringing the 1984 Games to Los Angeles, and Harry Usher. JAN BERLINER

From left, Bibis Samaranch, Mickey Ziffren, and Ginny. COURTESY OF JO USHER

In Cuba I met with Fidel Castro. At left is Mario Vázquez Rana. COURTESY OF THE AUTHOR

CHAPTER EIGHT

THE SILENT ARMY

SEX, AGE, RACE, education, and skills. Throw them out the window. Big corporations go for the cream of the crop—people who have "the right things going for them." They invariably miss some of the best talent. I go for the gems they miss. I hadn't followed conventional hiring practices at my travel company and had no intention of using them for the Olympic Games.

When it came to staffing key Olympic positions, previous experience was almost irrelevant. How many people had ever staged an Olympic swimming event? Or operated a sixteen-day, twenty-four-hour transportation service for more than twenty thousand people that covered an area of ten thousand square miles? Who had managed an Olympic Village? Who had ever designed a system to distribute more than five million tickets?

I believe in leadership and trust. People with those two qualities can manage anything.

It was with this in mind that I conceived the commissioner program, a sports management technique new to the Olympics. Each of the twenty-three Olympic sports was to be run by a commissioner whose function was chief operating officer. The commissioner was the LAOOC's counterpart to the president of the respective international sports federation.

The international sports federation presidents are powerful people who are treated as high-level dignitaries in the world of amateur sports. They're accustomed to pomp and circumstance and are extremely status conscious. Skilled negotiators, they could break us financially if we didn't treat them right. To deal with them, I sought individuals who had achieved success and could represent the LAOOC on an equal footing. I flipped through my Rolodex for men and women I knew and had seen in action over the years. By the summer of 1983 I'd filled every position.

Jay Flood was the first person I asked to become a commissioner and the first one to go into action. As commissioner for aquatic events—swimming, synchronized swimming, diving, and water polo—Flood ran four of the nine pre-Olympic competitions that summer. The first was the III FINA Water Polo Cup at Pepperdine University—the world championships of water polo under the auspices of the international swimming federation, the *Fédération Internationale de Natation Amateur.*

Harry Usher and I had both opposed pre-Olympic events at first. I saw them as no-win situations that would inevitably invite comparisons to the Moscow Olympic Games. Also, the slightest mistake would generate criticism all over the world. There'd been some discussion about USOC's holding its annual national sports festival at L.A. Olympic sites, but we didn't want to do that either. At a time when we had to begin building local support, negative publicity about our ability to stage events could be costly. Moreover, city officials and contractors could use their experience in the pre-Games competitions to leverage us into renegotiating agreements.

Flood came to me in February 1983 with plans to hold a swimming meet at the new McDonald's swim stadium at USC in conjunction with U.S. Swimming, the sport's national governing body. Flood argued that a dry run was needed to test the new facility as well as our operations and management techniques. He pointed out that the committee could use the event as a testing ground for all sports. As he made his pitch, I began to change my mind. Maybe he was right. No matter who might be named host of the event, the public would perceive it as belonging to the LAOOC.

Finally, I told him to go ahead. "On one condition," I said. "It has to be our event. Anyway you shake it, we're accountable, so we better make sure it's done right." We later expanded on the plan and decided to hold international events at all the new facilities.

This was where trust came in. My relationship with Flood dated back almost thirty years. We'd been water polo rivals in college and later teammates at the Olympic Club in San Francisco. We'd run into each other over the years and one of those times was at a Lake Placid hotel during the 1980 Winter Olympics. Flood, a successful architect in Santa Monica, had built several ski resorts around the country and was a spectator at Lake Placid. He congratulated me on my presidency of the LAOOC and then we talked about water polo. Toward the end of the conversation, I asked him if he had any interest in being involved in the Games. He said he did.

Flood agreed to become aquatics commissioner a few weeks later. Flood and aquatics, if you'll pardon the coincidence were a perfect match. Another good fit was Jim Easton and archery. Easton was the chief executive officer of Easton Aluminum, the largest manufacturer of aluminum arrows and bats in the country. His company was located across the street from my old company, First Travel, and we'd become good friends. When the president of the International Archery Federation, Francesco Gnecchi-Ruscone, first visited Los Angeles in 1980, I asked Easton to be his host on behalf of the LAOOC. Easton and archery were a match made in heaven.

Other commissioner assignments were a stretch—at least on the surface. When Swiss-born Willy Reich (who along with his wife, Babs, were old friends from the travel industry), was appointed judo commissioner, he had never seen a judo match. But he had other qualifications: He speaks four languages. Besides English and his mother tongue, German, he's fluent in French and Japanese. Those language skills made him the right man. The president of the International Judo Federation was Shigeyoshi Matsumae and the secretary-general was Heinz Kempa. Matsumae spoke only Japanese; Kempa only German.

The committee didn't ask commissioners to drop everything they were doing several years before the event. We couldn't because for the most part they were active in successful business ventures. Instead, I had appealed to their adventurous sides. I explained they would be the chief executive officers of the sports and would take full command at the time of the Games. Leading up to the Games, I had asked them to work part time—a few hours a month at the LAOOC office—for which they each would be paid an annual salary of $5,000. This was pocket change to most of them, but it was important they be paid. They had to be held accountable for their actions and a salary, regardless of the amount, served that purpose. It's very difficult to terminate a volunteer, much less a friend.

Each one's mission was to nurture friendships with key federation officials and become an expert on the sport. To accomplish this they had to travel extensively and weave themselves into the social fabric of amateur sport by attending federation congresses and world championships. They brought federation leaders into their homes, met their guests at the airport in their own cars, took them on personalized tours of Olympic facilities, and arranged extensive planning sessions for them at the LAOOC offices. In virtually every case they became good friends with federation presidents and secretarys-general and these relationships would pay off for us handsomely.

The commissioners, however, understood they had to clear federation requests through Usher and me and that they had to coordinate special events and meetings through organizing committee channels.

The buzz word was "control," which was difficult to achieve with this group. They were independent people accustomed to running their own shows and they frequently resented having to clear activities which, in some instances, they considered personal. But they represented our interests to the federations, not their own, and at no time were they to represent the special interests of the international federations.

The first major conflict occurred in September 1982 when Prince Philip, as president of the equestrian federation, visited Los Angeles to review the Santa Anita Race Track, the venue for the Olympic equestrian competition. Montgomery and Joanne Fisher, the equestrian co-commissioners, got carried away in planning the prince's social calendar. In addition to organizing various LAOOC events, they scheduled a dinner reception at their home in conjunction with the American Horse Shows Association. Although they had cleared it through an LAOOC sport manager, the LAOOC staffer had neglected to take the request through appropriate channels. Strict protocol requirements were in force for this visit, the security and diplomatic implications of an appearance by Prince Philip being paramount. As soon as Chuck Cale, our vice-president for sports, got wind of the party, he canceled it. The Fishers were furious. They resigned, claiming they'd been mistreated and that coordination with LAOOC senior staff was bad if not impossible.

We had another problem a week later. Robert Strub, president of the California Turf Club, which operates Santa Anita Race Track, had scheduled a dinner reception at the California Club in downtown Los Angeles. This one had been coordinated with the LAOOC, but we insisted Strub move the dinner because the club had a restrictive membership policy. Strub did: He moved the reception to a downtown restaurant. But when Strub learned that L.A.'s black mayor, Tom Bradley, and the LAOOC's Jewish chairman, Paul Ziffren, couldn't attend, he moved the party back to the California Club.

Since there was no longer an issue, Strub felt the reason for holding the event elsewhere had been negated. But LAOOC policy was clear: No Olympic events—social or otherwise—were to be held in locations where minorities were restricted from attending. The British consul, fearing its press would have a field day, brought pressure to bear as well. Strub had no choice. He moved it again.

The minority community gave us points for our stand on the California Club, which was a first. Staffing was another no-win situation and another example of how the Olympics were used as a visible forum for special interests. In some instances it was uglier and more counterproductive than I could have imagined.

Early in 1980, when the LAOOC was still very small, I

was accused of being "overly accommodating to Jews" and
then anti-Semitic—all within a period of a few hours. The first
incident took me completely by surprise. Apparently, there
were some on our board of directors who had assumed my
Germanic name and WASPish appearance confirmed I was a
fellow bigot and they sent a small delegation to make certain I
was in synch.

I met the delegation in my office in Century City. After
exchanging pleasantries, one got to the point of the visit.
"Didn't you know," he said, "that you were elected partially
to give balance to the organizing committee?"

"What do you mean?" I asked.

"Well," he continued, "with a Jew, Paul Ziffren, as chairman and with the International Olympic Committee never
having elected a Jewish member, it is important that you provide a certain balance which, we are disturbed to say, you
have not accomplished in your initial hiring."

I tensed and immediately became very quiet. Many employees call this my glazed-over look. I asked for clarification.

"It is not necessary for you to be overly accommodating
to Jews. We've noticed that your staff is weighed down with
them, particularly in responsible positions."

Joel Rubenstein, David Simon, and Joan Gilford were
the Jewish employees the delegation identified by name. They
were among the LAOOC's first dozen staff members and
were extremely talented. All would stay through the Games
and make important contributions.

"Can you go through this one more time?" I asked. I was
furious by this time, but I wanted to be absolutely certain I
was being told not to hire any more Jews for prominent positions.

The demand was repeated almost verbatim. I was struck
by how matter-of-factly these people, all of whom had good
reputations, could deliver this message of hate.

I stared at the message bearer for at least a full minute.
Then I stood up. I was in a rage.

"As far as I'm concerned," I said, "these last fifteen minutes have never taken place. But if I ever hear one word,
either directly or indirectly, about how I should conduct the

hiring practices of this committee, or about anti-Semitic ideas having to do with the Olympic Games, I will see to it that the identities of the participants at this meeting and the message you delivered are as widely known as possible."

Later that day, Irv Rubin, the leader of the Jewish Defense League, and about ten demonstrators burst into our offices carrying placards accusing us of being Olympic Nazi pigs and screaming obscenities. They were demonstrating because we didn't fully support Carter's boycott of the Moscow Games and therefore were pro-Soviet and anti-Semitic. Given the meeting I had had earlier, I couldn't help but note the irony of the situation.

Rubin tried to provoke me into a shouting match, which I resisted. Instead, I asked him and one of his lieutenants to join me in our glass-enclosed conference room. Meanwhile, Rieger, then the LAOOC press secretary, locked himself in an office and returned calls to all the local newspapers, wire services, and radio and television stations, telling each that the JDL had come and gone. This avoided a huge media turnout. The JDL, as was its custom, had tipped reporters in advance.

Rubin was much more reasonable out of earshot of his supporters. I told him he was demonstrating against the wrong Olympic committee. I explained that the LAOOC differed from the USOC, which as the national Olympic committee for the United States was responsible for training and fielding the team at the Pan American and Olympic Games, and that our committee had no formal connection with the Moscow Games.

This discussion, and the absence of news media, deflated Rubin's demonstration plans. He gathered his troops and left.

Affirmative action wasn't a mandate for Olympic hiring, but it was a natural outgrowth of my business experience. It was also an opportunity to involve L.A.'s diverse communities. This was important because variation is one of Los Angeles' strengths and we counted on these communities to welcome the athletes and the Olympic family. Every employee who worked for the committee had a public relations responsibility to share information with their neighbors and build support for the Games.

By law, affirmative action ensures equal job opportunities for minorities and women in the marketplace. I've found that if you hire the best people affirmative action falls into place.

One of our successes was Akasaka, Ortiz & Ciocatto, a local insurance company that handled our day-to-day insurance needs. When they learned of the difficulty we were having in signing a major carrier to handle all our insurance business, they interceded and brought us Transamerica. We signed Transamerica on December 16, 1982, as one of our last sponsors. As part of its contract, Transamerica agreed to ensure the Games with coverage of $200 million per incident and to provide group health coverage for the staff. We offered Akasaka, Ortiz & Ciocatto a generous finder's fee to show our appreciation for their efforts. They accepted only after we went to great lengths to talk them into it.

On the opposite side of the coin, when we tried in 1980 to make affirmative action work by specifically hiring a minority printing company, we had no luck. Two representatives of a firm that was listed with a minority business consortium paid an office call one day to offer their services. Both were well-dressed black men, and I was anxious to meet with them because we needed a printer. Joel Rubenstein had compiled a list of printing jobs we needed—stationery, envelopes, business cards, reports, scratch pads, and business forms—and brought it to the meeting.

"What are your printing capabilities?" I asked.

"Scratch pads," one said.

"What do you mean?"

"That's it," the other said. "That's the extent of our business."

"You mean that's your whole business, printing scratch pads?" Rubenstein asked in wonder. I was a little amazed myself.

"Yes," said the first one, "and no sample orders. We'll give you a year's supply for a flat fee. What's your offer?"

I wasn't about to make one and before I could say anything, he sweetened the deal.

"In addition," he said, "we'll go around and make speeches for you. We belong to certain associations. We'll tell everybody how well you treat minority firms. In fact, if you hire four or five more companies we work with, I can guarantee you will never have any problems."

I politely asked them to leave. We'd been prepared to give them hundreds of thousands of dollars' worth of printing business and all they wanted to sell us was protection.

A few months later I understood what they'd been talking about. Korn-Ferry had conducted a very thorough search for us to find a director of personnel. We interviewed ten solid candidates and finally decided on a talented black, Joe McKay. McKay, thirty-nine at the time, came to the LAOOC from Texas International Airlines, where he'd been vice-president of personnel. He was also an attorney and a member of the State Bar of California and the American Bar Association.

But McKay only lasted a few weeks before tendering a letter of resignation to Harry Usher. He told Usher over the telephone he'd been pulled aside and threatened while attending a business meeting. Thugs had told him he'd be sorry if he didn't cooperate and function as their inside man at the LAOOC. McKay quit rather than compromise himself, or us.

We then hired Priscilla Florence in November 1980, an attractive, vivacious black woman, who had extensive experience in hiring personnel for short-term defense projects at Northrup. She represented us beautifully in the community and ran a model affirmative action program.

One of Florence's first tasks was to find specialists to assess our operations and establish programs to take us through the Games. During this time Mike Mount, then an Arthur Young & Company consultant who later became one of our group vice-presidents responsible for bringing technology to the Games, told Usher of a computer program called PERT (Planning, Evaluation, Research, Technique), which was originally created to track the planning for the Polaris submarine and was later used for the MX missile system. Mount, with help from Lee Aurich, tried to adapt PERT to LAOOC uses. They identified more than ten thousand tasks and how each overlapped into various department functions. We continued experimenting with it for a year and a half before our planners became convinced its design was not compatible to solving illogical problems such as planning for an Olympic Games. According to PERT, we'd complete the tasks and be ready for the Games by 1988.

Other than putting all the data in one place, I hadn't placed great value in PERT, mainly because it has very negative potential. It makes people rigid in their thinking and serves as a replacement for creativity. Managers tend to rely on a plan, rather than judgment and momentum to get a project done. A plan says do this or that, and if something goes wrong, everybody is amazed. They ask, how can that be? It wasn't in the plan? That kind of thinking scared me, but I allowed Mount to go ahead and use PERT as a tool to specify the details so we wouldn't overlook anything.

This was where PERT was useful. It identified areas where accreditation overlapped into security, where both overlapped into sports, and where the entire personnel function overlapped into every department. These data were essential to the development of operational planning by venue rather than by department.

This planning was in high gear by the 1983 summer competition. Mike Mitchell, an experienced event consultant from Alaska, was in charge of developing the venues and reported to Usher.

Before the summer contests began, I told each commissioner I wouldn't attend unless asked. It was important they simulate Games conditions and have total autonomy without me or anyone else looking over their shoulders. I was available as the court of last resort.

On July 14, however, I attended the International Swim Meet at Jay Flood's request. He'd helped design the new swim stadium and was proud of it. He wasn't calling for help; he was anxious for me to see the stadium.

It was the smoggiest day of the year and it was hot. Doctors and air quality experts were out in force as were reporters curious to see how the heat and smog would affect the athletes—particularly the Soviets and East Germans, who had already criticized the outdoor pool.

I sat in the stands after Flood took me on a tour. I marveled at the beauty of the stadium, which was decorated with colorful flags, banners, and bunting. The stands were almost filled with spectators.

Just as the competition commenced, a light breeze blew away much of the smog, making downtown Los Angeles sparkle. Some of the best swimmers in the world competed that day and one of them, Vladimir Salnikoff of the Soviet Union, set a world record in the 800-meter freestyle. At a news conference the day before Salnikoff had called it "a simple pool . . . not fast." He sang a different tune after he set the record. He told reporters, "Now I think this is a fast pool for me because I swam the fastest in the world." When asked about smog, he said, "I've heard about it, but I haven't seen it."

The Soviets had been complaining for years about our facilities and poor air quality. It was appropriate that one of the Russian athletes set a world record in one of our so-called inferior facilities on the smoggiest day of the year. Complaints diminished somewhat after that.

All our venues passed the test that summer. So did the commissioners. Besides Flood, who carried the heaviest load, Peter Siracusa performed superbly at cycling and Hyla and Dick Bertea handled the difficult logistics of gymnastics competition. A few days after the gymnastics, our upbeat mood changed.

On the morning of September 1, the clock radio came on at 6 A.M., waking me.

"And the top story of the morning is . . ."

I was just shaking out the cobwebs and not really paying attention to what the announcer was saying.

". . . the Korean jetliner, thought to be missing last night, has been downed over the Kamchatka Peninsula in the Soviet Union . . ."

I bolted upright.

". . . We'll have more details as the story unfolds."

I started turning the dial for more details.

"What are you doing?" Ginny had just entered the bedroom with two cups of coffee.

I told her. She sat on the edge of the bed. I felt guilty thinking that four years of work had just gone down the drain.

"Maybe it was a forced landing," Ginny said.

"I hope so, but I doubt it."

The LAOOC staff, six hundred strong, had outgrown the Westwood office building and we were in the process of moving for the fourth time in as many years. The marina center, our final resting place, was a two-hundred-thousand-square-foot former helicopter-assembly plant in Culver City, California. I was knee deep in boxes, sorting through them with Sherry Cockle when Amy Quinn burst into my new office with the latest news on Korean Airlines jumbo jet Flight 007.

"Heat-seeking missiles," she said. "Two Soviet jets had been following it."

"Damn it!" I said. I turned away and immediately my thoughts began whirling. Olympics. North Korea. South Korea. International condemnation. Olympics. Soviet stonewall. Boycott. Our '83 events. Olympics. Reagan administration. Local reaction. Olympics.

"What's the toll?" I asked.

Quinn glanced over the wire copy. "There were two hundred sixty-nine passengers on board."

It was a terrible tragedy, which I sensed would cause us a lot of headaches.

I was right. The downing of Korean airliner # 007 threw a wild card into the Olympic deck. It pitted the emotions of people from around the world against the Soviets.

Within days the California State Legislature and the U.S. Congress unanimously approved legislation condemning the USSR and recommending that Soviet athletes be banned from participating in the 1984 Olympic Games. The hysteria grew.

On September 16, 1983, the USSR National Olympic Committee yanked its athletes from the LAOOC's remaining pre-Olympic events—rowing and canoeing at Lake Casitas and archery at El Dorado Park. A few days after that they canceled a tour with the U.S. hockey team.

I was angry that once again athletes suffered when governments made mistakes. I said in a press statement, "We remain opposed to any efforts to punish athletes. History has proven that the use and abuse of athletes for political purposes only hurts young individuals rather than achieving any political gain. Sports organizations and events should not be involved in disputes between governments."

Rather than wait for events to control us, I immediately dispatched an LAOOC delegation to the world wrestling championships in Kiev, to show the Olympic world that as far as we were concerned it was business as usual and that we were going to do our best to stay out of international politics.

I went to Washington at the end of September to testify before the House Subcommittee on Tourism. While there, I met with Michael Deaver; Speaker of the House Tip O'Neill; and House majority whip, Jim Wright of Texas, and was assured by each that efforts to keep any team from attending the Games would be blocked.

Back in Los Angeles, I gave Willy Reich (on his way to attend the world judo championships in the Soviet Union) a letter to deliver to Soviet sports officials. It said: "Your sportsmen and sportswomen will be accepted and welcomed in Los Angeles, not only in accordance with the Olympic Charter, but also in the spirit of friendship through sports."

A group called Ban the Soviets Coalition was born out of the ashes of the KAL tragedy. It claimed a membership of 155 conservative ethnic and religious groups and a sphere of influence that extended from 30 to 40 million people. Its sole objective was to keep the Soviet team from competing in the 1984 Olympic Games.

The media, however, reported that only two groups openly supported the coalition—the Baltic American Freedom League, led by Anthony Mazeika, and the Friends of Freedom Foundation, headed by Gene Voessler. The Ban the Soviets chief spokesperson was David Balsiger, who lived in Costa Mesa and had run twice for local office and lost. At various times he'd worked as an author, press agent, film executive, and real estate salesman.

In October, the coalition began circulating a petition to ban the Soviets from the Games. Originally, it had hoped to collect a million signatures, but eventually scaled down its goal to a hundred thousand. In the end, it obtained only ten thousand signatures.

As the uproar over KAL died down and Ban the Soviets faded away—for a while at least—an undercurrent of anxiety coursed through the LAOOC.

Department managers, confident from their successes at the L.A. '83 events, began pressing for additional staff. They wanted to get on with the final push. I stalled. The more people working on a project such as this, the less control you have.

I figured, too, that a shorter employment span would minimize employee burnout. It would also enable us to attract high caliber people who could only take short leaves of absence from their regular employment. Individuals who had jobs to return to presented greater stability to the committee than those who had to worry about unemployment at the end of the Games.

In Montreal, employees quit in droves immediately before the 1976 Games—at the most critical time—to take permanent employment opportunities. Their leaving devastated the organization and if we were to be faced with the same situation . . . what would happen?

Another reason I held back on hiring was my fear of infiltration by terrorist or criminal elements. I worried about everything: arson, bombings, leakage of confidential information.

I had hired generalists in the beginning because the LAOOC needed people capable of dealing with a multitude of issues and projects. When specialists were called for, Usher and I talked it over and agreed to open up the floodgates.

As we brought on more people and tasks were parceled out, problems inevitably developed. They first went to Usher, a master of detail who could sort out hundreds of items simultaneously. However, he'd never been a manager before and was reluctant to delegate authority: He kept his hands in everything and wouldn't allow decisions to be made without his input.

On occasion we discussed his management style. The job was taking its toll on him and one evening that October when he was looking particularly tired, I suggested he start looking for an alter ego.

"Suppose you get sick for a week or get run over by a car?" I said. "Who's going to carry the ball forward? You have to start sharing the responsibilities."

I had told every department head to bring on someone to take over in case of an emergency. I called them alter egos; the staff had begun calling it "the clone program."

"I don't need one, Peter," he said. "You know we have to keep control. It isn't time to let go. I'll be the first to give it up when the time comes."

I didn't need Usher to remind me about control—it was my middle name. Crisis management had been the order of the day from the very beginning. We had to be quick to stay one step ahead of the issues, not to mention the IOC, the sports federations, government, law enforcement, the media, and the public. Our organization charts were cast in sand: The one we created in the morning was outdated by the end of the day.

Usher felt he had to be the constant. He had a good point but I knew his system would eventually break down. The job was too big. He couldn't do it all by himself.

The commissioners were more than ready to point this out to him. Usher at times resisted the commissioners. He believed they lacked specific sports knowledge and were uncontrollable. Usher worked more closely with Chuck Cale, who relied on the managers to handle the nuts and bolts of each sport.

What evolved was confusion. Three different operational groups had little idea as to what the others were up to. Mike Mitchell was developing the venue plans, Chuck Cale and the sports managers were dealing with the federations and venue operators, and many commissioners were wondering when they were going to take over.

In their push to plan by venue, Mitchell and the venue development staff had excluded the commissioners from the early planning. Mitchell formed his group by collecting top staffers from each department and they dissected each venue and created blueprints for its management and operation. They covered everything from access to egress for athletes, spectators, staff, media, officials, and security personnel; they identified and located security stations, health stations, staff office space, placement of communications trucks and equipment, concessions, ticket booths, telephones, press areas, restrooms, and other temporary facilities. They developed the ultimate checklist and timeline to make sure everything was completed on schedule for the Games.

Sports managers, meanwhile, felt they were doing all the work and were resentful that the commissioners got all the travel benefits and would swoop in at the time of the Games and grab all the glory. There was an undercurrent of wishful thinking that the commissioners program would go away or be limited to a protocol function.

As for the commissioners, they feared they were being looped out of the planning process. One commissioner, who also had a list of personal gripes, took the lead and called a meeting of the commissioners at Jim Easton's home in Bel Air one summery evening that October.

This gathering became known as the commissioners' revolt. The main purpose of the meeting was to air grievances and form a list to present to Usher and me. I never would have known about it if Easton hadn't made a casual reference to it. He had assumed Usher and I had been invited.

Usher and I made plans to go as surprise guests and we discussed the problem on the drive to Easton's house. I faulted Harry for excluding commissioner input from the venue development program, but conceded that the commissioners, if unhappy, should have brought their complaints directly to us.

Easton, as planned, had left the door open. We went in and proceeded to the patio where the meeting had already begun. We took seats in the back. As the discussions continued, it became apparent that not all commissioners were there to complain.

Flood, who had the floor, was talking about how he and other full-time commissioners could help the part-timers get more involved. He offered the floor to us when he finished, but I told him we were there to listen. After a few more commissioners made brief comments, discussion came to a standstill. Several commissioners were obviously unnerved by our presence.

"Gripe sessions are counterproductive," I began. "If you have a problem, bring it to me or Harry.

"And if you don't like how we conduct business, quit. This is the time to do it. As a matter of fact, as I look around, I see a few who should."

My stomach was churning. The grievances were so petty I couldn't believe it. One wanted a private office and secretary, another wanted more Olympic pins to hand out, one wanted a particular sport manager assigned to him. The only request of substance was greater budget authority. At the time, Usher approved all expenditures exceeding $5,000.

Rather than let the ground swell grow, I told them to think about quitting overnight. As angry as I was, I knew that the whole situation had been overblown. There were only a few malcontents in the group. Mainly, there was a lack of communication between the staff and the commissioners, and it had to be fixed.

I called a meeting of commissioners and department heads at noon the next day. I made it very clear that the commissioners were there to stay and would run their respective sports with complete autonomy as planned. I reminded the department heads that the commissioners were leaders who possessed the skills necessary to make the Games a success.

"The commissioners are critical," I told the group, "and I am making it everyone's responsibility to bring them up to speed as quickly as possible. Regardless of the problems, make it work."

Then I addressed the commissioners. "You have your authority," I said. "If you have any questions or problems, see Harry or me. There are enough people taking pot shots at us from outside. An insurrection won't be tolerated."

Once the revolt blew over and all the commissioners started working full time and completed the venue development process, staff problems faded. The ranks closed and everyone rallied around the Games—well, almost everyone.

MENDING FENCES

"THE RUSSIANS ARE coming," I said. I looked up from reading the Telex. Sherry Cockle glanced at me inquisitively. I smiled. "At least for a visit."

It was the morning of November 11, 1983, and more than two months had elapsed since Soviet MiGs had downed the Korean airliner. The last time we'd heard from them—late September—they were withdrawing from the pre-Olympic archery, rowing, and canoeing events. I was happy that communications had resumed.

"Bring me my Soviet files," I asked Sherry, who returned with an armload. As I began thumbing through them, I wondered how extensive the fallout was from the KAL incident.

Knowing I couldn't count on the Reagan administration (which couldn't differentiate between its policy toward the Soviet Union and its views on the Olympic Games), I'd been working for a year and a half on my own foreign policy of repairing bridges between the national Olympic committees of the countries in the Eastern bloc.

I had begun planning my international offensive in late February 1982, when we completed a successful week of meetings with the high rollers of the International Sports Federations and the Executive Board. They felt confident of us. Now I had to turn my attention to the national Olympic committees—particularly those in the Eastern bloc—which were still smarting over the 1980 Carter boycott. Since I had planned to attend the IOC's eighty-fifth session in Rome at the end of May, I considered making a few stops along the way.

I discussed the trip with Ginny one night in the kitchen. She had prepared a late snack as I'd missed dinner once again. Family dinners had ended almost two weeks earlier on Valentine's Day. Vicki was away at college, but Heidi, Keri, and Joe were feeling left out and were angry that I rarely made it home in time for dinner anymore. To make matters worse, Ginny often accompanied me to Olympic-related social events.

So I promised Ginny and the kids that for Valentine's Day I'd be home for dinner by 7:30, no matter what. Murphy's Law prevailed. Once again I was held up and didn't arrive until 8:45. The kids had already eaten and none would even speak to me. Ginny had one succinct message.

"No more family dinners," she said, "at least during the week. It's too disappointing for the kids. I explained tonight that they can't count on having dinner with you until the Games are over. I hope they understand."

I was miserable. Ginny and I had discussed a hundred different ways to make it better. In the end, they arrived at their own solutions. Heidi and Keri said they'd like to attend school overseas, each for a year. Once Ginny and I decided to investigate the possibilities, Joe came along and said he'd like to try boarding school as well. He thought it would be boring to be at home alone. This wasn't easy. Neither Ginny nor I felt good about sending the children away to school, but it beat disappointing them on a regular basis.

As we talked about various itineraries for the trip, Ginny suggested we take a side trip to look at schools in Switzerland for Heidi and Keri. There was no time like the present, so we decided to go to Switzerland first and made plans to visit IOC headquarters in Lausanne.

I Telexed the NOC presidents of East Germany, Poland, the USSR, and Yugoslavia informing each that I'd be in Europe in May and would like to visit. Each responded with a formal invitation. I hoped to convince each to sign a protocol accord—an agreement in principle to attend the Games—and to send a delegation to Los Angeles.

Ginny and I arrived in Lausanne late on the afternoon of May 8, to meet with IOC Director Monique Berlioux. I needed her input and advice before meeting the Eastern European sports leaders.

Marie Chevalier, Berlioux's top aide, prepared a wonderful dinner for us at Berlioux's city flat, and over cocktails Berlioux briefed me on the leaders I'd be meeting, particularly Manfred Ewald, East Germany's sports minister, and Sergei Pavlov, the president of the Soviet National Olympic Committee.

Ginny and I visited Swiss boarding schools and enjoyed the countryside the next day. We were particularly impressed with L'Aiglon College, a secondary school for girls located in Villars, a two-hour drive from Lausanne. L'Aiglon, known for its academic excellence, had a beautiful campus, and I was impressed with its security. Before we left, we made arrangements for Heidi to begin attending in the fall.

That night we had dinner with Berlioux again, but this time we asked Horst Dassler to join us. Dassler, as the head of Adidas, is the premier sports outfitter in the world. I was told he inherited his business acumen and strong-willed, taciturn nature from his father, Adi Dassler, the founder of the company.

It's Berlioux's job to keep commercialism out of the Olympics; it's Dassler's to make sure every athlete bears the Adidas name in large letters on every piece of clothing and equipment. Therein lies the conflict. Along with Ewald, Pavlov, Samaranch, Dr. Primo Nebiolo, president of the International Track and Field Federation, and Mario Vazquez Rana, president of the Mexican NOC and the Pan American Sports Organization, Dassler is one of the most influential people in international sports. He carries a big checkbook and Adidas pays handsome licensing fees to NOCs and federations alike. Adidas also pays athletes to wear its goods.

Berlioux and Dassler were often at odds, but that night they put their differences aside to break bread together. Since the LAOOC was about to announce Adidas as one of its official licensees, I had hoped to get Berlioux's blessing on the deal as well as information for my trip. The conversation, though not especially jovial, was civil and, for me, worthwhile.

At one point Dassler took me aside to offer some advice. "Peter," he said, "I have known the presidents of every organizing committee since London in 1948. Each has had great strengths and great weaknesses."

I nodded, wondering what he was driving at.

"The day after the Games," he continued, "each was left out to dry on the dock like yesterday's fish."

"In my country we have another way of saying that," I said. "Here today, gone tomorrow."

I appreciated Dassler's words. He was letting me know that a lot of people would no longer give me the time of day once the Games ended. There was an unspoken message in what he was saying, too. He was telling me that he would be a friend for life. Before the evening was over, Berlioux approved our licensing agreement with Dassler.

On May 10, Michael O'Hara (the LAOOC vice-president for television) and Willy Reich met Ginny and me at the airport in West Berlin. I needed Reich's language capabilities for the German portion of the trip; I needed O'Hara because of his background as captain of the 1964 Olympic volleyball team and as a successful sports organizer and entrepreneur. This was also a good opportunity for O'Hara to begin negotiations with the Eastern bloc countries for television rights.

After a combination dinner/planning session the night we arrived, the four of us toured the Olympic stadium in West Berlin and walked through Checkpoint Charlie into East Berlin. You can take a taxi into East Berlin if it's authorized; ours wasn't. So we lugged our baggage across the border, through iron gates, groups of soldiers, and Customs officials. When we came out, a uniformed driver handed a huge bouquet of roses to Ginny and two limousines took us to our hotel.

The German Democratic Republic, a small nation of eighteen million, is one of the three most powerful sports countries in the world. On a per capita basis, it produces more fine athletes by far than any other nation. There's an undercurrent of suspicion, particularly in the Western press, that its superiority is gained through illegal means ranging from sophisticated doping techniques to genetic searches. I believe, however, its athletic success results directly from its restrictive political environment. There is little reason for happiness in that country other than sport, so the people take great pride in their athletic accomplishments and look forward to the Olympic Games.

We spent the next two days meeting with Ewald and other high-level GDR sports officials. They were interested in negotiating the finest possible arrangements for their athletes and they were tough but not petty. Our big breakthrough came when Ewald signed the protocol agreement that, providing we adhered to the Olympic Charter, committed the GDR to attend the '84 Games in full strength.

As one of the most powerful figures in sport, his signature practically guaranteed cooperation from the other Eastern European countries, as well as the Soviet Union. Ewald knew Sergei Pavlov well because they had served in their countries' Communist youth organizations in the 1950s and had become national leaders through sport.

After our meetings with Ewald, Ginny returned to the United States—she was anxious to get back to the children. O'Hara, Reich, and I headed north to Rostock near the Baltic Sea to attend the European Judo Championships. We were put up in a pleasant little resort hotel where the food, service, and ambience were excellent.

I had never had an opportunity to spend much time in East Germany's countryside. Frankly, I was surprised. There was a positive air about the area. The people—on the surface, at least—seemed happy and relatively prosperous, and development was going on everywhere. I was very impressed with the stadium in Rostock, as I was with other sports facilities I visited. East Germans don't skimp when it comes to sports. Whether training or competition facilities and equipment, they get the best of everything for their athletes.

There was a world boxing tournament in progress in Munich at the time, and I found it interesting that boxers from Jamaica and a few South American countries preferred to train for their events in the GDR. That's how highly regarded GDR sports facilities are by athletes the world over. East Germans effectively use sports as a tool for diplomacy.

We returned to East Berlin after the judo championships. While there I thought it wise to visit the U.S. embassy to advise the ambassador of my meetings with the sports officials and of their plans to visit Los Angeles. So I made an appointment with him.

In the embassy's reception area was a blow-up of a letter from the State Department, congratulating embassy personnel for doing a wonderful job in a hostile environment. I was amazed. This was an insult to the people of East Berlin and confirmation of State Department insensitivity. After a short wait, I was told the ambassador was busy giving dictation and couldn't be bothered to see me. Over the years, LAOOC representatives had always been welcomed with great hospitality in foreign countries. Heads of state often made themselves available to us; top leaders were always generous with their time and help. But during my five and a half years with the organizing committee never once did an American ambassador take time to see me.

Before leaving the country, we toured East Berlin and its suburbs by boat. We went through miles and miles of beautiful waterways, with magnificent homes and gardens lining the banks. O'Hara, Reich, and I were surprised by the apparent prosperity. We saw hundreds of homes on the waterfront, all different, all well cared for, and I wondered if they were owned by party members or private citizens.

The great differences that exist along the border between the GDR and the Federal Republic of Germany disappear the farther inland you go. I'm not speaking of freedom. The controlled society of the GDR is as stern as any Communist country in the world, but there is an affluence in that country which you don't see in most of the others.

We went to the airport after our boat ride, where O'Hara and I said goodbye to Reich. He returned home; we went on to Warsaw.

Reticent at first, Marian Renke, a sophisticated international sports leader, warmed to us and was a gracious host during our stay. He also signed a protocol agreement. Two for two. We were making progress in patching up relations with the Eastern bloc.

O'Hara and I had some free time one evening, so we wandered the streets of Warsaw on our own. I noticed how different the Poles were from the Germans. Poles are very physical and emotional people, and wherever we turned, people were holding hands or embracing. The emergence of spring following a severely cold winter seemed to ease the apparent shortages of essential foods and goods and the press of the ubiquitous and unwelcome military.

It was late when we returned to the hotel that night. The large park in front filled with people, who made a huge cross of flowers and illuminated it by candles. The cross was about twenty yards long and fifteen yards wide. Our interpreter told us that on his visit Pope John Paul II had knelt there and kissed the ground. Ever since, the people of Warsaw had made the square a shrine.

I was awakened a few hours later by the noise of trucks. From the window, I saw some soldiers dousing the candles and shoveling the flowers and ferns into the backs of the trucks. Other soldiers then washed down the area with a fire hose until there was nothing left. The whole site was razed in twenty minutes.

Saddened, I tried to go back to sleep but couldn't. I returned to the window and just as I did, I saw a single candle moving toward the center of the square. It must have been three in the morning. I saw a person—an old woman, I thought—set the candle where the heart of the cross had been. Slowly, from all directions, others carrying candles began to appear. Within an hour, the entire cross had been rebuilt and the people were quietly singing hymns.

There was a terrible sadness in Warsaw, which was everywhere, even in meetings with sports officials. At one, with a key leader of Polish sport, I was deeply moved by the dignity and strength with which he supported Solidarity. At the stroke of noon, he requested a few moments of silence as he turned on a small radio and tuned in a station that was playing church bells. "The bells of Krakow," he explained. He leaned forward in his chair, closing his eyes. A few moments later, he awakened from his meditation and told O'Hara and me how proud he was that Pope Paul, the first Polish pope, was such a great and beloved world leader.

Next stop Moscow. A protocol officer met us at the airport and escorted us to our hotel. On the way into town, we scanned the agenda that had been prepared for us. Our first meeting was with Sergei Pavlov at 11 o'clock the next morning.

Pavlov was a Soviet hard-liner and looked it. He was stocky, had a very muscular neck, and piercing blue eyes, and you could build a small bird's nest in each of his bushy eyebrows. Pavlov, long our most strident critic, once suggested that U.S. athletes be prohibited from participating in the L.A. Games as punishment for the 1980 Carter boycott.

We met Pavlov in his office at the Soviet Ministry of Sport. It was a long, narrow room with the standard photos of Breszhnev and Lenin as well as ones of the Moscow Games and of various Soviet athletes covering the walls. O'Hara, an interpreter, and I sat across a table from Victor Ivonin, Pavlov, Victor Khotochkin, and Alexandr Sereda. Ivonin and Sereda were NOC vice-presidents; Khotochkin was the secretary-general.

The meeting opened with an exchange of greetings: We thanked the Soviets for their hospitality; they thanked us for coming. That was the end of the pleasantries. Pavlov didn't waste any words.

"How can you expect us to attend your Games," he asked, "when at the hockey finals at Lake Placid you Americans kept chanting, 'Kill the Russians'? What kind of hospitality is that?"

"It is common at hockey games in the United States for spectators to get overexcited," I explained. "Chants of 'Kill the referee' or 'Kill the opposing team' or 'Kill the announcer' are heard all the time and are not intended to be taken literally."

I explained that there had been demonstrations in front of our offices in Los Angeles in which people carried signs criticizing my good relationship with the USSR. I purposely neglected to tell them the signs called me a "pinko" and a "commie pig."

Pavlov then unloaded: How did we expect him to bring his athletes to Los Angeles when we'd allowed "Lithuanian murderers to emigrate there and await the arrival of our children to slaughter"?

He went on. "You remember how you captured our Aeroflot stewardess, a young nineteen-year-old, and dismembered her, cutting her body into little pieces and sending them back to us."

"That's preposterous and you know it," I shot back. I'd recently read that an Aeroflot stewardess had been murdered in New York. Police investigators, however, had determined it was a senseless street crime; the murder had nothing to do with her nationality.

"Those same Lithuanians you are now protecting in Los Angeles are the ones who did it," he said. "Your government is protecting them."

I told him he was drinking too much vodka. That didn't stop him. He had more to say.

"How about in 1976," he continued, "when your CIA kidnapped our young athlete? You called him a defector. It wasn't until he escaped and returned home that we learned the true story."

As he ranted on, I quickly scribbled a note to O'Hara, telling him to stay silent but to get ready to move out.

I waited for Pavlov to run out of gas. Then I said, "Mr. Pavlov I think I have the perfect solution."

"What is that?" he replied.

"Don't come to the Games," I said. "If you think there will be Lithuanian killers hiding behind palm trees in Los Angeles to dismember your athletes, then don't come."

I was just warming up. I was also serious.

"And don't just skip the Olympic Games. You probably

shouldn't send your athletes to any U.S. competitions. You are scheduled to participate in eight different sporting events in the United States this year. Why don't you just give it a rest and sit this year out."

Pavlov steamed. I continued.

"Mr. Pavlov, declare that you are not coming to the Games. The USSR did not attend the Olympics prior to the Helsinki Games in 1952. The Olympics did not miss you then; we won't miss you now. Announce it today. I'll gladly participate in your news conference."

Calling Pavlov's bluff served its purpose: He was stunned into silence. Typically in Soviet meetings, the top guy calls the shots and does all the talking while the others sit silently until spoken to. From then on, Pavlov limited his vitriol to criticism of Los Angeles and the LAOOC's plans, preparations, and facilities. He did, however, agree to send a delegation to Los Angeles in the near future. Not wanting to appear totally obstinate and wanting to show solidarity with the GDR and Poland, he too signed a protocol agreement with the LAOOC, but noted that the USSR NOC was not yet convinced the U.S. government would ensure that the Games were organized in strict compliance with the rules of the Olympic Charter.

From Moscow, O'Hara and I flew to Sarajevo, Yugoslavia, to meet with our counterparts for the 1984 Winter Olympics. We shared a similar problem—we both faced the same thuggery from the NOCs and the federations—and I thought we could work together in the name of Olympic solidarity.

I had met my host, Anton Sucic, president of the 1984 Winter Games Organizing Committee, briefly at Lake Placid in 1980. Both committees had grown and changed since that time and I was eager to compare notes. The visit was a welcome respite from the tense activities of the past few weeks and I delighted in the warmth and hospitality of Sucic and his team of planners.

I was surprised to learn that the Sarajevo organizers faced some of the same difficulties we had in Los Angeles.

For example, their traffic congestion and smog easily equaled L.A.'s. Unlike Los Angeles, however, the people of Sarajevo and the state of Bosnia and Herzegovina, were enthralled with the idea of hosting the Games and, whether in the streets or the shops, talked of the upcoming event in glowing terms.

Our next and last stop was Rome for the IOC session. I got a wonderful surprise upon entering the Excelsior Hotel on the Via Veneto—Ginny was waiting for me.

We embraced. Even though it'd only been two weeks since we had separated in East Berlin, it seemed much longer.

"I'm glad you flew over," I told her. "I've missed your pretty face and starting the day without you hasn't been the same." I could tell she'd been lonely too.

That evening the entire twelve-person LAOOC delegation gathered for espresso and ice cream at an outdoor café. Joel Rubenstein and Richard Perelman, vice-president for press operations, had arrived in advance. They'd learned we were going to get raked over the coals on our village costs (we had planned to charge $55 per person per day). Perelman told me we had another problem.

"Madame Berlioux is livid over the size of our delegation," he said. "The charter says six only and she intends to enforce it."

"It's not a problem," I replied.

Before retiring for the night, Anton Sucic stopped by our table and I introduced him to the group.

"How much are you charging at the villages?" I asked.

"Forty-three dollars American for each athlete for each night," he said. "The IOC wants us to reduce the price to thirty-five dollars American, which we will do."

I told him the LAOOC was headed for a battle on this and I needed his help.

"Could you keep your price at forty-three dollars for now?" I asked. "This is very important."

He agreed and did. Later we both set the price at $35.

As Perelman predicted, Berlioux was furious the next morning when twelve of us appeared to report to the IOC session.

"Only six delegates, Mr. Ueberroth," Berlioux said.

"I didn't bring these people halfway around the world to sit outside," I said loud enough so everyone in the room could hear. "Please, bring me six more chairs."

She walked off in a huff. She returned a few minutes later with members of the hotel staff carrying the extra chairs.

Our report was well received. The village price issue was postponed, as was another issue that was potentially much more explosive: testing athletes for testosterone and caffeine.

The chairman of the IOC medical commission, Prince Alexandre de Merode, was insistent we test for these two banned substances while LAOOC's medical director, Dr. Anthony F. Daly, was strongly opposed. Daly pointed out that all other drug testing determined if a banned substance existed in the athlete's body but that the proposed testosterone and caffeine testing would show how much was present. According to him, not enough research had been done to determine how much was too much or unnatural. (Two years later we agreed to test for caffeine and testosterone.)

The extra events arranged by the organizers are part of the pomp and circumstance of every IOC meeting. At this one the highlight was an audience with Pope John Paul II on the last day of the meeting.

Chairs had been set up for the IOC delegation in a small but ornate auditorium at the Vatican. IOC Protocol Director Cornelis Kerdel instructed us that strict etiquette based on IOC seniority would be enforced. But by the time Kerdel got organized and made the seating assignments, we had only a few moments before the pope arrived.

Kerdel called out the first name—the oldest member of the IOC.

"Sir Reginald Honey," he said. Honey was the ninety-five-year-old member representing South Africa.

No response.

"Sir Reginald Honey," Kerdel said again, this time louder.

Still no response. People started looking around and there was muted laughter.

"Sir Reginald Honey," he said for a third time. People were getting restless.

Finally, Sir Reginald's man servant stepped forward. "I'm sorry to say that Sir Reginald is deceased," he said.

"Oh," Kerdel said. "Are you here to represent him?"

"Yes, sir," he said.

"Well then, sit here," Kerdel said, pointing to the first chair.

By this time the pope's arrival was imminent. There was no more time to continue with IOC protocol, so we sat where we could.

The pope gave the group his blessing, and then received each of us individually. When Ginny and I were introduced, I said, "Your Holiness, we would be honored if you would attend the Olympic Games in Los Angeles."

He smiled and explained that that wasn't a good idea. He said his appearance would cause security problems we didn't need, and he was right.

I wished he was wrong. I never had a stronger first impression of an individual. Here was a man who represented peace on earth and it was too bad he couldn't attend an event devoted to that cause. I had heard he had played soccer as a child and he had the firm handshake of an athlete.

We returned to Los Angeles the next day. Overall the trip had been a success. I had opened communications with three important Eastern bloc NOCs and had been assured there'd be further dialogue. Each country had promised to send a delegation to tour the Olympic sites and review our plans. At each stop, I pledged we would adhere to the Olympic Charter, even though our Games would be organized under a different set of rules. I believed Eastern bloc nations now had a better understanding of our committee and those rules and in each case would do everything possible to attend the Games. I also understood the unspoken reality: None of the sports officials I had met, regardless of how supportive, would make the final decision. That would be done in the Politburo of the USSR.

Pavlov fulfilled his pledge and sent a seven-person delegation to L.A. in December 1982, led by Anatoli Kolesov who brought along Victor Khotochkin, two sports department heads, the chief of Soviet sports medicine, the managing director of the sports committee, and an interpreter.

They toured the facilities from Santa Barbara to Long Beach and met with LAOOC department heads for updates on our planning. Mostly they listened to what we said. Although little of substance was accomplished during the visit, we were heartened by a handwritten note from the group's interpreter, Marina Kravchenko, and by a telegram from Pavlov.

Kravchenko wrote: "I do appreciate very highly everything that has been done to make our stay here very productive and enjoyable. I also think that now everybody in our group also thinks so. Perhaps you have noticed that the mood has changed greatly. . . . There may be some more questions, but I think we are now all of us more optimistic."

I was certain the Soviets would criticize the LAOOC and the 1984 Games after they returned home. Surprisingly, they didn't.

On December 24, Pavlov sent a cable praising our treatment of his delegates: "Allow me to express our gratitude to you and your colleagues in the LAOOC for the warm welcome and hospitality offered to the Soviet delegation during its short stay in Los Angeles. We consider the results of the visit as most successful for both parties, since the opportunity of a direct and frank exchange of opinions, I think, has helped, if not to resolve the majority of the questions finally then to at least define the correct approach to settling the problems. We hope that all these problems will find their positive solution in the very near future. . . . We can assure you that the experts of the USSR NOC and of the USSR Sports Committee are prepared to render the LAOOC any assistance they can in solving the various questions related to the organization of the Games, considering their experience."

He ended the message with a New Year's greeting. It was the last time I heard from Sergei Pavlov.

The December group was an advance team for the Soviets' appearance in Los Angeles for the International Olympic Committee Executive Board meetings with the national Olympic committees in January. In late December, I received a Telex requesting appropriate accommodations and government approvals for a fourteen-person delegation to be led by Pavlov. But on January 12, 1984, two days before the meetings began, I received another Telex from the USSR NOC advising me its delegation had been reduced by half and was to be led by Victor Ivonin. Pavlov had been deleted.

The switch didn't surprise IOC President Juan Antonio Samaranch or other IOC officials. Samaranch, a former ambassador to Moscow, had maintained reliable sources within the Soviet Union and he knew Pavlov wasn't close to the leadership in Yuri Andropov's government. That day in Samaranch's suite at the Biltmore Hotel, the IOC headquarters for the meeting, Samaranch told me that Pavlov's influence had been diminishing steadily since Andropov came to power a year earlier. Numerous rumors circulated about Pavlov's demise that week, one being he'd been caught dealing in hard currencies and another that he'd been dispatched as Soviet ambassador to Mongolia as punishment.

The meetings, attended by 560 delegates representing 141 nations, served as our first opportunity to set planning into operation. We tested meeting arrangements, protocol, transportation, security, health care, accreditation, press operations, language services, electronic message and results systems, uniforming, and venue operations. Perhaps the most important development from an organizing standpoint was the extensive and successful selection, training, and use of volunteers, who served as hosts and hostesses, drivers, interpreters, doctors, and tour guides. This was our first group of volunteers and it became the core of our program, which would grow to more than forty thousand for the Games.

The *pièce de résistance* of the week-long session was in-home hospitality. About two weeks before the international officials were to converge on Los Angeles, Joan Gilford, assistant to LAOOC Chairman Paul Ziffren and manager of the program, had assembled several hundred volunteers from the advisory commissions for a meeting.

I spoke to the group and laid out specific guidelines: Hosts were required to entertain delegates in their homes, they couldn't employ a caterer, they couldn't invite friends or relatives, they had to serve typically American cuisine, they could only serve wine and beer, they had to accept the delegations we assigned, and they had to chauffeur their guests.

A few were insulted that I dared tell them how to give a party and walked out of the meeting. Those who stayed and participated contributed to a smashing success. The delegations were hosted in sixty homes throughout the greater Los Angeles area, including Mayor Bradley's where the IOC Executive Board dined.

Ginny, I, and the Ushers began the evening at the mayor's home, then we separated. Each couple visited half a dozen dinner parties. Among those Ginny and I attended were for the Soviet delegation at the home of Jayne Morgan and Jerry Weintraub, an entertainment industry leader with close ties to the USSR through a business association with Dr. Armand Hammer; the Mexican delegation at the home of Margo and Eddie Albert; and the Italian delegation at the home of Dr. Tony Daly.

Toward the end of the evening, Daly pulled Ginny and me aside. "I thought having dinners all over town was a crazy idea," he said to us. "But it turned out great."

"I can see that," Ginny said. "The highest compliment you can pay is to invite someone into your home."

The Italian delegation was obviously enjoying the evening. Daly had served a typically American dish—pasta and chianti.

"Just watch," I said. "This will pay huge dividends down the line. The Olympic family will no longer consider us hardhearted, money-grubbing Americans. You don't say that about your friends."

By and large the NOC leaders were impressed with our sports and housing facilities and the thorough knowledge of our sports commissioners. Our accreditation and transportation systems worked flawlessly. Hospitality was impeccable. Most left Los Angeles convinced we could pull it off. The Russians, however, expressed doubts.

Reporters had constantly badgered the Soviet delegation throughout their stay for interviews. Finally, at 7:30 A.M. on January 20, only a few hours before we were scheduled to report to the IOC Executive Board, Victor Ivonin called a press conference in his room at the Biltmore Hotel. He had greatly underestimated media interest: At least forty journalists showed up, including television camera crews, and reporters overflowed into the hallway. Inside the room, reporters stood on chairs and tables.

Ivonin raised four issues: First was the cost of the athletes' stay in the villages; second was U.S. government recognition of Olympic identity cards as opposed to visas for entry into the country; third was permission for Aeroflot to transport Soviet athletes to Los Angeles; and last was permission for a Soviet ship to dock in the L.A. harbor. The Soviets had used a vessel as a warehouse and for additional housing at previous Games, most recently at Montreal in 1976.

I'd been prepared to address these items in our report to the IOC and did. We had already settled the cost for housing at $35 per athlete per day—charges consistent with Sarajevo's. I also said that in keeping with the Olympic Charter use of the Olympic identity card in conjunction with a valid passport would be all that was necessary to enter the United States for the Games. (David Simon, our government relations director, had already worked this out with the State Department.) As for the Aeroflot charters and the boat, I expressed confidence that we could make the necessary arrangements through the proper channels, even though Aeroflot landing rights in the United States had been revoked as part of Carter's sanctions against the USSR for its invasion of Afghanistan.

A few weeks later, the USSR NOC notified me that Marat Gramov, a veteran Soviet propagandist from the Ministry of Information, had replaced Pavlov. I sent a Telex congratulating Gramov on his new position and inviting him to Los Angeles.

He responded in March by inviting me to the Spartakiade that July. I declined. I wanted him to visit Los Angeles before I went to Moscow again.

In late July, IOC Director Monique Berlioux, on one of her periodic inspection visits to Los Angeles, had dinner with Ken Reich of the *Los Angeles Times.* Berlioux told him that she and Samaranch feared deployment of U.S. cruise and Pershing 2 missiles in Western Europe would spark a Soviet boycott.

I was outraged when I read the story and would have strangled her had she been sitting in my office that morning. But she was safely out of town in Colorado Springs. I'd spent many hours with Berlioux over the course of her three-day visit and never once had she broached the subject. I fired off a Telex to Samaranch and told him how damned angry I was. I wrote: "I must state that this type of counterproductive publicity is damaging to the Olympic Games and the Olympic Movement and I know you agree with me on this matter."

I issued a press statement saying the LAOOC had not received any such information and that I considered Berlioux's alleged remarks improper. I added that I expected the athletes of the Soviet Union to participate.

A few days later Gramov held a news conference on the eve of Spartakiade and criticized the LAOOC's plans for security transportation and housing. Gramov announced that the Soviet decision to compete in the Games wouldn't be made until May 24, 1984. According to a report filed out of Moscow by Bill Shirley of the *Los Angeles Times,* Gramov had said that our refusal to pay the expenses of foreign sports officials and referees would create a greater reliance on domestic officiating, inferring the judging would be biased. This was a complaint we hadn't heard before.

It was then that I decided to accept Gramov's invitation to go to Moscow. Usher went with me and Spartakiade was in progress when we arrived in Moscow. We attended competitions in gymnastics, equestrian, and swimming the first day and then met with Gramov and other sports officials the next.

Gramov began the meeting by referring to the recent comments made by Berlioux. He discussed the word "boycott" and explained how the word didn't exist in Russian.

"If we decide not to come, it will be a decision of the

national Olympic committee and will have nothing to do with
a so-called boycott," he said.

The meeting was extremely businesslike. Gramov didn't
rant and rave like Pavlov, though he did raise similar issues.
Gramov's concerns were security in general and anti-Soviet
demonstrations in particular. After reassuring him that every
security precaution imaginable would be taken to protect his
team, I carefully explained that peaceful demonstrations were
guaranteed by U.S. law. I promised, however, that demonstrations would not be permitted on the grounds of Olympic
venues.

Gramov then raised the issue of landing Aeroflot charter
planes and docking a Soviet cruise ship in L.A.'s harbor. He
explained the charters would carry the athletes, officials, and
spectators; the ship would transport equipment.

I told him we needed additional specific information in
order to process an official request through government channels. I didn't believe the Reagan administration would block
the requests and told him so.

On the subject of a Soviet attaché, I requested he ap-
point one as soon as possible. The Olympic Charter allows
each NOC to assign an attaché as a liaison to the organizing
committee to make last-minute preparations for the team. In
most cases, NOCs select a person who permanently resides in
the host city. On the other hand, if an attaché assigned to the
host city is to take up residence several months before the
Games, he must enter the country through normal channels.

The issue about the quality of judging did not come up
with Gramov. Soviet sports officials knew well that the selection of judges and referees was within the realm of the international sports federations and not that of the organizing
committee.

Before wrapping up the meeting, we agreed to terms on a
television rights contract for the Eastern bloc, and Gramov
accepted my invitation to visit Los Angeles. Again I was
hopeful that the Soviets would compete in the Games.
Gramov was impressive, both in stature and intellect, and had
obviously gone to great lengths to get up to speed on sports
issues. I left Moscow feeling his greatest concern was that we

abide by the Olympic Charter to the letter. I believed we could do that.

Now that Gramov had confirmed his visit, I felt we were back on track. On November 17, he sent another Telex listing the twelve-member team, which included a fellow named Oleg Yermishkin.

Ed Best came into my office two hours later and told me Yermishkin was a known KGB operative. He's been stationed in the Soviet embassy in Washington for several years.

"He's hotter than a pistol," he said.

Nevertheless, the State Department had approved his request for a visa.

Gramov's Telex also outlined an agenda: The delegates wanted to visit Mayor Bradley, the Olympic villages, and the venues for shooting, track and field, gymnastics, yachting, rowing, and canoeing. They also proposed discussions on housing arrangements for the Soviet delegation, payments, transportation, charter flights, docking of a ship, and plans for an Olympic attaché.

The Soviets arrived in two shifts—both through Mexico City since Aeroflot was prohibited from landing in the United States. We housed the delegates at the Marina City Club in Marina del Rey, near our offices. We wined and dined them. We took them to Disneyland. They shopped in Beverly Hills and Santa Monica. One night we escorted them to a Lakers basketball game at the Forum in Inglewood. Each social function was attended by different staff members so that the Soviets could meet the high-caliber people we had on the organizing committee.

Gramov told me at our first meeting in L.A. that Yermishkin was the USSR NOC's choice to be its Olympic attaché. According to his printed biography, Yermishkin was an administrative and logistical expert for the USSR Sports Committee and NOC. He traveled with the pack throughout the visit and was mostly unobtrusive.

On the delegation's last working day, December 5, Best gave a security briefing to the delegation. Yermishkin was there. Best later told me that during a break, he and Yermishkin chatted like old intelligence hands. Best said Yermishkin not only clung to the cover story that he was a sports expert, but also expressed excitement about coming back to Los Angeles to make preparations for the team. He asked Best to help him find an apartment with a well-equipped kitchen in the UCLA area. "I love to cook," he had said. He also told Best that when he returned he'd like to go tuna fishing and see the LAPD's SWAT operation in action.

During this visit, I called on my friend Dr. Armand Hammer and asked him to host the Soviet delegation for lunch. Hammer, chairman of Occidental Petroleum, had been a friend of Lenin and has a lifetime association with the Soviet Union and its leaders. His involvement with the Soviets is multifaceted, and he's the only American citizen I know who can come and go as freely in that country as he pleases.

One humorous aside I had with Hammer was his insistence that he be given an organizing committee title—special assistant to the president—and business cards and stationery printed to that effect. He scribbled a personal postscript on every note he sent me wondering where his office supplies were. I didn't think the title was necessary, so I finally told him: "You fly in on your private jet wherever you go and everybody knows who you are. I don't think LAOOC business cards can possibly enhance your international stature." But Hammer persisted, so we gave him the cards and stationery.

Lunch was a success. Hammer's support was an effective lead in to our last piece of unfinished business with Gramov— the signing of a protocol accord. That afternoon I met with the delegation in my office and began drafting a document acceptable to both parties. Gramov and I later refined it, and we both signed it at a farewell dinner at the Regency Club in Westwood.

We agreed that the USSR NOC would notify us of its participation by June 2, 1984; it would assign an Olympic attaché to take up residence in Los Angeles no later than March 1, 1984; we would process its request for landing rights and docking privileges; and we agreed that its team would live at Rieber Hall at the University of California, Los Angeles Olympic Village.

We covered the broad strokes of the agreement in a news conference. I said nice things about Gramov and he said nice things about me and the LAOOC. Questions of Soviet participation and Soviet concerns for security, transportation, and smog dominated the news conference.

Gramov's propaganda expertise came into play when he answered a question about his concerns over long-distance travel between venues by saying: "Dear friends, there are concerns not only about the distances between the Olympic venues. I think that jointly with the organizing committee we shall be working to overcome those obstacles and problems. But there are some concerns of a different nature. Here in Los Angeles we have only one journalist representing the Soviet Union. He is the correspondent of Tass news agency. As you know, the Tass news agency is one of the five IOC-recognized agencies which must be present during the Games. I do not see this journalist here."

Gramov was referring to Yuri Ustimenko who lived in San Francisco. In the 1950s, the Soviet Union restricted certain areas of its country to U.S. residents and the United States later followed suit with restrictions of its own. These cold war limitations still applied and were the target of Gramov's attack. We were aware of the numerous off-limit areas in southern California and had obtained a waiver for Ustimenko from the State Department before the delegation visit. He'd already accompanied the group to several prohibited areas, one being Disneyland, and knew he was cleared to attend the press conference, even though it was held at a hotel in a restricted area near the airport to accommodate the Soviets, who were departing immediately afterward.

It was a setup. The day before, Amy Quinn had reiterated to Ustimenko that he had permission to go with the delegation wherever it went. Ustimenko, however, had no intention of attending the press conference because Gramov had a point to make and Ustimenko was the vehicle by which Gramov would make it.

I immediately had the Soviet requests for the charter flights, mooring of a ship, and selection of Yermishkin as attaché forwarded by courier to Jay Moorhead, the LAOOC's Washington, D.C., liaison, who, in turn, hand carried the documents to Michael Deaver's office where he was promised swift action.

At my instruction, Moorhead sent a cover letter to Deaver's assistant, Michael A. McManus, Jr., clarifying the LAOOC's position on the Soviet requests. I wanted the White House to know that the proposals were consistent with the Olympic Charter and should be seen as a Soviet test of the Reagan administration's willingness to abide by it.

I hoped the administration would draw a distinction between its Olympics policy and its Soviet policy. A negative response would create an easy out for the Eastern bloc nations. While we supported the Soviet requests, however, we also understood the government's need to place conditions on its approval. We suggested the ship be periodically inspected in order to satisfy any objections that could be raised by government agencies.

I made it clear through Moorhead I wanted answers— regardless of what they were—to give Gramov at our next meeting at the Sarajevo Winter Games in early February.

The preliminary feedback Moorhead got from the State Department and the White House was mixed. He was told Yermishkin would probably be approved but to expect difficulties getting the ship and all the Aeroflot flights the Soviets wanted approved. The Reagan administration made it clear it wasn't going to roll over for the Soviets just because of an Olympic Games.

I was tired. The pressure was intense. I've always felt it's important to recognize fatigue and do something about it—it doesn't make any sense to plow ahead when weary. Part of my management style has always been to give those around me a week off when they needed it. I knew it was my time.

From Christmas to New Year's, I gathered my family and we went skiing with Jim Easton and his kids at Deer Valley, Utah. After some great skiing, we spent New Year's Eve playing Trivial Pursuit into the wee hours of the morning.

The next day, the kids scattered with the wind: Vicki returned to college for her last year and a half; Heidi hurried to Vanderbilt University in Nashville, Tennessee, eager to join a sorority; Keri flew to Villars, Switzerland, for her last year at

L'Aiglon College; and Joe went back to Cate School in Santa Barbara to finish his freshman year of high school. Although Ginny and I would occasionally see the children during the coming months, we wouldn't be together again as a family until right before the Games.

It was time to return to Los Angeles to start the final and hardest lap.

DOUBLE TIME

CONTRARY TO POPULAR BELIEF, the Olympic flame and the torch relay did not begin in ancient Greece. The idea of a flame-lighting ceremony was suggested to the International Olympic Committee by one of its members, Theodore Lewald of Germany, in 1928. The IOC approved Lewald's plan to light the flame in Olympia, Greece, the site of the ancient Games, and transport it by relay to the country hosting the Games. Although the relay wasn't run that year, the planners of the Amsterdam Games did ignite a flame, which burned throughout the Games, at the entrance to the stadium. A flame was ignited again four years later in Los Angeles.

Carl Diem, the founder of the Graduate School of Sports in Cologne, Germany, organized the first Olympic torch relay for the 1936 Berlin Games. As suggested by Lewald, the flame was lit in Olympia and hand carried through Europe to Berlin for the opening ceremonies.

Torch relays have been part of the Olympics ever since. In 1964, 101,473 runners carried the flame more than five thousand miles in and around Japan to start the Tokyo Games. The final torchbearer, a man named Yoshinori Sakai, was born in Hiroshima the day the atom bomb was dropped. In 1968 the flame reached the shores of the Americas via the sea route Christopher Columbus took to the New World. The torch relay took fifty days to Mexico City and involved 2,279 runners, the last being Enriqueta Basilio, the first woman to light the stadium torch. For the 1976 Montreal Games, the flame was lit by remote control: Its energy was coded by a sensor in Athens and then beamed to a satellite, which transmitted the energy to Ottawa. Seven hundred runners then carried the flame from Ottawa to Montreal. On the final leg, two fifteen-year-old students brought the flame to the top of the stadium, where it remained throughout the Games. Those two runners subsequently married.

I had started thinking about the torch relay as early as 1980. I knew our relay would have to be something very special to attract the attention of the American people. At that time, only southern California was interested in the Games—and most of that interest was negative. To make the Games a success, the American people had to be proud that they were being held in their country, and a torch relay might spark that interest.

There were several ways to go. The best, I was convinced, was to fly the flame into New York City from Greece and run it across the width of the country. It was a good idea that needed polishing. I waited two years before going forward with the planning.

There was stiff resistance the first time I broached the subject to senior LAOOC staff members, who viewed it as a logistical nightmare and gave more reasons to drop the concept than develop it.

Priscilla Florence, our director of personnel, worried about its effect on the Games staffing. "It'll take hundreds of employees away at a time when we need every ounce of manpower available to get ready for the Games," she said.

Harry Usher had his eye on the bottom line as usual. He said, "It'll be too costly and won't be worth the effort from a public relations standpoint."

"Why don't we just fly it to San Francisco and run it from there?" Dick Sargent suggested. Being the trouble shooter, Sargent saw this project coming his way and wanted to narrow the margin for error.

"It's a security nightmare," Ed Best said. "What if some maniac douses a torchbearer with a bucket of gasoline? Or a lunatic starts firing from a hillside?"

They hadn't raised any issues I hadn't thought of. In fact, I could add a few more to the list: obstinate city officials holding us up for permits, local politicians grandstanding along the way, logistical breakdowns and total uninterest on the part of the American people.

Nonetheless, I believed that with good planning we could eliminate the negatives and create a relay Americans would remember for the rest of their lives. I put it to a vote and was outvoted seven to one. My instinct is to go with the majority, but in this case I knew deep in my gut the majority was wrong. I needed time to think it over, so I let it sit for a week.

The more I thought about it, the more I knew it was the right thing to do. After the week was up, I pulled the same group together.

"Sorry," I said. "We're going to run the torch across the country." No one tried to talk me out of it—they knew better.

Since this was a high-cost, high-risk project, our first priority was to line up another sponsor. Only a corporation in a position to benefit greatly from a national campaign and which had the resources to back it to the hilt would do. AT&T immediately came to mind. It had the depth, reach, and nationwide network of affiliates unmatched by any other company.

Jerry Foster, region vice-president of Pacific Bell, the western affiliate of AT&T, was wild about the relay and convinced AT&T executives in New York to sponsor it.

In the middle of our negotiations, a federal judge ruling on an antitrust lawsuit ordered AT&T to deregulate. This enormous entity was carved up into several smaller regional and autonomous parts. The judge's ruling, however, gave AT&T greater incentive to go forward with the relay. It was a means for AT&T to retain a national, united image during its restructuring process.

Foster diligently went to work on each division—AT&T, Pacific Bell, AT&T Directory Services, AT&T Long Lines Division, and Western Electric Company—and helped us lock each into the sponsorship deal.

On September 29, 1982, we announced AT&T as the official sponsor of the 1984 Olympic torch relay. AT&T agreed to pay for all logistical costs including vehicles, maintenance, and manpower, and to provide a cadre of runners to carry the torch in areas where there were no local runners. In addition, it offered the services of the Telephone Pioneers of America, an active group of phone-company employees who had worked for the company a minimum of eighteen years, as a resource for logistics and planning.

With AT&T on board, the plan moved ahead. But something was still missing. We needed a strong, emotional hook.

Whenever I wanted to bat ideas around, I sought out the original idea man, David Wolper. This was no exception. We'd already spent many hours discussing ways to get people from all walks of life involved in the relay when, over breakfast one morning, Wolper suggested we use the relay to raise money for the organizing committee. By donating money to run, Wolper explained, people would be making a commitment to the Games. That wasn't the hook I was looking for but it was close. I suggested it might work if the funds stayed in the communities.

I refined that idea and opened the relay to all Americans who wanted to participate and donate $3,000 to a charity— not to the LAOCC—in their community. Everybody said that was too much money, but a large donation gave the plan meaning. If 3,350 people across America each donated $3,000, the relay would raise $10 million. That's a good fundraiser.

Dan Cruz, who ran our Olympic youth programs, lined up the Boys and Girls Clubs of America and the family YMCAs as the original beneficiaries of the relay. Those organizations were selected because of their grass-roots memberships—you can find one or all three in practically every community in the country. Also, they agreed that all funds raised would go to Olympic-type sports programs; none of the funds would be used for capital improvements. A fourth beneficiary—Special Olympics—was added later.

The final step was to clear the decks with our international partners. The IOC was easy. Both IOC President Juan Antonio Samaranch and IOC Director Monique Berlioux expressed concern about apparent commercialization of the relay, but changed their minds when they learned that not one penny would go to the LAOOC or to eligible Olympic athletes: The money would stay in the communities and help kids become better acquainted with Olympic sports programs. Samaranch and Berlioux considered this positive, long-range support for the Olympic Movement.

The Greeks weren't as understanding. At the IOC's eighty-sixth session in New Delhi in March 1983, Harry Usher outlined the torch-relay concept to the entire IOC membership. The Greek IOC members, Nikos Filaretos and Nikolaos Nissiotis, objected, claiming we were commercializing the flame. Samaranch interceded on our behalf and persuaded them to support the relay, and the Greeks, as part of the IOC membership, signed off on the project before the end of the session.

I then sent Sargent to Greece to hammer out the details of the 500-kilometer relay that we would finance from Olympia to Athens. Sargent made sure we would get the flame in time to start our relay in New York.

Although the twenty-page agreement didn't outline the scope of our relay, the Greeks clearly understood our plan. The contract focused on the number of uniforms, shoes, torches, and flags they would need for their portion of the relay. It also specified the size of the LAOOC delegation to witness the flame ceremony and accompany the flame to the United States.

I figured the Greek issue was resolved. We stated our plans for the 1984 Olympic torch relay on July 28, 1983—one year before the start of the Games—in a bicoastal press conference. I went to New York City and shared the announcement honors with Mayor Ed Koch and the AT&T brass, while Usher, Paul Ziffren, and Mayor Bradley made a similar announcement in Los Angeles.

We said the relay would start in New York on May 8, 1984, travel twelve thousand miles, and pass through all fifty

states. Any individual, community organization, group, or business making a commitment of $3,000 could designate a torchbearer to run a kilometer. We called these Youth Legacy Kilometers (YLKs) and set a goal of ten thousand YLKs, which would net $30 million for America's youth.

The New York press conference was held at the Madison Square Boys Club. One reporter addressing Mayor Koch asked, "Mayor Koch, how are you going to allow this torch to go through New York? Who's going to pay for the security costs?"

This was typical, I thought. Here we are, standing in a Boys Club trying to raise money for kids and the press was already skeptical.

"We won't charge them a dime," Koch said without missing a beat. "They are trying to help youth and help the city. We are proud to have the torch here. It won't be a problem for New York."

After explaining the sponsorship program, I announced how the relay would start.

"You probably don't know the name Gina Hemphill," I said, "but you might remember her grandfather. The torch-relay idea started in Berlin, Germany, during the time of Hitler. It was during those Games that a little known American athlete went to Berlin and made the best possible statement anyone could make against Hitler's racist policies. His name was Jesse Owens. He won four gold medals.

"Gina will share the first kilometer with a young man who is a Native American. His grandfather was once proclaimed the athlete of the half-century. He competed in the 1912 Stockholm Olympics where he won two gold medals. His name was Jim Thorpe and we are proud to have his grandson Bill run alongside Gina."

Hemphill and Thorpe came to the front of the room to meet the press. They provided the necessary spark. Reporters loved the idea and wrote great stories about it. Suddenly I was certain the program would sell itself from then on.

I had other business besides the torch relay in New York that day. After the press conference, I met Bob Lurie and John McMullen—the owners of the San Francisco Giants and the Houston Astros—for lunch. Lurie, an old friend, and McMullen were on the major league baseball search committee for a new commissioner. Bowie Kuhn, baseball's commissioner since 1969, had already gotten word that the owners were looking for a replacement.

Lurie and I had been partners a few months earlier in a foursome at the Bing Crosby Pro-Am golf tournament at Pebble Beach, California. There he had first floated the idea by me and I had expressed interest.

During lunch Lurie and McMullen made it clear the owners were interested in my succeeding Kuhn, providing I was willing to start right away. That was out of the question and I told them so. I returned to Los Angeles thinking baseball was behind me and to begin dealing with the logistics of carrying the torch across the country.

We'd put the cart before the horse by announcing the torch relay before figuring out how to do it. The man most responsible for eventually putting it together was Wally McGuire, a San Francisco-based political consultant. Before he joined us in September 1983, nobody at the LAOOC had a clue how to schedule or advance a cross-country relay.

McGuire was recommended to me by Amy Quinn, who'd worked with him on two political campaigns—Governor Edmund G. Brown, Jr.'s gubernatorial campaign in 1978 and Brown's presidential campaign two years later. McGuire had also advanced numerous international trips for President Jimmy Carter, including the Jerusalem portion of Carter's shuttle diplomacy between Israel and Egypt. He'd also taught training seminars to advance people who worked on the presidential campaigns of George McGovern in 1972, Brown in 1976 and 1980, and Carter in 1980. (He later taught training seminars for advance people working for Vice President Walter Mondale in 1984).

McGuire was the perfect choice for the job. I had persuaded AT&T to pay his salary and only met with him five times before the relay began. The first time, he told me that going through fifty states was too ambitious and too difficult given the time constraints. He recommended scaling back. I

Carl Lewis (USA), winner of four gold medals, sprints to victory in the 200 meter.

Above, Alex Bannian (CAN) establishes an Olympic record in the 400-meter individual medley, the first gold medal in swimming for his country in seventy-two years.

Left, all-round Olympic champion Mary Lou Retton won five medals, including one gold, two silver, and two bronze.

Above, Randy Lewis (USA) outpoints Chris Brown (AUS) in freestyle wrestling.

Right, Zola Budd (GBR) and Mary Decker (USA) leading eventual winner, Maricica Puica (ROM), in the 3000-meter final.

Above, Joan Benoit (USA) is the winner of the first women's marathon.

Left, Greg Louganis (USA) won gold medals in both springboard and platform diving.

Overleaf, the U.S. men's volleyball team wins the gold medal, America's first-ever medal in the sport.

told him to go ahead and shorten the route and asked him for three alternatives—so long as we took the flame to areas where people supported the concept—by the first of the year. I gave him one directive: "When you set the route, be an artist. Paint a picture across this country." I never worried again about the logistics.

Meanwhile, the Greeks had the torch relay on their minds too. On December 19, Angelo Lembessis, president of the Greek NOC, and Filaretos, the NOC secretary-general in addition to being an IOC member, fired off a scathing telegram accusing the LAOOC of using the Olympic torch relay "as a tool for collection of money for athletic resources." They went on to say that "our protest reflects also the entire Greek public opinion which has the unshaken belief that a 'sacrilege' is attempted against an institution which Greece considers as sacred and is determined to protect by all possible means." They claimed we never explained the nature of our relay and demanded we make a public announcement abandoning the plan.

The accusation that they knew nothing of our plans was not true. Usher had explained it to Filaretos and Nissiotis in New Delhi, and Sargent had explained it again during his visit to Greece in July. Additionally, we had extended an invitation to the Greek NOC to participate in our press conference announcing the relay, which it declined.

I resented the charges. I replied immediately by reminding them that our objectives—to present a symbol to the youth of the world, to educate young people to the Olympic Movement through participation in Olympic sports on a continuing basis, to expose the significance of the Olympic flame and its part in the Olympic Games worldwide, and to provide all torchbearers and their friends and families an opportunity to participate in Olympic history through the torch relay— were entirely consistent with the objectives of the IOC and the Greek Olympic Committee. I couldn't figure out where we'd gone wrong.

Lastly, I wondered who the Greeks thought they were to raise complaints about the commercialization of the Olympic Games. They affected great umbrage, yet the economy of

Olympia was largely dependent on commercializing the flame. There's a hotel there called the Olympic Flame Hotel and there are shops that sell plastic Olympic torches and other memorabilia. The national airlines of Greece is called Olympic Airlines and uses the Olympic rings as its logo.

Filaretos wired back suggesting we resolve this "deadlock" at the Winter Games in Sarajevo in February. I liked Nissiotis, a university professor, and believed him to be an honest man. I wasn't so sure about Filaretos. I had no reason to believe we'd settle anything with him in Sarajevo, since we'd already signed two deals. Filaretos knew exactly what we were doing, and I believed he had changed his mind for political reasons.

On Tuesday, January 3, my first meeting of the day was with Wally McGuire. He presented only one torch-relay route—a winding, nine-thousand-mile trek that took the flame to every region of the country but to only thirty-three states and the District of Columbia.

McGuire assured me the route would achieve our goals and, most important, would work. I gave him the green light to hire people to advance the route.

The announced scale-back the next day didn't appease the Greeks, who still wanted to meet in Sarajevo. So did the Soviets. Between the two of them we had our hands full. It wouldn't be long before I'd begin to wonder about a connection.

Later that week Marat Gramov sent a Telex complaining that the U.S. government was blocking their requests for the attaché, charter flights, and transport ship. If he could expect better results by going directly to the U.S. government, he wanted to know about it. By reply, I told him that in keeping with the Olympic Charter he should continue to work through the committee.

I went to Washington the following week to push things along. The Games were right around the corner—we didn't have time to dawdle as government moved at its normal slow pace.

First I met with Ed Derwinski, counselor to Secretary of

State George Schultz. Jay Moorhead, our man in Washington, was with me. Derwinski, a former congressman from Illinois, seemed to be a pleasant man with a full face and a crewcut. He looked like a retired marine sergeant.

He'd brought along a group of security and foreign relations experts to brief us on international terrorism. I didn't need that; I'd read the *New York Times* that morning. Besides, the villains they identified had long been the subjects of cheap dimestore novels. I expected a lot more from a high-ranking State Department official.

I became impatient as they rambled on. Finally I said, "You know, I can see that the only purpose of this meeting is to put us on notice that there is a potential for problems. I already know about Carlos and FALN. Tell me something new."

I was damned disappointed with their lack of commitment and insulted they'd try to snow me with a show-and-tell game. As difficult as it was, I stayed civil. But my frustration carried over to the next meeting, with Mike Deaver and his staff at the White House.

Ken Hill, the White House security liaison, and Deaver's two assistants, Bill Sittman and Mike McManus, joined Deaver, Moorhead, and me for lunch. I said that bureaucratic foot dragging was almost as high as terrorism on my list of chief concerns for the Games. Hill, who'd been with the State Department, offered to help. Deaver added that Sittman had replaced McManus as Olympic liaison and was our new White House contact. McManus had been promoted to White House director of communications.

Deaver's main concern that day was to make sure we rolled out the red carpet and had tickets available for ambassadors. I told Deaver that Mayor Bradley had already made those kinds of arrangements with the State Department and assured him that the key ambassadors would be treated well.

We then discussed the Soviet requests. Deaver said they were moving along.

"You have nothing to worry about," he said. "The Russians will be here."

"Mike," I replied, "if I were a gambler I'd say there is a

good chance they'll come. But by no means are they a sure thing. After listening to you, I'm more concerned than ever. I firmly believe the Soviets are testing the Reagan administration's sincerity about abiding by the Olympic Charter—every bit as much as they are testing a private group's ability to stage the Games. They won't make it easy on us. One slipup is the only excuse they'll need to boycott the Games."

Deaver thought I was being overly dramatic, but I wasn't. I'd become politically savvy enough to know that in an election year the Reagan people might come to us for help down the line and there would be room for trading. I didn't have to tell Deaver that the outcome of the Games might have a profound effect on the election.

My last meeting of the day turned out to be the most enjoyable. Moorhead and I paid a visit to the ambassador from the Soviet Union, Anatoli Dobrynin, late that afternoon. We arrived at the Soviet embassy on 16th Street at 5 P.M. and were escorted upstairs where two ministers met us.

One asked, "Is this your first time to our embassy?"

I nodded.

"Welcome," he said. We were then led inside to the main parlor, a beautifully ornate room filled with nineteenth-century Russian furnishings. The ceiling was trimmed with gold and a tray filled with fruits, candies, cookies, coffee, and tea was laid out on the table.

Dobrynin entered the room and introduced himself. I introduced Moorhead. We sat down.

"So tell me," he began, "how goes your Olympic Games?"

I gave him a five-minute overview, emphasizing that we were a small private committee and that I was in Washington to push along the Soviet requests for the cargo ship, airplanes, and attaché. Dobrynin admitted he wasn't an avid sportsman. He said he could barely ride a bicycle.

"I'd be a more devoted follower of sports if chess were a part of the Olympic Games," he said. "Chess is a sport, isn't it?"

"It is a very demanding sport," I said. "Unfortunately, it is not part of the Olympic program."

"One of your staff members was in to see me at lunch," he said. "He gave me this card." He handed me Armand Hammer's LAOOC business card." I promised him I would tell you that he is working hard."

We discussed Hammer and his friendship with the Russians. Dobrynin's fondness, high regard, and trust for Hammer were evident. He told me how his daughter had joined them for lunch and had discussed politics at length with Hammer. Dobrynin said he was impressed that his thirteen-year-old daughter was able to hold her own. He said with a smile, "She did so well I may leave her in charge of the embassy the next time I go to Moscow."

Dobrynin explained the girl he called his daughter was actually his granddaughter. The child's mother, Dobrynin's daughter, had divorced her husband many years earlier when the child was six. Dobrynin had brought the child to Washington, where they developed a strong relationship. In time, he adopted her. "Now I have two daughters, one a thirteen-year-old and the other a forty-year-old," he said laughing. Jay and I laughed with him.

I told him about my daughters and said that thirteen-year-old girls can be difficult and wonderful at the same time. Dobrynin said he knew what I meant. Against his will, his daughter had been experimenting with makeup, going to great lengths to hide it from him. Dobrynin, while imitating how his daughter would try to hide the makeup, made some wonderful facial expressions.

Just then she entered the room. She was thirteen years old going on seventeen, a pretty and extremely poised blonde. I gave her some Olympic memorabilia and invited her to the Games.

"I have a fourteen-year-old son who'd be happy to escort you to the events," I said. She thanked me. But, she said, she was going to Moscow for the summer and didn't expect to return in time. We got down to Olympic business after she left.

"There are a few things I would like you to hear directly from me," I began. "First, all Soviet athletes, officials, and guests will be treated fairly. Second, I have always kept my

word in negotiations with the USSR officials. From my years
in the travel business, I feel I know your people well and I
have the utmost respect for them. Third, I will work hard to
get an early decision on the requests made by your national
Olympic committee."

I reminded him that his people had to be patient because
we were only a small and insignificant committee. A good
working relationship between the LAOOC and the USSR was
essential to the success of the Games, and, I told him, Soviet
officials should bring all their questions and concerns straight
to me.

"I know all about business," I said, "but I don't know
much about how government works. You probably understand the U.S. government much better than I."

Dobrynin laughed. "Yes, I know the U.S. government
quite well."

We ended the meeting by arranging for Jay Moorhead to
work directly with one of Dobrynin's assistants, Viktor Cherkashin, on relevant issues.

It was an uplifting meeting. We had talked as fathers and
that led me to believe we had talked as friends. Since
Dobrynin had the ear of those in power within the Politburo,
I hoped my message of LAOOC's sincerity in hosting the Soviets would reach Moscow.

I hadn't been back in Los Angeles thirty-six hours when
Moorhead called. He was in a snit. "Peter," he said, "you
won't believe this."

"Trust me, Jay," I replied.

"The Soviet requests have been sitting on Mike
McManus's desk ever since I delivered them last month. No
one in the State Department has even seen them. Nothing has
been done."

Sittman had discovered the oversight when McManus
turned over the Olympic portfolio to him.

"You're right," I said, "I don't believe it." I paused for a
moment. "Jay,." I said, trying to keep my voice steady and
controlled, "take another set of requests over to Sittman and
find out who at State will make the decision on each item.

Then I want you to check daily until the decisions are made. I need answers to give Gramov by the time I leave for Sarajevo."

That was in less than three weeks.

I wasn't too surprised on January 19 when Gramov again went public with his complaints, charging that the State Department did not recognize LAOOC's authority and was blocking Soviet requests.

Publicly, I covered for White House inefficiency. We had a long way to go and would need much White House assistance before the Games were over. I told reporters I understood Gramov's concern, but I also understood why the Soviet NOC's requests had to go through appropriate government channels. Given the myriad important issues with which government must deal, I said, there were times when Olympic issues took a backseat.

Privately, I resented remarks made by State Department officials that I was out of line for making deals with the USSR National Olympic Committee. Before the Soviet press conference in December, Deaver and I had made a deal that the Reagan administration would comply with Olympic Charter rules that NOC requests go through the LAOOC. It was up to Deaver to share information about our deal with the appropriate agencies, including State.

This lack of coordination and communication among government agencies continued to plague me as it affected every important facet of the Games, particularly security. I had believed that government cooperation would naturally get stronger as the Games approached. This episode proved there was reason to worry. The Olympic Games were obviously not a high priority for either the Reagan administration or the State Department, and I couldn't imagine how priorities would change over the next six months.

While the Russians simmered, the Greeks boiled. Two days after Gramov's announcement, Spyros Foteinos, the Communist mayor of Olympia, said he wouldn't let the flame leave his town unless we canceled the Youth Legacy Kilometer program. We were trapped in a revolving door: first the

Soviets, then our government, then the Greeks. It made my week when I read in the paper that Iran was boycotting the Games. Prime Minister Hussein Musavi had said their reason was "to expose the criminal acts of the world-devouring U.S. government."

A week before going to Sarajevo, I pressured Moorhead for answers to the Soviet requests. Moorhead met with John Matlock of the National Security Council and Ken Hill on Thursday, January 26. The next day he flew to Los Angeles to give me a report. I wanted the news in person, the issues were that sensitive.

Also, Jay no longer trusted the telephones in his Washington office. Shortly before Christmas, a secretary had seen a well-dressed man carrying a briefcase leaving Moorhead's office early one morning. She had exchanged greetings with the mystery man, assuming he was leaving a meeting with Moorhead. She went about her business for a few minutes, then she became curious and opened the door to Moorhead's office. Nobody was in there.

We immediately had the offices swept for bugging devices. Nothing turned up, and Moorhead couldn't find that anything was missing. We assumed the mystery man had photographed documents.

First thing Friday morning, Moorhead and I had coffee in my office while he recounted his meeting at the White House.

"What specifically can I tell Gramov," I asked.

"Matlock is very optimistic," Moorhead replied. "He said that privately you can tell Gramov he can dock the ship, land the planes, and he'll get an attaché."

"What do you mean by 'an' attaché?" I pressed. "What about Yermishkin?"

Moorhead hedged. "He didn't mention Yermishkin by name but stated the attaché was acceptable."

Jay had more faith than I did. I wasn't at all convinced. If Yermishkin was acceptable, why didn't Matlock mention him by name? I decided on impulse not to pass the information on to Gramov.

Before leaving for Sarajevo, Ginny and I went to Pebble Beach on February 2 for the Bing Crosby Pro-Am golf tournament. Ever since I'd met with Bob Lurie and John McMullen, Lurie, Bud Selig, the owner of the Milwaukee Brewers and head of the baseball commissioner search committee, Los Angeles Dodgers owner Peter O'Malley, and Seattle Mariner owner George Argyros had been encouraging me to take over major league baseball.

Lurie wanted to talk to me again, so we made arrangements to meet in Pebble Beach. There I told him a few close friends had been urging me to go to baseball right away rather than stay with the Olympics and take the chance of failure. While I appreciated their concern, there was no way I would do that. Lurie asked me what it would take. I told him I'd be interested if baseball could wait until the Games were over.

Lurie called Bud Selig who immediately flew to Pebble Beach with Lou Hoynes, the National League's attorney, and a partner of the well-known Willkie, Farr & Gallagher law firm. The four of us then mapped out a few preliminary ground rules to consider upon my return from Sarajevo.

Reporters covering the Crosby tournament must have heard we were getting together because they converged on me as I approached the first tee. I confirmed that I had met with Lurie and other members of the search committee, but added that I was with the Games through the Games.

Ginny and I discussed baseball and our lives after the Games on the flight to Sarajevo from San Francisco. For the first time in our lives, we'd be independent. The kids were settled in their various schools and were happy. Finances were no problem, and New York appealed to both of us.

We'd often discussed how media scrutiny, which had intensified each year, had become a brutal invasion of our privacy. A major change, besides being welcome, was inevitable and New York and baseball provided that. We decided we'd do it if we could dictate the terms. Talking about baseball and our future had a soothing effect on me and by the time we arrived in Sarajevo, I was clear-headed and prepared to tackle the issues with the Greeks and the Soviets.

After checking into the Holiday Inn, Sarajevo's swankiest and most modern hotel, Harry Usher briefed me on a meeting he'd already had with Filaretos, Nissiotis, and Samaranch. IOC Executive Board member Alexandru Siperco of Romania had joined the discussions as an intermediary at Samaranch's request. Usher, in an effort to appease the Greeks, had agreed to halt Youth Legacy Kilometer sales in early April. Siperco was preparing the written document which was to be signed by both parties that evening at an IOC Executive Board meeting.

Usher then told me about Bill Hussey's trip to Greece. Hussey was a retired State Department official who handled international relations for David Simon, our director of government relations. He'd gone to Greece to feel the pulse of government and Greek Olympic Committee leaders. En route to Yugoslavia, Usher had rendezvoused with Hussey at the Frankfurt airport, where Hussey reported that the Papandreou government figured the conflict over our torch relay would soon dissipate and planned to stay out of it. Mayor Spyros Foteinos continued to take a hard line and told Hussey that the only way we were going to get the flame out of Olympia was for me to go get it.

That wasn't good news and neither, as it turned out, was Usher's agreement with the Greeks. The one Siperco drafted and that was already signed by Filaretos and Nissiotis didn't reflect the oral agreement Usher had made earlier in the day. It was much more restrictive and would have created chaos for us and the program. We refused to sign.

Branko Mikulic, chairman of the Sarajevo Organizing Committee and president of the state of Bosnia and Herzegovina, gave me one of the torches used in the Sarajevo torch relay. The torch was nothing special, and certainly not as handsome as ours. Joel Rubenstein, who was with me at the time, noticed the "Mizuno" name and logo inscribed on the handle and on the bowl of the torch in bold letters. Mizuno, a Japanese sporting goods company, was the official sponsor of the Sarajevo torch relay.

We howled with laughter. Talk about double standards. We were getting slammed by the Greeks for raising millions of dollars for children and they didn't say a word to the Yugoslavs for putting advertising on the actual torch.

Between meetings Ginny and I toured the city and the venues. The organizers and the government had done a wonderful job. I had visited the city a year before and it had been smoggy and crowded. Traffic was unbelievably congested and I wondered how they would manage during the Games. The solution was easy: The government said no traffic during the Winter Games and—like magic—traffic disappeared!

The people were incredibly friendly and hospitable and everything ran like clockwork. The entire effort was a tribute to the people of Yugoslavia—it was a triumph of will. They were proud of their country and their city and wanted to present them in the best possible light to visitors from around the world. Taxi drivers carried tape recorders and language tapes to practice phrases in English, French, and Spanish. The total commitment was impressive. I hoped we could duplicate it in Los Angeles.

Ginny and I visited the Olympic villages and as many delegations as possible. The personality of each team was evident in its facilities, all of which were excellent. The Italians brought extra staff, a pasta chef, and lived in a very relaxed atmosphere. They were almost as open as the U.S. team, which allowed media to run up and down the floors of its village conducting interviews.

The most organized by far were the Canadians and East Germans. Both these countries, despite their relatively small populations, always seem to get the most out of their athletes. I renewed my acquaintance with Manfred Ewald, president of the GDR National Olympic Committee. Unlike other NOC presidents who lived the posh life in Sarajevo's best hotels, Ewald lived in the village with his team.

Ewald and I met one afternoon at the GDR's hospitality center, which had been converted from an athlete's room by the wives of GDR sports officials. There we talked about preparations for the L.A. Games and toasted one another with schnapps. Ewald, his staff, and his athletes went to great pains to be sure their facilities were first rate. There was a great sense of camaraderie within the delegation. GDR victories were shared by all athletes, not just the winners, and it was common for a GDR medal winner to share journalists' interviews with less successful teammates.

I had invited Mayor Tom Bradley to be part of our official delegation and to report to the International Olympic Committee during the Sarajevo Games. He was the best possible person to answer questions about hospitality in Los Angeles. Hannah Carter, an LAOOC board member and a 1936 Winter Olympian, reported on the Olympic arts festival, Ed Best covered security, Dr. Tony Daly gave a medical report, and Usher and I reviewed the nuts-and-bolts planning.

I expected a good roasting from the Greeks and the Soviets, but neither occurred. Nissiotis and Filaretos spoke for the record against the torch relay, but—for Filaretos, anyway—in relatively mild tones. When Soviet IOC member Constantin Andrianov took the floor, I turned to Mayor Bradley and told him to put on his earphones and hold on tight. I thought he'd be interested to hear how the Soviets viewed his fine city.

Incredibly, Andrianov, who read from a prepared text, was downright laudatory. I kept waiting for the kicker, but it never came. He told the IOC that "the LAOOC should be congratulated for doing an excellent job." Usher and I exchanged puzzled but appreciative glances.

The day before, OIRT, the consortium representing Soviet and Eastern bloc television, had signed a contract for television rights and handed me a $300,000 check as a down payment. I sensed we had turned the corner.

I was determined to maintain those good feelings with Gramov. His requests, I told him, were going through government channels and I expected final approval in a week or so, but certainly in time for Yermishkin to take up residence, in the apartment we had found for him, on March 1, the day he was scheduled to arrive in Los Angeles.

On February 10, Samaranch called me into his hotel suite to inform me that Yuri Andropov had died. Bad news, I thought. I had a good rapport with Marat Gramov; that plus Andrianov's speech and the signing of the television contract were all good signs. I feared a new administration in Moscow would mean big changes in its sports administration, and I might have to start all over.

The Soviets lowered the flag in front of their residence at the village to half mast. I sent Gramov a condolence note and Ginny and I paid our respects in person. On February 11, we returned to Los Angeles. There were 168 days to go before the Games.

One lasting impression I had of Sarajevo was a conversation with Branko Mikulic. He was a bear of a man, warmhearted, and rightfully proud of the accomplishments of his fellow citizens. While offering me a few words of advice one day, he became emotional and grabbed me by the cheeks and shouted in Serbo-Croation.

His interpreter, Ada Gregoric, was a tiny young woman with a high-pitched voice that carried his words in English.

"Listen here," Mikulic said, "these next six months will be a blur. Everything will happen so fast, you won't think you'll have time enough to get everything done. Then, five days before the Games open, time will stop. A thirty-minute meeting will seem to last for hours."

SEVENTH INNING STRETCH

MIKULIC KNEW WHAT he was talking about. Back in Los Angeles, I could feel the pace quicken. This was especially evident at our Marina Center office building, where the LAOOC staff had increased by 500 percent in less than six months. We had had three hundred people when we moved in the previous September, and I didn't think we would ever fill the space. Now we had fifteen hundred workers and all two hundred thousand square feet were filled.

The entire ambience was Olympic. A walk through the building gave one a strong sense of the intensity and vastness of the operation. On the east side of the building was the Café de Coubertin, the in-place for the LAOOC staff. Named after the founder of the modern Olympics, the café had been set up to test the food services for the Games, and it served the same menus we would have for the athletes—nothing fancy, just good, wholesome food. The café was also an informal setting for employees from all departments to meet and trade information. I ate breakfast and lunch there almost every day, and I made it a point to eat with different groups to see how people were doing and to make new friends.

Entering from the parking lot next to the café, I would pass by the press operations and technology departments before going into a huge area called the bullpen. Normally, I'd cut across a diagonal walkway through the bullpen on my way to my second-floor office. Each department had its own area. On the right were medical, arts festival, accreditation, travel, Olympic family operations, food services, language services, and personnel; on the left were architecture and construction, design, transportation, and material logistics. The bullpen led to a narrow hallway that divided ticketing on the left and news, security, and community relations on the right. Upstairs, a smaller bullpen contained corporate relations, torch relay, sports, and venue development.

Usher and I were tucked in the back of the building with our secretaries. During these February days, managers lined up outside Harry's door as though they were waiting for service at the local delicatessen. There was usually a line outside my door too, but never as long as Usher's. Although I frequently held meetings in my office, I preferred being a mobile manager, visiting the various departments as much as possible. It was important that staff members see me and talk to me about virtually anything. And they did—from the quality of the food in the café to rumors about my becoming commissioner of major league baseball.

The nature of organizing the Games had by this time clearly defined the roles between Usher and me. Usher was Mr. Inside; I was Mr. Outside. Usher managed everybody: He was responsible for all the minutiae involved with staging the Games and keeping them on track and integrated by departments (he was a master at that); he supervised all contract negotiations and enforced those we had with suppliers and vendors; and he also supervised the "look" of the Games. In concert with sixty of the finest design talents in southern California, the major ones being Sussman/Prezja and Jon Jerde and Associates, Usher and LAOOC design director Larry Klein approved colors for the Games that reflected the dynamics and versatility of southern California.

Being color blind I stayed out of it, but Harry assured me that hot magenta, vermilion, chrome yellow, vivid green, and aqua would work, especially as background for television. Usher called them environmental colors. "They suggest Mex-

ican markets, mariachi, Los Angeles, and the Pacific rim," he
said. I didn't argue. The overall design concept was named
festive federalism and was adapted to all physical elements of
the Games, including uniforms, tickets, programs, tents, concession stands, signs, flags, and banners.

Usher and I always popped into each other's offices to
keep one another advised of what was going on. I got directly
involved in his domain only to discuss decisions or to develop
a negotiating strategy. I was occupied by all levels of government, international relations, public relations, and the Olympic family.

During the last two weeks of February, as I anxiously
awaited word from the White House on the Soviet requests, I
put the pressure on Usher and everybody else to nail down
outstanding items and agreements. We were in constant motion and moving in what seemed to be thousands of different
directions at once.

The Olympic Family Services Department had begun
pressing national Olympic committees, international sports
federations, and IOC members for information on specific
housing and transportation requirements. Corporate relations
and press operations were also gathering similar information
from their clients. The appropriate data went to the accommodations department, which processed them and made
housing assignments for the Olympic family. The accommodations department had reserved nearly twenty thousand rooms
in seventy-three hotels throughout southern California.

The athletes, of course, were assigned to one of the three
villages: UCLA; USC in downtown Los Angeles; or UC at
Santa Barbara, which was a satellite village for the rowing and
canoeing athletes.

Games staffing had set its wheels in motion and was can-
vassing southern California for volunteers for all phases of
Olympic operations. Transportation planners from the Olympic committee and government agencies were in the final process of developing plans to prevent massive traffic congestion
from disrupting the Games.

Ticketing was preparing letters of confirmation for more
than three hundred thousand purchasers; Ed Best's security

department had begun riding herd on the private security companies to recruit and train approximately twenty thousand guards; Charley Bear began the difficult task of implementing a system to accredit more than one hundred thousand people; the arts festival, under the direction of Bob Fitzpatrick, had announced its ticket program in January and was actively promoting the festival.

Everybody at the committee got involved in taking visiting NOC and IF delegations and journalists on tours of our Olympic facilities. Each LAOOC staff member was required to have a working knowledge of organizing committee operations, the International Olympic Committee organization and history, the Olympic sports, and our facilities. Each was also assigned a nation to study and was expected to use that knowledge while hosting a delegation from that nation.

Those were just some of the nuts-and-bolts items. Every item on our critical list involved government. Most important on the local front was wrapping up our negotiations for supplemental and in-transit security for the athletes with the L.A. Sheriff's Department.

The Olympic Law Enforcement Coordinating Committee (OLECC) had assigned in-transit security and supplemental law enforcement responsibilities to the sheriff while parceling out security tasks. Since the county board of supervisors had budgetary review over the sheriff, we had to negotiate a contract with them. They weren't easy, particularly Republican supervisor Mike Antonovich, an outspoken opponent of the Olympic Games. I believe he'd convinced himself early on that being anti-Olympics was the politically correct stand to take, so he'd been forced to stick to his guns when most other critics had come over to our side. Antonovich sought more than adequate reimbursement for the services we requested and turned negotiations into a personal crusade. It was impossible to satisfy him; he balked at everything. The more we resisted, the more recalcitrant he became and the more negotiations dragged on.

On the federal level, I was growing tired of waiting for the decision on the Soviet requests, and it didn't help that Moscow stayed silent. The Soviets hadn't uttered a word since

Sarajevo. Constantin Chernenko had succeeded Yuri Andropov, which I viewed as a negative development. Chernenko, according to news reports, had been a close adviser to Leonid Brezhnev, Andropov's predecessor and the premier of the Soviet Union during the 1980 Carter boycott, and had witnessed Brezhnev's great anger over the American-led pullout. I hoped this wouldn't have any bearing on our Olympic Games.

Both Bill Hussey and Jay Moorhead had informed me that a bitter struggle was brewing at State over Oleg Yermishkin's nomination as Soviet attaché. There was a hard-line anti-Soviet faction that vehemently opposed allowing Yermishkin a diplomatic passport, claiming he was too dangerous to be given a free run through southern California.

Interestingly enough, Ed Best told me that many in the FBI supported the Soviet request because Yermishkin gave them a rare opportunity to play spy games with a known quantity. The FBI, like everybody else, assumed whomever the Soviets chose as an attaché would be KGB.

Moorhead also learned the president would be directly involved in the planes and ships decision because it concerned foreign policy and that the White House wanted nothing to do with the Yermishkin decision. The White House considered it a national security matter. That decision would be made by the State Department with input from intelligence services.

Best was convinced Yermishkin had been handpicked at the highest level of the Soviet Union for a specific reason: to bring the entire delegation home. Best's sources had reported that the Soviets had surveyed and profiled their athletes for likely defectors and were alarmed by the results. During their December visit, the Soviets had made inquiries into leasing a house high in the Hollywood hills—not far from UCLA, the village of their choice—ostensibly to use as a resting place for their top medal contenders. Best was certain they would also use it as a holding tank for potential defectors. They wanted a professional shepherd for the team and Yermishkin allegedly had the experience to do the job.

In the middle of February, Mike Deaver, Bill Sittman, and a cadre of Secret Service agents flew to Los Angeles to survey the Coliseum for President Reagan's participation in the opening ceremony. Before advancing the site, they came to our offices for a brief meeting and, later, a quick game of tennis.

Deaver, Sittman, and I were joined by David Simon, Moorhead, and Hussey in my office. The focus of the meeting was the opening ceremony and the seating options for the president's party at the Coliseum. But we also talked about the ships and planes proposals, which Deaver said were moving along nicely through channels and would be approved in principle. To my question about the Soviet attaché, Deaver responded with basically the same response Moorhead had been getting in Washington—that the request was moving forward and it looked good.

Moorhead continued to make inquiries over the next ten days at both the White House and the State Department but got nowhere.

The first of March was busy. This was the day Yermishkin was scheduled to arrive in Los Angeles to begin his duties as the USSR attaché, and we still hadn't heard from Washington. I was really angry. How could our government be so insensitive and rude? They'd been playing with the requests now for two and a half months. That was wrong. I had Simon and Hussey get to the office early to make calls and man the telephones until we got results one way or another.

While waiting, I joined a press conference with Manolo Guerra who, as president of the Cuban National Olympic Committee, had led a delegation of sports leaders from his country on an inspection tour of our facilities. Guerra told the media he was impressed with our preparations for the Games and was eager to return to Los Angeles with a full team of Cuban athletes in July. When questioned about Soviet participation, he said he assumed they would come, providing we abided by the Olympic Charter. When reporters began asking me about taking the job as baseball commissioner, I said I'd answer those questions after the press conference. The Cuban delegation had to catch a flight and I didn't want to delay them.

Rumors had been flying for days that I was about to accept the baseball job. Although I had not formally signed any papers, the prospects were getting better. As I had before, I confirmed to reporters that I had met with the search committee but had not reached a deal. Most important, I reiterated my long-standing comment: "I'm with the Games through the Games."

As I returned to my office following the press conference, I was met by Bill Hussey at the top of the stairs. He was paler than usual.

"I have some very bad news, Peter," he said.

I waited. "Well?" I asked.

He hemmed and hawed for another minute and then said, "Yermishkin's visa has been denied by the State Department."

We went on to my office and I shut the door behind Hussey.

"Sit down," I said.

I sat behind my desk and he grabbed a chair and pulled it up next to me and sat down.

"What's their reason, Bill?" I asked. "And what the hell took them so long to make the decision?"

"Peter, let me tell you the worst part."

I leaned back in my seat, rested my right foot against an open drawer, and took a deep breath. I stared at Bill.

"The State Department has already communicated the decision to the Soviets—on its own," Hussey said.

I slammed my foot against the drawer and felt the wood splinter. *"What?"* I shouted.

I stood up. I didn't know what to do with myself.

"What in the hell went wrong?"

Hussey remained silent.

"What the hell is Jay doing in Washington? He's been talking to those guys daily. How could he let this happen?"

I walked briskly to the office door and snapped it open.

"Sherry," I said as calmly as possible, "get Moorhead on the line."

I immediately understood the repercussions of this blunder. The State Department had blatantly violated the

Olympic Charter by circumventing the LAOOC in communicating directly to the USSR NOC. I knew we'd have to work quickly and forcefully to mitigate the damage.

"Bill," I said to Hussey, "do you know anything about the planes and the ships?"

"Only what they've been saying all along," he said, "that both will be approved in principle."

By this time, Moorhead was on the line. I put him on the speaker phone.

"Jay," I said, "I have Hussey here with me. He just told me the State Department has denied Yermishkin's request for a visa and has communicated that directly to the Soviets."

Moorhead went on a tirade. He felt deceived. He had worked with Deaver and others at the White House and considered them his friends. He was shocked they would betray us. I asked him to follow up and explain to both the White House and State that by violating the Olympic Charter they had placed the Games in jeopardy.

"One last thing," I told Moorhead, "tell those bastards back there that I'm going to Telex Gramov and apologize for the government's slow and sloppy handling of the requests, and I'm going to make a public statement within the hour.

"Jay, make it clear to them I'm not criticizing the substance of the decision. I understand that's a government matter."

It was essential I take the lead in criticizing the government for its poor handling of the requests and prevent IOC officials from criticizing the United States violation of the Olympic Charter. I hoped this smokescreen would deflect Soviet reaction to the news and limit international outrage over the charter breach. I could only wish my comments would beat the Soviets and their allies to the punch.

We issued a statement within two hours at the second press conference of the day, this one held outside at the public entrance to the building. It was strange to see our neighbors in front of their homes curiously watching the spectacle of television crews and reporters surrounding Usher and me. I found it humorous that just as I began my statement, someone in the rear began singing "Take Me Out to the Ball

Game." Before long the entire press corps, some of whom had covered the LAOOC for four years, chimed in. After the singing, I delivered my version of a fastball and criticized the U.S. government.

One reporter asked the inevitable question, "How will this affect the Soviets' participation in the Games?"

"Obviously, this doesn't help," I said. "I sent a Telex to Marat Gramov today, asking him to submit another candidate for the attaché position and promised we would hand carry the paperwork through government. I've also been assured by government officials that we can expect a speedy response on the planes and transport ship issue."

While Usher stayed outside to answer further questions, I returned alone to my office. It was late by then and many of the staff had gone home for the day. I wanted to think about the next steps I would need to take. Would I have to go to Moscow again and reinforce our relationship? Should I go to Washington and light a fire under officials on the remaining two requests and emphasize how we'd need their help on hundreds of other things down the line?

And then there was baseball. For the past few weeks I had laid every deal breaker I could think of on the table and each of my demands had been met by the owners. It was obvious they wanted me badly. But making this decision was tearing me apart. I was also concerned about staff morale. I knew there'd be resentment among some of the staff, that there would be those saying I was deserting them and thinking only of myself. I had already sensed that in a few of the remarks some staff members had made about baseball as I wandered through the building.

It had been lonely at home. Ginny and Joe were visiting Keri at school in Switzerland over Joe's spring break; Vicki and Heidi were away at college. The night before, Ginny had called from overseas and we'd discussed the pros and cons of baseball.

"It's up to you to take the lead and demonstrate that the Olympic Games won't last forever," she said. "You have to set that example for everybody else."

As usual Ginny was right. We decided to go for it if the

owners met my final terms. They were meeting in Tampa that weekend and I was going down there, prepared to accept the position.

On my way out that evening, I popped my head into David Israel's office.

"Feel like a quick trip to Tampa tomorrow?" I asked.

Israel smiled and said, "You're going to do it, huh?"

I smiled back. Israel, formerly a columnist with the *Los Angeles Herald Examiner,* had joined the committee in January as my assistant. He had many connections in baseball and even owned a small piece of a minor league baseball team. Israel was also knowledgeable about baseball and I knew he'd be helpful with last-minute advice in Tampa.

I left Los Angeles on Friday afternoon, March 2, on a private plane belonging to George Argyros. Argyros, Israel, Bob Lurie, and I talked baseball as we flew across the country. The only reference made to the Olympics was by me. I told Israel I was surprised the Soviets hadn't yet reacted to Yermishkin's denial.

Bill Schulz, an LAOOC advance man, greeted us at the airport and whisked us to the Hyatt Regency in town, away from the reporters covering the owners' meeting at the Airport Marriott. Ginny and Joe, who had just arrived from Switzerland, were waiting for me at the hotel. I was thrilled when Vicki flew in from Colorado later that night. Heidi couldn't make it as she was busy at Vanderbilt.

The kids were as excited as Ginny and I about the baseball job, especially Joe who's an avid fan.

Later that evening Lou Hoynes and Bud Selig came to my room, contract in hand. I signed the two-page typewritten agreement that was contingent on the owners' meeting the next morning. I was 95 percent sure the owners would approve my terms, even though they had to change baseball's by-laws to meet one of them. Instead of the commissioner needing a two-thirds vote to be retained by the owners, I demanded a simple majority. The other conditions were to raise the fining powers of the commissioner from $50,000 to $250,000; to bring the league presidents under the umbrella of the commissioner's office; and to retain Bowie Kuhn as commissioner until I finished my Olympic assignment.

After breakfast the next morning with American League President Bobby Brown and National League President Chub Feeney, we went to the Marriott where Schulz led us through a rear entrance to one of the owner's suites to await the outcome of the vote. Ginny and I were in one room with Bowie and Luisa Kuhn; the kids were with Schulz and Israel in another. I got a call at about 11:30 from Selig telling me I was in. The vote had been unanimous. I hugged Ginny and called the kids to give them the news.

Ginny and I took a freight elevator downstairs to meet the owners. Kuhn and Israel were with us. As I collected my thoughts, Bowie turned to me and said, "I don't know whether to offer my congratulations or condolences." Israel and I exchanged bewildered glances. I shrugged and said, "That remains to be seen." I felt bad for Bowie: The owners had treated him shabbily.

I met the owners and afterward joined Kuhn and Selig at a press conference where Selig announced the terms of my contract. Everybody assumed the commissioner's position had been substantially strengthened. That wasn't true. The changes were more window dressing than substance. I took the job because I felt I could do something about the problems facing baseball: economic viability, resolving market infringements of the television superstations, and cleaning up drug abuse. I hoped to restore its traditional values. The task would be very difficult but worth the effort. Baseball is an important part of the fabric of our country.

That done I flew back to Los Angeles with Ginny and the kids. I spent a lot of time on the long flight studying each and knew I'd made the right decision—they were happy.

I met with the southern California press corps the next morning and reiterated my commitment to the 1984 Games. I told them these would be my last words about baseball until October 1.

The hardest group to face, I knew, would be the LAOOC staff. After seeing some long faces the previous Monday, I decided I had better address the entire group as soon as possible. The next morning I had Sherry Cockle distribute a memo asking everybody to assemble in one of two groups, a half hour apart. The news department set up microphones and a sound system in the bullpen of each floor. I stood on a desk top.

I told each group that my attention would remain totally focused on the job we all had to do; I wasn't abandoning them and nothing would change. Since I had been successful in finding a post-Games job, I promised we'd create a program that would be totally devoted to finding staff members good jobs immediately after the Olympics. Collectively, we breathed a sigh of relief and went back to work.

CHAPTER TWELVE

VODKA ON THE ROCKS

THE ISSUE OF my becoming the commissioner of baseball and the conflict with the Greeks in a number of ways camouflaged my primary concern: the question of Soviet participation in the Games. Few seemed to notice how strangely quiet the Soviets had been, especially those in the media. I hoped it would stay that way.

The torch relay had become one of those good news-bad news scenarios. I didn't purposely fan the fires of controversy—the Greeks saw to that—but neither did I have any intention of capitulating when I was right.

Besides, I knew we'd get the flame one way or another. By approving our torch relay, Juan Antonio Samaranch was already committed to providing us with a bona fide Olympic flame. Still, Samaranch had asked me to appease the Greeks, and I tried. I wanted them on our side. Otherwise they would foment unhappiness and unrest within the Olympic family.

I had sent Samaranch a Telex on February 28 outlining an accord I thought would satisfy everyone. As a face-saving gesture to the Greeks, I agreed to end kilometer sales thirty days after the date the accord was signed and to include a Greek sports organization among our beneficiaries.

In return I asked for a joint press communiqué issued

simultaneously by the LAOOC, the IOC, and the Greek NOC reaffirming the torch relay as a noncommercial venture and promising no further interference from any Greek officials—federal, municipal, or Olympic. Also, I wanted it spelled out in the accord that the transfer of the flame from Olympia to New York City on May 8 would be accomplished electronically to avoid demonstrations along the relay route in Greece.

Samaranch wanted to stay above the fray and he asked that I continue my attempts to resolve it directly with the Greeks. Samaranch, always concerned with his power base, never wanted to get his hands dirty. I gladly played the game. I had a few aces up my sleeve, one being our approval of the Greek National Theatre's participation in the 1984 Olympic arts festival—the cultural component of the Olympics that was to run at various theaters in the Los Angeles area from June 1, 1984, until the end of the Games.

The theater group was a pet project of Margaret Papandreou, Prime Minister Andreas Papandreou's wife, and she desperately wanted it included in our festival. Arts festival director Robert Fitzpatrick decided to play our hand in early March when she visited the United States accompanied by actress Melina Mercouri, the Greek minister of culture. Fitzpatrick led a delegation that included Bill Hussey and Joel Fishman, LAAOC torch relay administrator, to meet Madame Papandreou in New York to persuade her to trade Greek government support for the relay for a spot in the arts festival for her troupe. During conversations with Fitzpatrick, Madame Papandreou promised an orderly transfer of the flame to the LAOOC, repeating that promise on network television the next day.

Unfortunately, neither the Greek NOC nor Mayor Foteinos paid any attention to what she said. They continued the worldwide publicity campaign against our torch relay. We traded Telexes daily for a few weeks. They promised to stop criticizing us if we'd put an immediate stop to the Youth Legacy Kilometer sales; we promised to cut off sales after a grace period if they would sign our accord.

From time to time during the impasse, a few of us would

have a little fun brainstorming various ways of getting an Olympic flame from Greece to Los Angeles. At one point, I even had David Israel prepare a letter over my signature outlining the most intricate and grandiose flame-lighting ceremony imaginable.

For openers, the plan specified that the IOC would establish a permanent Olympic flame at its Château de Vidy headquarters. This would take the Greeks out of the Olympic flame business. Then, starting with a kindling of the flame in Lausanne, Israel's scenario called for a relay to be run in each of the previous ten Olympic cities, from Berlin to Moscow— the last city to host the Games. There, Samaranch would be presented the flame and he would personally bring it to New York for the start of the U.S. portion of the relay. In an appeal to Samaranch's self-interest, Israel added this thought to the letter: "This would be the International Olympic Committee's grand and meaningful gesture for peace, one that would truly qualify the IOC for the rightful awarding of the Nobel Peace Prize." I don't know how we would have done it had Samaranch approved the plan, but fortunately he didn't. He did, however, get off the dime, and he started applying pressure on the Greeks to be more reasonable.

One pleasant diversion during this time came in early March when Ginny and I helped recommission the *Angelita,* the beautiful, sleek, gold-medal-winning yacht in the 8-meter class at the 1932 Olympics. It was a picture-perfect southern California day: about 80 degrees, not a hint of smog, and a gentle breeze crossing Marina del Rey where the ceremony took place at the California Yacht Club. It was the first time Ginny and I had sailed on the vessel and we were joined by three surviving members of the *Angelita*'s crew, Owen Churchill, John E. Biby, Jr., and Richard Moore. Churchill, who was eighty-eight years old, had been the owner and skipper of the *Angelita* in 1932.

It wasn't my love of sailing that roped me into the *Angelita*'s restoration; it was Dick Sargent, my old sailing partner. Recognizing my weakness for Olympic memorabilia and using Churchill's tearful reminiscences as an effective backdrop, Sargent had persuaded me to tackle the project.

He found the hull of the *Angelita* lying in a San Jose boat yard, and then he teamed up with Churchill. They figured it would be a piece of cake to restore it to its original specifications and would only cost $10,000. The *Angelita* was as beautiful as she ever was $100,000 later, and I made her the flagship of the 1984 Olympic yachting events.

By the middle of March I was growing weary of the daily Greek grind and I asked Hussey, Israel, Fishman, and Peter Caloyeras to wrap it up. Caloyeras, a successful Los Angeles businessman fluent in Greek, was the volunteer envoy to Greece who handled our numerous conversations with Nikos Filaretos and other Greek officials.

As they tried to settle with the Greeks, we finally heard from the U.S. government about the Soviet requests for the Aeroflot charter flights and the berthing of the *Gruzia,* both of which were approved in principle as Washington had been promising for months. In keeping with the Olympic Charter this time, the State Department allowed us to notify the Soviets. It gave me a chance to Telex Marat Gramov the good news and to resume the dialogue that had ceased after Sarajevo. I waited for a reply, but didn't get one. However, I *did* hear from the Coalition to Ban the Soviets.

The coalition had been keeping quiet too, but the day after the State Department approved the Soviet requests, David Balsiger announced the coalition had infiltrated the LAOOC, which it could easily have done given the speed with which we were growing.

Balsiger also said his organization had planned an aggressive campaign to encourage Eastern bloc athletes to defect. He set the coalition's goal at fifty defectors, though he said he'd be satisfied with five or ten. I thought it was wrong to encourage young athletes to leave their homes and considered Balsiger's attempts a grandstand play and not a patriotic act.

Then it was back to the Greeks. The revolving door was turning swiftly. At a press conference on March 20, I announced we had made peace with the Greeks and issued a statement made jointly with the Greek NOC. I set April 10 as the deadline for accepting contributions for torch-relay kilo-

meters and said the Greeks had promised full cooperation for
a smooth transfer of the flame.

Peace lasted a day. Filaretos betrayed us again. In negotiating the truce, we explained through Caloyeras that we
needed a grace period of several weeks to wind down the
torch sales operation. At first, Filaretos balked, demanding
we limit it to two weeks, but we refused to be pinned down.
In deference to Filaretos, we made no reference to a grace
period in the joint statement, saying only that we had "decided to call a halt to accepting the charitable contributions
in connection with the running of the flame in the United
States."

Apparently, Filaretos had neglected to inform his associates at the full plenary session of the Greek NOC about the
grace period, because the next day he accused us of violating
the agreement. It took a week, and at least another dozen
Telexes, to explain sales had already ceased in New York and
Los Angeles—our two largest markets—and we were only
accepting those kilometer contributions already being processed. Sales had increased significantly during the controversy, but the relay had by no means sold out.

Filaretos was satisfied, but not Mayor Foteinos, who was
making too much political hay to let us off the hook. He said
the only way he would permit a peaceful transfer of the flame
was if we returned all the money we had received for the relay. It was obvious Filaretos and the Greek NOC had no control over the mayor of Olympia, and that the Papandreou
government had no influence over either.

I didn't waste much time worrying about the Greeks,
however. Other things were happening. The closer we got to
the Games, the greater our needs became for specific information from more than 150 national Olympic committees and
23 international sports federations. The logistics we were
dealing with were staggering, considering we were obligated
to host more than 20,000 people.

We needed numbers: number of athletes, officials,
coaches, trainers, journalists, technicians, delegates, and
guests. We needed data on how many rooms were needed and
where; what kind of equipment and how much. We needed

training schedules by sport. We needed information about dietary, religious, and entertainment preferences. Lastly, we needed accurate arrival and departure schedules among the many other items of minutia.

While we were successful in obtaining much of the information requested, we also received a long list of complaints, the majority about our services and costs. As was to be expected, members of the Olympic family wanted more tickets than those already allotted. They wanted more free cars, more hotel rooms, and more accreditations. In short, more perquisites, more clout, more stroking.

Samaranch had been receiving the same complaints—but more. Unlike his predecessors, who were remote and preferred to govern the Olympics from their homes in their own countries, Samaranch threw his whole being into Olympic service when he took office. In 1981, he surprised everybody in the Olympic Movement by moving to a third-floor suite at the Lausanne Palace Hotel instead of returning to Barcelona when he retired from the diplomatic corps.

From an office there, and from another at IOC headquarters, he launched a worldwide campaign to generate greater interest in the Olympic Movement and began restructuring the IOC to enhance his power. One of those who suffered was Berlioux, whom he put on a tight leash. During his first three years as IOC president, Samaranch visited more than one hundred countries and met more heads of state and ministers of sport than any human alive. During each visit he reinforced the need to separate the Olympic Games from political interference. He made it a point to take copious notes of legitimate complaints and concerns and promised to do something about them. He was now bringing them to me.

Samaranch and I talked almost daily on the telephone, but that was a poor substitute for personal contact. My knowledge of Spanish is limited to only a few words, so we couldn't use Spanish. Although Samaranch's command of English was good, his thick accent made it difficult to communicate over the long-distance phone. I therefore welcomed his invitation to meet him in San Juan, Puerto Rico, where he was attending a conference of the Pan American Sports Organization. I carried my own agenda, which covered a list of thirty-eight items of Olympic business.

One of the most important was working out a foolproof solution to bar the Palestine Liberation Organization from our Olympics. On March 15, a PLO spokesman had said the PLO was considering applying to the IOC and forming a national Olympic committee in time to participate in the Los Angeles Games. There was no way I was going to let that happen. I remembered how Yasser Arafat had been treated at the Moscow Games and how I was repelled by the kingly treatment the organizers had given him.

There is a provision in the Olympic Charter that states an NOC must represent a specific, recognized territory, but I doubted that this provision would weather public scrutiny, especially since the PLO was recognized by the United Nations. The resolution was a simple one: Get Samaranch to decree he would not recognize any additional NOCs until after the 1984 Olympics.

I also lobbied Samaranch to make an exception to the charter's rules on the opening ceremonies. According to the charter, I, as president, was the only member of the organizing committee permitted to participate. That wasn't fair. Paul Ziffren and Harry Usher were equally as important and deserved to be part of the opening ceremonies. Lukewarm at first, Samaranch signed off on my scheme that they participate in the passing of the Antwerp flag on the Coliseum field, but my attempt to get a speaking part for Ziffren wasn't successful.

Overall, Samaranch was very cooperative. He approved in principle an Olympic family member ticket-reservation system replacing the one specified in the charter, which is one of the great examples of Olympic waste.

Usually at past Olympics, tens of thousands of the best seats at events often went unused every day. Not only were seats reserved for Olympic family members who had no intention of using them, but in many cases they reserved seats at several events going on at the same time. At Sarajevo, it distressed me to see entire sections of empty seats at most events (including the ice hockey finals) because Olympic family members, in their arrogance, preferred it that way. I hoped a new reservation system would change that, but I knew it would be difficult, even with Samaranch's blessing, to persuade Olympic family members to give up their free tickets.

For example, Primo Nebiolo, the president of the International Track and Field Federation, had been pressuring Samaranch daily for special treatment and additional accreditations; Samaranch asked me to help him out. Although I had vowed for years there would be no special treatment, I knew I'd eventually be forced to relent. Not all sports federations, or NOCs, for that matter—so it turns out—are created equal. But holding firm for so long allowed us to open the store from a bargain-basement level, meaning that anything we conceded was viewed as something of value by the recipient.

In Nebiolo's case, I intended to give him all the accreditations he needed, but I told Samaranch he'd have to wait until we got closer to the Games. If I gave Nebiolo the green light right away, he'd tell people who would tell others and before we knew it we'd have an insurrection with everybody demanding special privileges.

We then discussed two trouble areas, the first being the Greeks. I told Samaranch time was running short for our torch relay and we needed to resolve the flame question.

He said, "Do not worry. The IOC owns the flame and we will get it, if need be."

I asked him how and he replied with a mischievous grin. "I will let you know when to come and get it."

That was good enough for me. I then told him I was very upset I hadn't heard anything from Marat Gramov since Sarajevo.

"Don't be concerned," Samaranch said. "I am in touch with the whole Olympic family and I have no reason to believe there are any serious problems."

"Do you think they'll submit another name for attaché soon?" I asked.

"I am certain. That is why you have heard nothing. They are trying to decide whom to select."

"People on my government relations staff worry that Andrei Gromyko will use his influence to persuade Chernenko to boycott the Games. I am told that if anybody is looking to retaliate for the Carter boycott, it is he."

Gromyko, long a senior statesman of the Soviet Union, had been personally affronted by the Carter boycott, I had been told. He had misread the Carter administration and had had to account for this failure to his friend Brezhnev. Gromyko hadn't forgotten, nor had he forgiven the United States.

Samaranch had been absentmindedly shaking his head during my comments about Gromyko. "I think you are worrying needlessly," he said.

"I hope you're right," I replied.

A few days later, on April 6, 1984, we heard indirectly from the Soviets. The news was not good. Robert Gillette, the *Los Angeles Times*'s Moscow correspondent, reported that the state-controlled press had harshly criticized security preparations for the games and had also accused the White House of encouraging anti-Soviet groups to try to stop Soviet athletes from participating in the Olympics.

The latter charge was in reference to a January 10 letter that the White House had sent to the organizers of the Ban the Soviets Coalition over Mike Deaver's signature. The coalition had sent Reagan a letter seeking support for its efforts. Through an oversight that reflected the government's insensitivity to Olympic issues, one of Deaver's staff automatically sent the letter to the National Security Council, where another staff person wrote a bland response of support. Deaver hadn't seen either letter. It was an endorsement for the coalition that they gladly advertised. Now the damn thing had come back to haunt us. It had struck me from the outset that the letter inadvertently seemed like a remarkably convenient propaganda tool for the Soviets.

According to Gillette, Western diplomats in Moscow interpreted the Soviet charges as a pressure campaign to extract more favorable treatment for their athletes, rather than as a threat to boycott the Games. I hoped he was right, but I had an empty feeling in my stomach that night as I flew to Colo-

rado Springs to address the United States Olympic Committee
at its annual meeting the next day. There I told reporters I
was still optimistic about Soviet participation, but not as much
as before. I would even consider going to Moscow to personally assure Soviet leaders that their athletes could expect
equal treatment, warm hospitality from the people of Los Angeles, and a secure environment in which to compete, train,
and live during the Games. I was beginning to smell a rat. As
with Carter in 1980, the Olympics could become an easy target for Chernenko to make himself look strong.

Until then, the only contact we had had with the Soviet
Union was through Jay Moorhead's meetings with Viktor
Cherkashin, whom Moorhead and I had met the previous January at the Soviet embassy in Washington during our visit
with Dobrynin. Two FBI agents came to Moorhead's home
after one of their meetings and told him Cherkashin was
KGB. Although they didn't object to his meetings with Cherkashin, the agents wanted him to know the meetings were
under surveillance. They debriefed Moorhead, instructed him
to be careful, and left, saying they would visit again.

Moorhead filed a report to me after every meeting. After
one on March 28, Moorhead wrote there were two problems
the Soviets wanted resolved before they would commit their
athletes to participating in the Games. First, they wanted free
movement of Soviet embassy and consulate personnel in Los
Angeles, which Cherkashin claimed was guaranteed in the
protocol accord. The second problem was the "environment,"
a catchall that covered three specific Soviet worries: anti-Soviet bumper stickers, anti-Soviet demonstrations, and an organized effort by anti-Soviet groups supported by the FBI and
the State Department to find fifty potential defectors from
Eastern bloc countries. The Soviets wanted assurances that
their athletes wouldn't be subjected to a hostile atmosphere.

As I reread the report, I noted Moorhead's conclusion:
"It was clear that the 'environment' question would never be
fully resolved." I wondered if these words would be pro-
phetic.

Over the next few days, sports officials from East Germany, Bulgaria, Czechoslovakia, and Hungary joined the at-

tack, using rhetoric identical to that of the Soviets. On April 9, the Soviet National Olympic Committee issued a public statement that contained their strongest charges to date, and I quote them extensively because it's interesting to see how the Russians tried to politicize the Olympic Movement, and how our government unwittingly helped them achieve their goal.

The statement began with a general charge that the Reagan administration was violating guarantees to abide by the Olympic charter. It accused Reagan of "trying to use the Olympic Games on the eve of the elections for [his] selfish political ends."

It claimed that "a large-scale campaign against the Soviet Union's participation in the Olympic Games has been mounted in the USA. Different reactionary political, émigré and religious groupings are teaming up on an anti-Olympic basis. In particular, a coalition called 'Ban the Soviets,' enjoying the support of U.S. official services, has been set up. Open threats of physical victimization and provocative actions are made to sportsmen and officials of the USSR and other socialist countries. Slanderous allegations are being made that the participation of a Soviet delegation in the Olympic Games would presumably threaten U.S. security. . . .

"It is known that the country hosting the Olympics assumes the commitment to ensure the full security of the national delegations. The situation, which is taking shape at present in Los Angeles, makes one doubt the effectiveness of undertaken measures. The American press reports that preparations are under way in the city of staging political demonstrations and rallies . . . slogans and posters with contents hostile to socialist countries are being hung out. . . ."

The Soviets specifically charged us with two Olympic Charter violations, one for accrediting Radio Free Europe and Radio Liberty, which "are financed by U.S. intelligence services and engaged in subversive activities against the peoples of the socialist countries," and another for rejecting the Olympic identity card for entry into the United States for Olympic family members. In early April, the Soviets explained, the U.S. embassy in Moscow had ordered the Soviet NOC to submit a list of its delegation for visa applications.

Citing the State Department's denial of Oleg Yermishkin as their Olympic attaché, they accused the State Department of its "right to constantly correct the actions of the LAOOC," and they went on to charge the LAOOC for "flaunting" the charter by using the Olympic flame for commercial purposes. Furthermore, they predicted there would be price gouging in Los Angeles during the Games and that we were charging NOCs "big sums of money" for traditionally free services. The statement didn't specify what they were or what kind of price gouging they expected.

They summed up the statement with this: "Violation of the Olympic Charter and the anti-Soviet campaign unleashed by the U.S. reactionary forces with the connivance of the official authorities are creating an abnormal situation. In this connection, the NOC of the USSR addresses the IOC and its president, Juan Antonio Samaranch, with the request immediately to review the situation on the eve of the Los Angeles Games at an emergency meeting of the Executive Board of the International Olympic Committee and demand that the U.S. side strictly respects the Olympic Charter and takes effective measures to guarantee proper security to the participants and visitors to the Games. . . ."

Whew! The telephone rang. It was Samaranch.

"It's a pack of lies," I told him. Accrediting Radio Free Europe, I explained, was an IOC and a United States Olympic Committee decision over which the LAOOC had no influence. The only charge that caught me unaware was the item about the embassy in Moscow demanding a delegation list from the Soviet NOC. That wasn't right. Our agreement with government to use Olympic identity cards for entry into the United States still stood. NOCs were required to submit lists, but those lists were to be used only as a means to weed out known terrorists and not as applications for visas. The key word was "visa." Visas would not be required for Olympic family members to enter the United States for the Olympics. I told Samaranch I'd get to the bottom of it.

I called David Simon into my office. "Soviet participation in the Games hinges on the answer," I told him. "And I need it in ten minutes."

Nine minutes later Simon entered my office along with Bill Hussey. "It was a screw-up," Simon said. "Bill's State Department contacts told him a minor functionary at the embassy in Moscow mistakenly told the Soviet NOC the embassy needed the list for visa purposes."

"Apparently, he was unfamiliar with the Olympics and Olympic terminology," Hussey added.

I wondered.

This was another manifestation of the low regard with which government in general and the State Department in particular held the Olympic Games.

About eighteen months earlier, State had approved Simon and Hussey's plan to establish Olympic liaisons at every U.S. embassy and consulate in the world. It made sense. State would have Olympic experts to handle its requests and we'd have people to contact when we needed help. State failed to follow up. The liaisons it appointed rarely took their jobs seriously, and, in many cases where liaisons were transferred, the post remained vacant. At our embassy in Moscow, where we desperately needed a liaison and where one certainly would have averted this diplomatic blunder, we had nobody.

Samaranch called me on April 11 to inform me he had received a Telex from Marat Gramov officially requesting an emergency session of the IOC Executive Board.

Samaranch forwarded the Telex. The request read in part: "In view of the U.S. administration's incessant interference into the affairs of the LAOOC, flagrant deliberate violation of the Olympic Charter by the American side, attempts to use the Games in the interests that are alien to the noble Olympic ideals, we are requesting you to consider the possibility of convening an extraordinary meeting of the IOC Executive Board in order to discuss the situation. . . ."

Samaranch was inclined to call the meeting. He said it would give us an opportunity to answer their questions once and for all and pave the way for their participation in the Games.

I received a lengthy Telex from Gramov two days later, enumerating the same old complaints: security and the Ban the Soviets, visas, Yermishkin, accreditation for Radio Free

Europe and Radio Liberty, and demonstrations. But this time he added specific questions about the Aeroflot charter flights and the mooring of the *Gruzia* in Long Beach, none of which presented any problems.

I immediately wired the Telex to Samaranch and he responded with one of his own, informing me he had decided to convene a meeting at IOC headquarters on April 24 with IOC vice-presidents Louis Guirandou-N'Diaye of the Ivory Coast, Alexandru Siperco of Romania, and Ashwini Kumar of India; IOC Director Monique Berlioux; and a delegation from the USSR National Olympic Committee. He asked me to head a delegation from the LAOOC.

Muddling the situation even further was an announcement that the Soviet Union had withdrawn from Olympic tennis. Optimists dismissed this development, pointing out that the top Soviet player didn't rank within the top two hundred on the Association of Tennis Professionals list and wouldn't have been a factor in the competition anyway. Besides, tennis was only a demonstration sport, the results of which were not included in the medal count.

I issued a statement calling the Soviet complaints "for the most part baseless.

"The issues raised in the USSR NOC communication are by and large easy to answer," I said. "In fact, we have answered many of them on numerous occasions. There are no violations of the Olympic Charter—I'm not sure how many different ways there are to say that."

I left the decision open about the IOC meeting. I was waiting for the Soviets to confirm they would attend and wanted to know who they'd send. If Gramov was going, the situation was serious. If a lower-level sports official led the delegation, it meant the Soviets were merely positioning for better treatment for their athletes. When Samaranch told me on April 17 that it was Gramov, I began assembling a small LAOOC delegation.

On Sunday evening, April 22, David Simon, Amy Quinn, and Jerry Welsh, the LAOOC envoy to the USSR, joined me and my youngest daughter, Keri, at LAX for the long, twelve-hour red-eye flight to Lausanne. Keri had been home for spring break and was returning to L'Aiglon College.

I sat next to her on the plane, and we chatted about family and school during the meal. She'd enjoyed being home with the family for a few weeks and was excited that Heidi would be joining her in Switzerland within a few weeks to start a summer job at the International Olympic Committee.

Keri was growing up so quickly, and it saddened me to realize how much I was missing of her childhood. So I was glad to have this opportunity to be with her, even though it was short and I had a lot of work to do on the plane. She asked me about the latest Olympic developments and I explained how serious they were.

"I want to warn you to expect some pretty nasty press about the Games from here on in," I said. "Also, be prepared to read some bad things about me."

She laughed. I turned to her, surprised.

"What's so funny?" I asked.

"You forget I know French," she said. "I've already read many of the bad things they've said about you in the French press, and they don't know the half of it."

I hugged her. "You'd better not spill the beans." I was happy she was able to take the tension of the Games in stride.

While I was spending time with Keri, Quinn and Simon briefed Welsh. Welsh was a top executive with the American Express Company, and I had met him a month earlier when Louis Gerstner, president of American Express Travel Related Services, and he had visited the LAOOC offices. Welsh had taught courses in Russian and Soviet studies at Vanderbilt University before joining American Express. I needed him brought up to speed because he understood the Russians and would serve as my adviser and interpreter during the meetings. After Keri drifted off to sleep, I joined them in the food-service compartment.

"How are you going to save U.S.-Soviet relations?" I asked Welsh.

"I'm going to have two glasses of vodka and get some sleep so I can think like they do tomorrow morning," he replied.

We transferred planes in Paris and took a Swissair flight to Switzerland where we arrived in the late evening. We were driven to the Lausanne Palace Hotel, and I was immediately escorted to Samaranch's suite for a briefing on the next day's agenda. Everyone else went to sleep.

Everybody gathered for breakfast in the morning, including Keri. We were in good spirits. Simon was excited to be in Switzerland for the first time and ordered hot chocolate expecting a culinary experience. His smile drooped when the waiter produced with great fanfare a cup of hot water and an envelope of premixed instant cocoa.

While Samaranch, Monique Berlioux, and the three IOC vice-presidents met with the Soviet delegation first, we walked through the streets near the hotel to stretch our legs and get our bearings. It was a beautiful spring day and obviously it was better to be outside.

"I don't want any of you to be intimidated," I said to the group. "The IOC runs very formal meetings, but we don't have to play by their rules. We can do whatever we want. If you have something to add to the discussion, don't hesitate—speak up."

I wanted to spend the remainder of the morning with Keri, who was leaving that afternoon. We said goodbye to the group and headed off in search of a gift. Her seventeenth birthday was a few days away and I was sad I wouldn't be able to be with her. We combed the shops of Lausanne for about an hour before settling on a jewelry store where we bought a pretty gold ring.

Our preliminary meeting followed the Soviets'. We met upstairs in the Executive Board conference room at Château de Vidy. There were translation booths equipped for service in five languages lining one wall, and a long rectangular conference table in the center that was large enough to comfortably seat twenty. The IOC had set out note pads and pencils at each seat and bottles of two brands of mineral water. There were photographs of Olympic scenes and portraits of IOC presidents on the walls. At this morning session, Samaranch and Berlioux sat at one end of the table and I sat opposite them.

Samaranch listed the Soviet complaints and we answered them. There were no surprises. He gave each of the vice-presidents an opportunity to raise issues. Kumar asked about the Coalition to Ban the Soviets and handed us leaflets and letters that the coalition had sent to Gramov in Moscow. The literature used inflammatory language and promised to greet the Soviet athletes with anti-Soviet demonstrations. One handout, which the Soviets claimed had been distributed at a Soviet-U.S. wrestling meet, graphically depicted an American eagle clawing the back of a Russian bear.

I explained to Kumar that the Ban the Soviets was a group of nobodies who got increased media attention each time the Soviets complained. "They don't have any support," I said. "Not the LAOOC's and not the U.S. government's."

Siperco then questioned us about the U.S. embassy in Moscow demanding a delegation list from the Soviet National Olympic Committee to process visas.

Simon responded to Siperco. He said, "The State Department erroneously used the word 'visa' in a communiqué to the Soviet Foreign Office from the U.S. embassy. They have withdrawn this language and issued an official apology. It was a mistake."

The final issue was the *Gruzia*. Samaranch took this point on himself.

"The Soviets would like international regulations to be followed and only have one inspection of the boat when it reaches Los Angeles. Not an inspection every day, which is normal status," Samaranch said.

"The boat will be handled very carefully with normal inspections," I said. "We will assure special security arrangements for the ship."

"Then we will tell them that the boat will be inspected under normal international regulations?" Samaranch asked.

I nodded. I was grateful that Samaranch understood the LAOOC's precarious position in this matter. We had no control over the number of inspections, only that the inspections be carried out through normal international procedures. By telling the Russians that normal international procedures would be adhered to, he was walking a diplomatic fine line. From the U.S. government's point of view, the Soviets were lucky to have obtained permission to dock the boat in the first place. Our government wasn't about to allow the Soviets to dictate procedures and didn't care how they interpreted international law.

That afternoon I had the opportunity to respond directly to Gramov. He questioned me about the same points Samaranch had raised in the morning. However, while discussing the *Gruzia,* he surprised me with a new issue.

"What will be the LAOOC's attitude if the athletes are housed on the boat?" he asked.

I shrugged. "The IOC says all athletes are required to stay in the Olympic villages," I responded. "If they want to visit the boat, that is something different."

"The athletes would be more comfortable on the boat," he said.

"After competition," I said, "any athlete is free to go on the boat. However, conditions will be much better in the villages."

"American food is different from Soviet food," Gramov added. "Our athletes have special requirements."

"We will make every attempt to meet your needs. As you said before, it is important for the Soviet athletes to meet and mix with athletes from the other nations."

"During the Montreal Games, the American athletes lived in a hotel."

I didn't like the direction he was taking. "This is not true," I replied.

He continued, "During the Sarajevo Games, the U.S. team did not stay in the Olympic Village."

"If you are interested we can research this question," I said. "The U.S. athletes stayed at the village with the exception of a few skaters. The U.S. athletes will stay in the village at the Los Angeles Games."

"Athletes from other countries didn't stay in the village, either," Gramov said in an attempt to be conciliatory.

Samaranch interjected, "The IOC view is according to the charter. Whatever the charter allows, we will enforce."

The charter only mandates that the organizing committee provide villages to house the athletes and officials. It doesn't require anyone to stay there. However, the charter *does* state that the NOC is liable for all housing costs, whether the housing is used or not.

I then said, "This situation would present other problems. We would need entirely separate transportation and security systems. It would be like an Olympic Games within an Olympic Games. Suppose every team made the same request?" I didn't want to end it there. I wanted to talk to Gramov privately. This request had the potential of being negotiable. "This is a new subject," I added. Then looking directly at Gramov, who was sifting through papers, I said, "We will study this if you would like us to."

"Yes," he replied without looking up.

Samaranch then began summing up the issue. "All athletes would live on the boat? How many? I don't think everybody should live on the ship. Perhaps just the athletes the days prior to their competitions and then a few additional rest days. The USSR NOC should send a formal request to the LAOOC and Peter should respond."

"Will we discuss this at the press conference or is this a private matter for study?" I asked.

"There is no secret about it," Gramov shot back.

Samaranch said, "This question will not be raised during the press conference. If a question does arise, I will respond."

Gramov started to change the subject, but I wanted to make sure it was perfectly clear that this issue was *not* to be made public. The request had to be cleared through government officials in Washington and I didn't want them to be in a position where it was easy to deny yet another Soviet request.

"I'd like to go back to the ship issue," I said. "It is important that we all agree on this being a private matter. Potentially it has far-reaching implications for the Los Angeles Games and could be precedent setting for the Olympic Movement. The costs would be very high and worldwide reaction very negative. We have been criticized by the USSR NOC for

years for having two Olympic villages and a satellite village
for the rowers and canoeists in Santa Barbara. It is essential
that this remain private. If it is already public, I would like to
know."

Gramov assured me it wasn't and that he would keep it
confidential.

Samaranch was handed a wire-service report by a member of the IOC secretariat as he ended the meeting. He
brightened visibly as he read. He showed it to Gramov first.
As he handed it to me, he said, "We have just had very good
news."

The report, datelined Moscow, quoted Italian Prime
Minister Giulio Andreotti speaking optimistically about Soviet participation in the 1984 Games following a discussion
with Soviet Premier Constantin Chernenko. This contributed
to Samaranch's optimism.

While Samaranch prepared for the press conference, I
strolled through the gardens behind Château de Vidy with
Gramov and our interpreters, Welsh and Stanislaus Belianov.
I thanked Gramov for his forthright manner at the meetings
and let him know I understood his deep concerns for the welfare of his athletes.

"If it would be helpful," I said, "I will travel to Moscow
to reinforce the U.S. government's support of the Games and
the LAOOC's commitment to safeguarding all athletes of the
world."

Gramov, walking with his hands clasped behind his back,
nodded. His inner feelings were hidden by the dark sun-
glasses, which he always wore outdoors and sometimes even
indoors.

"However," I continued, "a meeting with Premier Chernenko would be necessary if the trip were to have a chance at
success."

Gramov didn't respond at first. Then he said, "Mr.
Ueberroth, we in the Soviet Union regard you with the highest esteem. I will let you know if it is a good idea for you to
come to Moscow. Soviet participation will be decided at the

highest levels of my government. Please understand, whatever decision is reached will not be a reflection on your efforts."

When I entered the large meeting room on the first floor of the Lausanne Palace Hotel for the press conference twenty minutes later, I certainly didn't share Samaranch's optimism. Gramov's message could only be interpreted one way, and the only hope to which I clung was the slim chance I'd be invited to Moscow to appeal directly to Chernenko. It was clear to me that Soviet participation would be a political decision and probably a negative one. I privately wondered if this entire meeting had been staged by the Soviets as another step in that direction. Gramov didn't have the authority to go beyond the rhetoric he had delivered throughout the course of the day. I feared the worst, but I made a conscious decision to stay as upbeat as possible and support Samaranch's positive characterization of the meetings.

Journalists had converged on the hotel from all over Europe and more than two hundred had asssembled in the room.

Samaranch said, "The black clouds which have accumulated in the Olympic sky have vanished or are very soon to vanish. Both parties showed a desire to safeguard the Olympic Movement."

I found his hyperbole a little hard to swallow, let alone support. I was more reserved in my optimism, saying we'd made some headway in addressing the Soviet complaints and would continue to try to resolve any differences. I said we had agreed to communicate regularly and that consistent with the IOC Charter, we would allow the Soviet NOC to submit its delegation list directly to the LAOOC. Gramov, for his part, stuck to the party line.

Before leaving the hotel early the next morning, I stopped by Samaranch's suite to say goodbye and to thank him. As a parting shot, I asked him if he'd made any progress on obtaining the Olympic flame from Greece. Our torch relay was to begin in only two weeks and we still hadn't reached peace with the Greeks. He smiled wearily and said, "I am working on it. I haven't forgotten and I will notify you as soon as I have it."

At the airport, I thought my eyes were deceiving me as they focused on the approach of a short, white-haired gentleman.

"Is that Nissiotis?" Quinn asked.

"I'm so tired, I hope not," I said.

It was. Nissiotis had read I was in Switzerland and had flown there specifically to talk to me.

"Peter, do you have a few moments to talk about your torch relay?" Nissiotis asked.

We found an isolated spot across from our departure gate.

"I am humiliated by our treatment of your program," he said, "and I want to explain the problem to you in person. The politics in my country have shifted dramatically to the left in recent months and we are being pressured by those elements to criticize and, if possible, force you to terminate your program."

"I appreciate your candor," I told him. "We're not going to cancel it, but we must figure out a solution that saves face for your country and gets the Olympic flame to New York on time for the relay."

"I want you to know I will do everything I can," he said. "I think a private ceremony would be best. I am sure that can be arranged."

"I know you'll do the best you can," I said. I said good-bye to Nissiotis and we boarded the plane.

I returned to Los Angeles and kept my end of the bargain. I sent three Telexes to Gramov over the next five days. In the first, I answered specific questions regarding the Aeroflot charters and the *Gruzia* raised in Lausanne. In the second, I followed up on the possibility of my visit to Moscow. On May 2, I sent a wire wishing him well on the Soviets' May Day holiday and requesting a response to my earlier Telex.

That same day Samaranch called with news that the Olympic flame was in Lausanne. Two Swiss students working on an Olympic project had driven to Olympia with a miner's lamp and a manual describing the ceremony for lighting the Olympic flame. They lit the flame by the sun's rays and

brought it to Château de Vidy. To verify the flame's authen-
ticity they had photographed the ceremony from start to finish. Chuckling, Samaranch said, "Come and get it."

I knew Richard Perelman, the LAOOC vice-president for
press operations, was sending a two-man delegation to Paris
that weekend to address an international press group on our
press preparations for the Games. I asked him if either one
could handle a clandestine assignment and he assured me
Greg Harney could do the job. He was a young, hardworking
guy from New York, who'd been the sports information director at Arizona State University before joining Perelman's
group. I called Harney into my office and gave him the assignment and then told Dick Sargent to arrange the logistics.

My next step was to huddle with Hussey and Caloyeras.
Now that we had an official flame, it was time to play the final
card.

"Get Filaretos on the phone," I told them, "and make
one last request for his help to arrange a flame-lighting ceremony in Olympia. If he refuses, tell him fine. Tell him we
already have a flame and we'd be pleased to tell the world
how we snuck into Olympia and got it, if that's how he wants
it. Also, mention we've decided that Greece will march in
alphabetical order at the opening ceremonies, instead of in its
customary place—first in line."

An hour later, Hussey and Caloyeras returned. Both
were grinning from ear to ear.

"I don't think you'll be surprised to learn the Greeks are
looking forward to Sunday's flame-lighting ceremony in
Olympia," Hussey said. "Filaretos even guaranteed Greek
government support."

Rather than take a chance on the Greeks' falling
through, I decided to let Harney bring back the flame from
Lausanne and have Sargent, Hussey, and Caloyeras bring
back the other.

Meanwhile, still nothing from the Soviets. The only information we received from Gramov during the next few days
came indirectly from Mario Vázquez Raña, president of the
Association of National Olympic Committees and the Mexican Olympic Committee.

On May 5, Gramov wired Vázquez that "he was not quite sure that the organizers of the Games could follow the rules of the Olympic Charter. . . ." He invited Vázquez to Moscow to discuss ideas to strengthen the role of the national Olympic committees for future Olympic Games. This was a clear signal they wanted to maintain their level of influence in the Olympic Movement regardless of their upcoming decision on participation.

Samaranch was troubled by this development. I had already arranged a meeting for him with President Reagan in Washington following the start of our torch relay in New York, Tuesday morning, May 8. He thought a letter from Reagan to Chernenko guaranteeing U.S. support of the Olympic Charter would help, as would a meeting with Ambassador Dobrynin. Samaranch had just returned from a visit to Romania where Nicolae Ceausescu, the Romanian president, had told him that a Reagan letter might be helpful. I told him I'd do what I could.

I left for New York the morning of May 7. I'd already been informed that Harney's mission was successful and that Sargent and his crew were en route to New York with the other flame.

I arrived feeling wonderful and excited. Seeing the relay begin would be the culmination of a dream. Wally McGuire assured me the relay was logistically sound, as was the agenda for the ceremony. Everything looked good, everybody in place. Dick Sargent called, telling me he'd arrived in New York. I then touched base with Monique Berlioux and Juan Antonio Samaranch to let them know we had more than enough Olympic flames in New York. I told Samaranch that Reagan was amenable to drafting a letter to Chernenko, but Dobrynin had canceled his appointment because of a Soviet holiday. I never did find out which holiday it was.

I joined Dick Sargent, Jay Moorhead, David Israel, and Amy Quinn at Elaine's for dinner. We celebrated. Sargent regaled us with his heroic adventures in Greece. He, Hussey, and Caloyeras had flown to Athens on Air Force G3, an eleven-passenger Gulfstream jet normally assigned to Secretary of State Shultz.

"Just as I was about to get on the helicopter for Olympia," said Dick, "one of the Greek NOC guys told me the cost was twenty-eight hundred dollars. I looked at Caloyeras and he just shrugged. He said, 'Let me talk to the gentleman for a moment.'

"As Caloyeras took the guy off, I asked Hussey what was going on. 'I thought we had a deal,' I said. 'Twenty-four hundred bucks for two helicopters to take us from Athens to Olympia and back.' Hussey smiled that silly smile of his and said, 'I thought so, too.'

"Caloyeras came back frowning. He said, 'The price is twenty-eight hundred.' I knew I had to be careful with the Greeks. I also remembered Ueberroth lesson number ten: Don't show more money than you are prepared to spend. So, being prepared for a swindle, I had twenty-four one-hundred-dollar bills clipped together in my pocket. I pulled out the wad of money and told the NOC representative, 'This is all I have, take it or leave it.'

"This guy was a real hustler. He shook his head and said, 'I am sorry, Mr. Sargent, but you must pay us twenty-eight hundred American.' I said, 'This is it. We'll just have to find another ride to Olympia.'

"But as I started walking away, he stopped me. 'In the spirit of Olympic brotherhood,' he said, 'the national Olympic committee will pay the outstanding balance out of its own funds.' Can you imagine that? Olympic brotherhood, after the ordeal they put us through?"

We laughed and continued eating. Sargent described the actual flame-lighting ceremony and got misty-eyed. He took a crumbled piece of paper out of his pocket and read us the comments he had made upon receiving the flame on behalf of the LAOOC: "All nations and athletes should come to this sacred place and experience the ceremony. Then they would better know and understand the importance of the Olympic Movement and the great part it plays in generating peace throughout the world."

Top, photographic evidence of the back-up Olympic flame being ignited by the heat of the sun, according to Olympic tradition, in Olympia, Greece. *Center,* the flame is transferred to an official LAOOC miner's lamp before being transported by a group of students to IOC headquarters in Lausanne, Switzerland. *Bottom,* IOC President Juan Antonio Samaranch (left) hands Olympic flame to LAOOC press officer Greg Harney, who brought the back-up flame to the United States.
COURTESY OF THE IOC

Left, LAOOC Vice-president Dick Sargent carries the flame in Colorado. *Below,* a lone torch relay runner in the Smokey Mountains of Tennessee.

Bottom, O. J. Simpson holds the torch high as he reaches the top of the California Incline in Santa Monica. LAOOC PHOTOS BY PAUL SLAUGHTER

Top, a crowd awaits the arrival of the torch-relay caravan at the Santa Fe Plaza, New Mexico. *Above,* LAOOC Executive Vice-president Harry L. Usher (center) on board the press truck as it followed the torch in Santa Monica. At left is Angie Rios, a member of the LAOOC news department. *Below,* thousands gather to witness the torch relay in Santa Monica. LAOOC PHOTOS BY PAUL SLAUGHTER

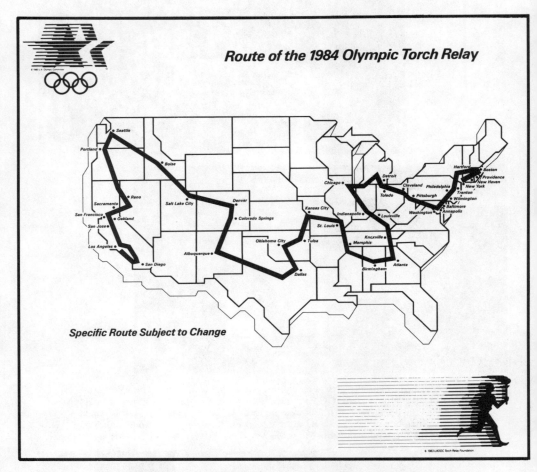

Route of the 1984 Olympic Torch Relay

Seattle
Portland
Boise
Reno
Sacramento
San Francisco
Oakland
San Jose
Los Angeles
San Diego
Salt Lake City
Denver
Colorado Springs
Albuquerque
Oklahoma City
Tulsa
Dallas
Kansas City
St. Louis
Indianapolis
Chicago
Detroit
Cleveland
Toledo
Pittsburgh
Louisville
Knoxville
Memphis
Birmingham
Atlanta
Philadelphia
Trenton
New York
Wilmington
Baltimore
Annapolis
Washington
Hartford
Boston
Providence
New Haven

Specific Route Subject to Change

© 1983 LAOOC Torch Relay Foundation

The Olympic torch relay passed through thirty-three states and the District of Columbia. COURTESY OF THE LAOOC

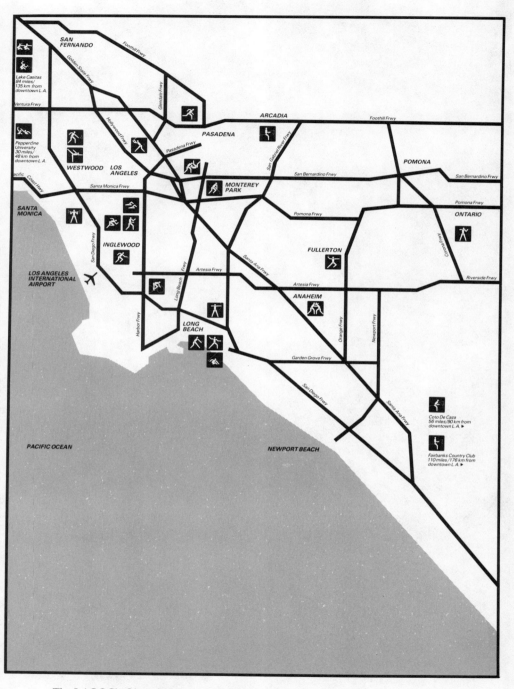

The LAOOC's Olympic venue map. COURTESY OF THE LAOOC

Balloons fill the sky over the Los Angeles Memorial Coliseum during the opening ceremonies. PHOTO BY BOB KUHN

Top, carrying the Olympic flag during opening ceremonies are (front row, left to right) John Naber, Parry O'Brien, Wyomia Tyus, and Bruce Jenner; (back row, left to right) Al Oerter, Mack Robinson, Billy Mills, and Bill Thorpe, Jr. Each flag bearer devoted thousands of hours to the Olympic Games as members of the Olympic spirit team. *Below,* LAOOC Executive Vice-president Harry L. Usher carries the Antwerp flag at opening ceremonies followed by LAOOC Chairman of the Board Paul Ziffren, and Los Angeles Mayor Tom Bradley. LAOOC PHOTOS BY PAUL SLAUGHTER

The jubilant Romanian gymnastics team responds to the cheers. LPI/84 PHOTO BY
MICHAEL YADA

Left, members of the U.S. 4 × 100 meter freestyle relay team celebrate their victory with high fives. NOPP PHOTO BY DAVE GATLEY/*Los Angeles Times*

Above, Ecaterina Szabo of Romania shyly receives a silver medal in the gymnastics competition. LAOOC PHOTO BY PAUL SLAUGHTER

Left, Peter Vidmar of the United States and Koji Gushiken of Japan celebrate on the gymnastics award stand. LPI/84 PHOTO BY ROBERT LONG

Decathlon gold medalist Daley Thompson participating in the long jump. LAOOC PHOTO BY PAUL SLAUGHTER

Right, Gabriela Anderson-Scheiss of Switzerland struggles to complete the women's marathon. LPI/84 PHOTO BY JOE DIMAGGIO

The U.S. team marches into the Coliseum during the opening ceremonies. LPI/84
PHOTO BY MICHAEL YADA

The Ueberroths in the stands at closing ceremonies. From left: Joe, Heidi, Keri, me, Ginny, and Vicki. COURTESY OF THE AUTHOR

IOC President Juan Antonio Samaranch hangs the gold medal of the Olympic Order around my neck during closing ceremonies. LAOOC PHOTO BY PAUL SLAUGHTER

Harry Usher (first row, second from left) and I (third row, second from left) gather with the
LAOOC commissioners after the Games. COURTESY OF THE AUTHOR

The Ueberroths at the surprise twenty-fifth anniversary party given by the kids. From left: Joe, me, Ginny, Vicki, Keri, and Heidi. COURTESY OF THE AUTHOR

Ginny (far left) and I (far right) join (from left) Mrs. George Bush, former Detroit Tiger stars George Kell and Al Kaline, and Vice-president George Bush as Kell throws out the first ball of a World Series game between Detroit and the Chicago Cubs in October 1984. COURTESY OF MAJOR LEAGUE BASEBALL

THE LONGEST DAY

IT WAS MAY 8, 1984, and I got up at 6 A.M. I opened the curtains to my suite at the United Nations Plaza Hotel and looked outside. It was gray and drizzly. Little did I realize what was going to happen that day would cause me to remember it as being the worst day in my life.

I called Dick Sargent. Room service had already delivered coffee, fresh fruit, and cereal when he arrived.

"Help yourself, Dick," I said.

"Are you worried that it's going to rain on your parade?" he asked while pouring coffee.

"The weather is the least of my worries," I said. "I'm more concerned about the torch-relay staff overreacting to problems along the route."

"How can I help?" Sargent asked.

"I'd like you to travel with the relay for a week. Keep it running smoothly. Work with the staff—advance and security particularly—and make sure they're friendly to everyone they come in contact with. I also need you there to avert a general panic in case it falls behind schedule."

We talked for a few more minutes, then I worked on my speech which I hoped would set the tone for the relay. Before leaving, Sargent listened to it and offered a few suggestions.

"One last thing, Dick," I said. "Make sure we have enough umbrellas for the dignitaries. Especially Monique."

An hour later I walked a half block through a light drizzle to visit United Nations Plaza, where the torch ceremony would take place. The LAOOC advance people were there in force, scurrying about and taking care of myriad last-minute details, one of which was erecting a tent over the platform to protect the VIPs from the rain.

To one side of the stage was a large caldron. It was empty then, but in a few hours it would contain the Olympic flame Sargent had brought from Greece. I stood on the perimeter and watched as television crews set up equipment and the New York police put up barricades along the start of the torch route. Despite the rain, everything was falling into place.

Back at the hotel, I met Samaranch and Monique Berlioux in the lobby on our way to a breakfast AT&T was hosting for the dignitaries. As we took our places around a large, U-shaped table, I noticed that an incredibly eclectic group had gathered: L.A. Mayor Tom Bradley, New York Mayor Edward I Koch, AT&T Chairman Charles Brown, U.S. IOC member Julian Roosevelt, USOC President William E. Simon, Olympian Rafer Johnson, and the first torchbearers, Gina Hemphill and Bill Thorpe, Jr.

We gathered promptly at 8:40 A.M. in the hotel lobby after breakfast. By this time the rain was steady and we needed our umbrellas for the short walk to UN Plaza. Jay Moorhead carried the miner's lamp containing the Olympic flame for Berlioux, who would be its caretaker during the ceremony. We had created this role for her at the last minute, but she still seemed miffed that she didn't have a speaking part.

We took our places on the stage and the speeches began. Mayor Koch welcomed the flame and the Olympics to New York; Mayor Bradley talked about how this was a proud moment and how he was anxious for the flame to reach Los Angeles; and Samaranch proclaimed that in Spain rain was a good omen. "It brings good luck," he said.

I was thrilled to see several hundred people there and they were cheering each speaker enthusiastically. When it was my turn, I looked over the wall of television cameras to the crowd. "This is the beginning of the Olympic Games," I said. "Americans from all walks of life will have a chance to participate in the Games as torchbearers in this history-making, cross-country relay. All of America will benefit because the funds raised from this relay will go toward strengthening the youth of our nation."

Monique Berlioux, Rafer Johnson, Gina Hemphill, and Bill Thorpe, Jr., joined me at the caldron after my remarks. Johnson lit a sparkler from the miner's lamp held by Berlioux and plunged it into the caldron, igniting the Olympic flame. I dipped the first torch into the flame and was stunned when it lit. I couldn't believe I was actually holding it. I was tongue-tied and felt a chill run up my spine as I handed the torch to Gina and Bill.

I'll never forget their wonderfully warm smiles as they grasped the torch together. They paused, held the flame aloft for all to see, and took off running up First Avenue to Forty-fourth Street. The relay was on and it wouldn't stop for eighty-two days.

I said goodbye to Berlioux, who was returning to Switzerland, and to mayors Bradley and Koch. Samaranch and I were hustled off the stage and rushed to Butler Aviation at LaGuardia Airport. There we would take a chartered Lear jet to Washington for our meeting with President Reagan.

The heavens really let loose as we sped toward the airport.

The flame, meanwhile, was making its way through Manhattan. The second runner was ninety-one-year-old Abel Kiviat, who had won a silver medal in the 1,500 meter at the 1912 Stockholm Olympics. The flame arrived at the entrance to Central Park at Columbus Circle and was carried along Central Park Drive, leaving the park at Seventh Avenue. From there, it headed east to Fifth Avenue, turned south, and passed St. Patrick's Cathedral and Rockefeller Center on its way to the Empire State Building. It circled Union Square, traveled south on Broadway to city hall, and arrived at the World Trade Center at 12:30 P.M. before leaving Manhattan.

"I think this torch relay was a very good idea," Samaranch said during the drive. "It will be good for the Games and good for the Olympic Movement. I hope our Washington meetings will also be productive."

Samaranch was a master at switching gears. But he couldn't do a thing about the weather: The airport was fogged in and we were told our plane would be delayed until it cleared.

"I already notified the White House," Moorhead told us.

"Can we still see the president?" I asked.

"Deaver doesn't think it'll be a problem," he replied.

"Good," Samaranch said.

"I thought you said rain was good luck," I said turning to Samaranch.

"It's good luck in Spain," he said.

Moorhead returned to the terminal. Twenty minutes later he came back and said, "It looks like it's going to be awhile. Come inside and have some coffee."

Samaranch and I had coffee with David Israel and Amy Quinn while Moorhead checked in with his Washington office. The waiting area of the terminal was a big, bleak room, musty and damp. There were dozens of plastic chairs banked along the walls. Two vending machines—one for hot drinks, one for cold—stood in one corner of the room. We were the only ones there.

"President Samaranch," Moorhead said, "my secretary tells me your assistant at Château de Vidy is trying to reach you."

Samaranch walked over to the pay telephones and made several attempts to place an overseas call. The long-distance operator told him all circuits were busy.

Moorhead then called his office and instructed his secretary to call IOC headquarters and give somebody there the number of the pay telephone Samaranch was using.

Samaranch answered the telephone himself when the call finally came through. He spoke softly into the receiver for about two minutes, showing little emotion throughout the conversation. After he hung up, he walked toward us slowly.

"The Soviets are at it again," he said.

"What do you mean 'at it again'?" I asked.

"The reports are vague, but one says they will not participate in the Los Angeles Games," he said grimly.

Quinn said, "Peter, I better call the office and tell them to batten down the hatches until we get some definitive information."

Samaranch and I sat down. Neither of us spoke. We were lost in our own thoughts.

It was another twenty minutes before we received clearance to take off. We hadn't received any further word about the Soviets by the time we boarded the aircraft.

Samaranch and I talked quietly on the plane and we revised our White House strategy. It was more important than ever now to obtain a letter from Reagan for Samaranch to hand deliver to Chernenko. At first, we were reluctant to accept the sketchy report as the Soviets' final decision to boycott the Games. After all, the Soviets, like all other participants, had until June 2 to decide. We wondered why they would make a decision so early. Deep down, however, we knew this was no idle threat, even though it hadn't been confirmed.

I asked Samaranch about going directly to Moscow that night; take a few high-level U.S. government officials with me, sit down with the Russians face to face, and persuade them that their fears were unjustified. But Samaranch didn't think it would be a wise thing to do. The USSR was dangerously close to repeating the same mistakes the U.S. government had made in 1980.

As we began our approach into Washington's National Airport, the weather cleared and the sun shone through. We went directly to the Hay-Adams Hotel where Moorhead had already arranged a working suite and accommodations for us. Reporters were there waiting. I had nothing to say. I told them I'd only heard the news moments earlier and the reports were vague.

I was anxious to get to the suite and make a few telephone calls to find out what in the hell was going on. I picked up the phone and got nothing. The bellboy told me the phone lines were down but that they'd be fixed within the hour.

Moorhead ran up the street to the LAOOC office to reschedule the meeting with Reagan. Israel arranged for lunch, and Quinn went searching for a working phone. She returned ten minutes later. It was 1:30 P.M.

"There's a wire report out of Paris," she said, "saying that the Soviets won't participate under existing circumstances—citing the usual security and government intervention reasons. The source is a journalist named Victor Louis who frequently writes for European newspapers."

"I know this Louis," Samaranch said. "The Soviets use him frequently to break news in the West."

"What's going on at the office?" I asked.

"The phones are ringing off the hook," she said. "But I think it's important for you to call Paul Ziffren. He's already made some statements, and you probably ought to coordinate a game plan."

"Where's Harry?" I asked.

"He's meeting with Gates on the security agreement," she replied. Usher was still negotiating with Los Angeles Police Chief Daryl Gates on the staffing levels LAPD would provide for the Games. It seemed the Russians picked an opportune time to make this announcement: We had no one minding the store.

Moorhead entered with news that we could meet with the president in an hour. He also told us the phones were working.

I called Ziffren and told him about our meeting with Reagan and asked him to refrain from making any further statements until we got a better reading from the Soviets and the White House. I had the LAOOC press office issue a statement that Samaranch and I would be available for comment outside the White House immediately following our meeting with Reagan. I hoped that would stem the uncontrolled flow of information for the time being.

Before we went to the White House, Quinn read me the formal Soviet statement she'd received from her office. Based on the usual complaints, the Soviets concluded: "In these conditions the National Olympic Committee of the USSR is compelled to declare that participation of Soviet sportsmen in the Games of the XXIIIrd Olympiad in Los Angeles is impossible."

Samaranch was outraged over their cavalier remarks regarding the April 24 meeting in Lausanne. The Soviets claimed that "the IOC found the stand of the USSR National Olympic Committee to be just and substantiated."

This was typical Soviet propaganda and I shrugged it off.

Samaranch and I met with Mike Deaver first, and he gave us more information. He asked if the boycott was for real; we assured him it was. After a few minutes we were ushered into the Oval Office. We were told Secretary of State Shultz was running behind schedule and would arrive later.

President Reagan readily agreed to draft a letter for Samaranch to hand deliver to Chernenko. But Samaranch changed his mind during the course of the meeting and asked the president to address the letter to him, Samaranch, rather than to Chernenko for protocol purposes. Samaranch felt the position of president of the IOC would be diminished, and the Olympic Movement undermined, if heads of state began communicating among themselves on Olympic issues rather than through him.

I suggested that the president perhaps ought to invite Chernenko to attend the Games as his personal guest. It would be a marvelous gesture of statesmanship, I said, whether he accepted or not, and might allay Soviet fears and criticism.

It was my impression the idea appealed to the president, but I noticed Deaver stiffen. He immediately excused himself and left the room. Samaranch continued to outline the points he thought the president should make in the letter. When Deaver returned, Shultz was with him. Shultz immediately vetoed the idea of Reagan inviting Chernenko to the Games, saying it would complicate other existing issues. That was the end of that idea—and the meeting. We were told Deaver's assistant, Bill Sittman, would notify Moorhead when the letter was ready to be picked up.

We waited for Israel, Quinn, and White House deputy press secretary Peter Roussell in Sittman's office for a few minutes. Roussell said the press corps had gathered outside the East Wing of the White House and was ready for a statement. I decided to call it for what it was—retaliation for the

1980 Carter boycott. Samaranch offered to address the meeting with Reagan and leave the rest for me. From an international point of view, the Reagan meeting would appear less staged coming from him. He looked drained.

Walking outside was like walking into quicksand. A huge press corps encircled Samaranch and me so tightly we had to gasp for air. It was a physical battle just to stand up. There was no order. Reporters fired questions from every direction and none could be heard clearly. I tried to take control over the din.

"I would like to make a couple of quick statements," I said. "Then I'd be pleased to answer your questions."

There were several interruptions and one voice was clear as a bell. "Before you answer any questions," the unknown woman said, "could you tell us who you are?"

I identified myself and continued, saying, "Basically, the charges are unfounded. We were very disappointed to learn of the Soviets' decision. It appears we're paying the price for 1980. That's our interpretation. Those who will be hurt the most, once again, will be the athletes. We will expend every last ounce of energy to reverse this decision on behalf of the athletes of the world."

Samaranch said, "I was with President Reagan some minutes ago, and he assured me the Olympic Charter during the Games will be fully respected. All athletes and officials will be treated well and in the same way."

Most of the questions were predictable. Who else might boycott? How would the Russian announcement affect our preparations? What ideas did I have to reverse the decision? How would it affect competition?

I didn't have any answers.

We walked wearily across Lafayette Square to the Hay-Adams. Samaranch was anxious to return to Lausanne, but we spent an hour conferring before he left for the airport.

I called Harry Usher in Los Angeles. He'd just returned to the LAOOC offices from his downtown meeting. The negotiations with Gates and the LAPD were still stalemated.

I asked him about office morale. He said the shock was

beginning to wear off, and everyone was banding together. The Los Angeles media were clamoring for a local LAOOC reaction. He told me that Bradley, LAPD Chief Gates, and City Council President Pat Russell had already issued lengthy statements. His sense was that local civic leaders were rallying around us. Then he laid one on me. The Coalition to Ban the Soviets had held a news conference and had taken credit for the Soviet boycott.

I hit the roof. "What did they say this time?"

Usher said, "Let me go through this wire copy." He was quiet for a moment, then said, "That guy Balsiger said, 'We're definitely responsible [for the boycott], no matter what they say. I'm sure they decided to pull out because the United States would not muzzle our coalition and agree to turn defectors back over to the KGB, which was probably the major reason they withdrew.' Balsiger and his associates took turns patting each other on the back."

"I hope they are proud that they're able to hurt so many young athletes," I replied.

We discussed damage control. I told Usher I was going to send our envoys into the field right away to nail down as many early NOC acceptances as possible. I had formed the envoy program two years earlier, modeling it after the commissioners. But instead of working with the international sports federations, the envoys were our ambassadors to the national Olympic committees. We'd lined up envoys for more than half the NOCs—Peter Caloyeras for Greece and Jerry Welsh for the USSR, for example—and now it was especially important that we complete the roster.

Usher was about to go into a meeting with the LAOOC senior staff where he would ask them to revise operational scenarios. He said he'd scheduled a news conference after the management meeting and would tell the Los Angeles press it was business as usual at the LAOOC.

I still had to deal with ABC. There was a clause in our contract that allowed ABC to arbitrate its final payments in the event of a boycott. At this time, ABC still owed us $90 million. All of it was now in jeopardy. Roone Arledge was in Los Angeles presiding over a meeting of ABC affiliates and I put his name on my list of people to call. But I felt better after talking to Usher. I knew he would handle the situation well.

Next I talked to Tom Megonigal, the LAOOC commissioner for handball who had recently agreed to run the envoy program. I told Megonigal assigning envoys and getting them in contact with their respective NOCs was top priority.

"Have a list of people with their credentials waiting for me when I get back tomorrow," I told him. "Have home telephone numbers. I want Tony Frank and Charles Lee to get ready to go overseas."

Frank, a Bay Area banker, was our envoy to the German Democratic Republic; Lee, an attorney with LAOOC's law firm, Latham & Watkins, was assigned to the People's Republic of China. The GDR and PRC were key, and we had to make every effort to keep them in the Games. But I knew the GDR would be tough.

I then called Roone Arledge. He said he had resisted intense pressure from the ABC board to call the boycott a catastrophe for the Games. The board also had wanted him to announce he was holding up final payment. Arledge had refused. In fact, he did the opposite and publicly said the boycott was not cataclysmic in terms of American viewership. He pointed out that the U.S. would win more gold medals, which would appeal to the American people. I thanked him for his support.

I had Moorhead follow up with the White House to make sure Samaranch received the letter before leaving for Switzerland. I worked with Quinn to develop a press strategy. We had to show the world we weren't panicking and that we were continuing to do everything possible to assure maximum participation at the Games. At the same time, I didn't want it to appear we would kow-tow to the Soviets. Therefore, we planned that I would make myself as available as possible to the media before returning to Los Angeles the next day.

Conscious about reporters' deadlines, I returned calls to the print media—working my way east to west—throughout the remainder of the afternoon. Before dinner, I was interviewed live by Patrick Buchanan and Tom Braden for their show, *Cross-Fire,* on Cable News Network. Then I rushed back to the hotel to appear live on the *McNeil-Lehrer News-hour* and *NBC Nightly News.*

After a brief dinner at Duke Ziebert's, Moorhead and I walked to his apartment where I did a few telephone interviews. I had two more to do late that evening: CBS with Dan Rather and ABC's *Nightline* with Ted Koppel.

Nightline was in progress when I arrived, and during a commercial break I was seated between Georgi Arbatov and Richard Burt, neither of whom I knew. I was struck by the coldness with which Burt stared at Arbatov, who was head of the Canadian-Soviet trade mission and one of the leading Soviet spokesmen in the West. Burt was the number-three person at State.

The discussion was lively, and I felt like a referee arbitrating the future of the Olympic Games. They battled it out, using the same tired rhetoric. Knowing that Arbatov's presence meant the Soviets were closely monitoring the show, I appealed that they reconsider.

It had started to drizzle and the ABC producer offered us a ride back to the Hay-Adams after the show. While driving through the streets of Washington, I remembered we were in the middle of an election year and I wondered if the Soviets thought their announcement would negatively affect Reagan's reelection campaign. If so, would the Reagan administration go any further publicly than it already had to help us control the damage? I thought not. The Soviet decision would surely help Reagan in the long run.

When I entered my room at 12:15 A.M., the message light was blinking. Ginny had called and so had Sargent. I was anxious to talk to her, but I wanted to leave the best for last. I stretched out on the bed and dialed Sargent in Connecticut. He told me crowds of people had lined the torch-relay route all day long, waving American flags and cheering the torchbearers on.

"Along Highway One, they were three deep in the pouring rain," Sargent said. "Along one stretch between Greenwich and Stamford, just before we put the flame to rest, a group of eight-year-old kids, all wearing raincoats over their pajamas, got together with their instruments and tried to play the ABC Olympic theme.

"It's unbelievably heartwarming," he added. "I may stay on for the next eighty-one days."

That cheered me up. I placed a call to Ginny. She'd been worried about me. She had first heard the news of the boycott at the Los Angeles Music Center where she was attending a fundraiser.

"It looks grim," I said. "But we are going to keep on trying."

"What can I do?" she asked.

"Try to reach the kids and tell them everything's all right."

Talking about the kids must have triggered something. She asked me what she'd always asked them before tucking them in for the night: "What's the best thing that happened to you today?"

"Besides this phone call, it was the torch relay," I said. "It's a smash."

CHAPTER FOURTEEN

CUTTING
OUR
LOSSES

THE MOST IMPORTANT thing now was to break the Soviet boycott. Although we'd been preparing for such a crisis, I had a sinking feeling that our own government would be unable to help, especially since the record was so bad in 1980 when the Carter administration got only half the number of nations it predicted would boycott Moscow. The LAOOC would have to attack. We had to convince the national Olympic committees to accept their invitations to go to the Games before the Soviets beat us to the punch.

The afternoon I returned to Los Angeles, I sent Tony Frank and Charles Lee with their delegations to the GDR and PRC. Bulgaria had already announced it was boycotting, and I was afraid it would spread to the rest of the Eastern bloc and beyond. The envoys had instructions to contact NOCs and bring in written confirmations quickly. Our goal was 123 NOCs, one more than the all-time record for participating nations set in the 1972 Munich Games.

Frank had an impossible assignment. The East Germans were the best prepared team in the world and I knew they were eagerly looking forward to competing in Los Angeles. They weren't worried about security, but they were worried about the Russians. Frank's job was to assure GDR officials that their athletes would be welcome and safe in Los Angeles. While I didn't expect to beat the odds, I thought a visit by Tony and his delegation might stall the inevitable. At least it would give the countries that were wavering something to think about.

Lee's task was to secure a firm commitment from the Chinese, who were skittish about attending the Games and were being pressured by the Soviets to join the boycott. During a visit in January, the president of the Chinese NOC had indicated his country's desire to participate, but much had happened since then.

Joel Rubenstein and Bea Nemlaha, director of NOC relations, assembled the envoys and created a task force of twelve staff members to operate a twenty-four-hour telephone bank and began calling every NOC in the world. Bill Hussey and Jay Moorhead were added to the project: Hussey, because of his State Department background, was to contact U.S. embassies in those countries where communications were difficult, and Moorhead was assigned to pound the pavements on Embassy Row in Washington. We might have been guilty of overlapping assignments, but I wanted to make sure we covered all the bases.

Tony Frank called from East Germany during the early morning hours of May 10 with bad news: The GDR had pulled out of the Games. Frank reported the Germans were cordial but obviously uncomfortable with his delegation. "I'm sorry, but the four hundred thousand Russian troops stationed on East Germany's soil were more persuasive than I was," Frank told me. His impression was that the sports leaders of the GDR were devastated.

Three days and three NOCs, I thought. I didn't like the mathematics. More than a hundred local reporters, photographers, broadcasters, and cameramen had packed a first-floor room at the LAOOC's Westwood headquarters that morning for our first press conference since the Soviet announcement.

"It's like receiving a one-a-day bitter pill," I said. I assured the media we'd make every effort to contain the boycott on behalf of the athletes of the world. President Reagan, I disclosed, had guaranteed his support of the Games in a letter to IOC President Samaranch, which Samaranch hoped would help reverse the Soviet decision. I also knew that Mario Vázquez Raña, president of the Association of National Olympic Committees, was in Moscow at Samaranch's request to meet with Marat Gramov. Samaranch had to play out the scenario, but I didn't have much hope.

In the meantime, Moorhead was conducting a farewell session in Washington with his acquaintance from the Soviet embassy, Viktor Cherkashin. "Cherkashin doesn't paint a pretty picture, Peter," Moorhead reported later that afternoon. "He says their complaints about commercialization, smog, transportation, security, Ban the Soviets, and whatever are all overshadowed by a much larger problem—the attitude of the United States government and, specifically, the State Department."

"That comes as no surprise. What else did he say?" I asked.

"He ridiculed the State Department for saying it had done everything possible to accommodate the Soviets. State's concessions, he said, were actually thinly disguised penalties against the Soviet Union. He claimed the USSR only wanted equal treatment; it never asked for concessions and was offended by State saying it had offered the Soviets special handling. Cherkashin pointed out that special handling was an Olympic Charter violation."

"Something doesn't ring true here, Jay," I said. "We must be missing a key point somewhere along the line. See if you can find out what it is."

As Usher and I had discussed earlier, when the Soviets first announced their boycott, we had to demonstrate that the LAOOC was moving forward at a fast pace. Part of this meant going to social functions. We discovered that long before doubling up at events was wasteful, so we shared the responsibility.

Ginny and I attended a dinner that evening at the Century Plaza Hotel to raise money for the Children's Museum. This event was the culmination of months of hard work by Ginny and other volunteers and I knew it was very important to her that I attend. This was also special because my sister,

Jill, flew out from Washington for the event. Jill was radiant
that night and about as happy as I had ever seen her. It was a
thrill for her to talk to Burt Reynolds and hear Neil Diamond
sing, and I could see the excitement in her eyes when I introduced her to them.

Afterward, she kissed me and said, "I'm really proud of
you, little brother." That touched me. I had never told her
how important she was to me, and I wish I had that night. Six
months later she died of cancer.

Vietnam and Mongolia joined the boycott on Friday. The
next day, before meeting with David Wolper at our Westwood
headquarters, I learned that Laos and Czechoslovakia had
also announced their intentions to boycott the Games. That
made seven. Vietnam, Mongolia, and Laos were not great
losses, but I regretted losing Czechoslovakia.

David Wolper, who'd become our commissioner of the
opening and closing ceremonies in August 1983, asked me to
his office to approve some plans, which I did. Originally, Walt
Disney Productions had agreed to produce the ceremonies
and had hired Bob Jani to plan and direct them. Jani had
produced hundreds of special events including Super Bowls,
Rose Bowls, other college bowl games and presidential inau-
gurations.

The first time I saw Jani in action—at the opening of the
Epcot Center at Disney World in Orlando, Florida—I had my
doubts. Harry Usher and I had been invited by Card Walker,
chairman, and Ron Miller, president, of Disney at the time.

We were in a VIP suite at the park before the ceremony
and watched the key players panic over last-minute problems.
Walker and Miller, two gentlemen, intervened and calmed
everybody down. I never wanted to see Usher or me in that
situation. Also, having seen Jani's work, I was never confident he could capture the imaginations of two and a half
billion people.

We had set a budget of $5 million for the ceremonies,
which Disney believed was too low. When they rejected my
suggestion that they become a sponsor and pick up all additional costs, we all agreed it was best to part. I had kept

Wolper involved throughout Disney's preliminary planning and when they bowed out I asked Wolper to take it over. I must admit I always felt that Wolper was the only person alive who had the creative talents to produce a show that would turn on the world.

His only condition was that I trust him. If I hadn't, I wouldn't have asked him.

That Saturday, Wolper was in his usual good humor and he made hilarious comments about how unfortunate it was that the world wouldn't see the sensational athletes from Vietnam, Laos, and Mongolia.

"Peter," Wolper said, "now that we have some extra time, can we fit in the Buicks?"

"That's not a bad idea; that's the worst idea I've ever heard," I said, borrowing one of his pet phrases.

One of Wolper's first brainstorms as commissioner was to begin the opening ceremony with 150 white Buick convertibles (the official car of the Games) parked on the Coliseum infield and positioned in such a way that they spelled the word "Welcome." The convertible tops would open when the music started, releasing thousands of helium balloons. Then they'd be driven off the field.

I had asked Wolper at the time, "What happens if a car stalls on the way out?"

Wolper hadn't blinked an eye but had said, "I'll have a tow truck come out with a sign that says NOBODY'S PERFECT."

As we laughed once again over the synchronized Buicks, I realized he was just what the doctor ordered. Then, just as the meeting ended, Joel Rubenstein called with good news.

"Pete, I just got a call from Charles Lee," he said. "The PRC has confirmed in writing."

"Can we make it public?" I asked.

"Lee said they preferred to make the announcement," Rubenstein said.

"Today?"

"I don't know."

After a moment's thought, I decided. "I'm going to announce it today," I said.

I placed a call to Lee in Beijing and fortunately got right through. Lee assured me we could go ahead with our plans.

That morning I had kept a golf date with Los Angeles Police Chief Daryl Gates at a police charity tournament at Riviera Country Club in Pacific Palisades. Afterward, I'd returned to the Westwood office for the press conference.

The first PRC participation in the Games was major news. The Chinese Olympic Committee had formally withdrawn from the IOC in 1958 in protest over the International Olympic Committee's recognition of athletes from Taiwan. Eleven years later at Nagoya, Japan, the IOC Executive Board readmitted the Chinese Olympic Committee as the representative of the PRC. To accommodate the new member, the IOC redesignated the national Olympic committee in Taiwan the Chinese Taipei Olympic Committee. The PRC sent a team to the 1980 Olympic Winter Games at Lake Placid but didn't attend the Moscow Games.

Overall our relationship with the PRC was excellent, but there had been a few snags along the way. On New Year's Day 1982, for example, millions watched the Rose Bowl parade on television and saw the float of one of our sponsors, ARCO. The float had an Olympic theme—as many of our sponsor's floats did that year—and the national flags of each Olympic country. Among the millions watching was an angry member of the PRC's embassy in Washington. Somehow he got my unlisted home telephone number and called.

"Mr. Ueberroth," he said, "what do you have to say about the incident that just occurred on television?"

I didn't know the caller or what he was talking about. He explained that the ARCO float flew the Taiwan national flag instead of its Olympic flag and didn't fly the PRC flag at all.

"This is a great insult and there will be repercussions," he said.

I apologized and pointed out that we'd had nothing to do with the float. "I'll do whatever I can to rectify the situation and make sure it never happens again."

David Simon told me the PRC immediately called a halt to ARCO's offshore drilling rights and kept the wells capped for several months until the appropriate—and expensive—

apologies were made. It took an inordinate amount of time to get the right ARCO people to make the right apologies and concessions, and through it all I worried that this incident might give the Chinese reason not to participate in the Games.

The most serious conflict with the People's Republic of China took place in April 1983, when the U.S. government granted political asylum to Chinese tennis star Hu Na. The Chinese immediately called a halt to all Sino-U.S. sport and cultural exchanges, including their participation in the LAOOC's 1983 pre-Olympic cycling, rowing, and canoeing events. There are many ways the State Department and the Immigration and Naturalization Service allow foreign citizens to take up permanent residence in the United States. Political asylum is the one that implies the individual has fled in fear of persecution.

Through diplomatic channels, I was told, the PRC had notified the U.S. government it would accept its decision to grant Hu Na U.S. residency, providing it wasn't under the guise of political asylum, a notice the U.S. government ignored.

Harry Usher, who'd just returned from a visit to Beijing, fired off a Telex to Zhong Shitong, president of the Chinese Olympic Committee, explaining that we didn't agree with the government decision and hoped the Chinese would reconsider and send their athletes to our 1983 events. Shitong replied saying they would not, but he assured us the Hu Na controversy wouldn't have any bearing on Chinese participation in 1984.

Shitong was true to his word. The PRC announcement on May 12 gave us our first public victory over the Soviets.

Samaranch, meanwhile, began mobilizing the Olympic family for yet another attempt to persuade the Soviets to reconsider. He called a meeting in Lausanne of the Commission on the Olympic Movement, which consists of representatives of the NOCs, sports federations, and the IOC Executive Board. He timed it to follow a Soviet press conference in Moscow where Gramov would announce the pro forma results of its national Olympic committee meeting. The press conference would begin at midnight, May 13, Los Angeles time. Cable News Network had arranged to broadcast the Soviets' press conference live, and Usher and I planned to watch it with representatives from the Los Angeles press corps at CNN's studios in Hollywood.

I looked forward to reading the *Los Angeles Times* that Sunday morning. China was a big plus and the news from the torch relay was also uplifting. The torch was going through New Jersey en route to Washington and drawing enormous crowds. If nothing else, it appeared the Soviet boycott was beginning to galvanize public support for the Games.

I padded barefoot to the front gate, wearing jeans and a T-shirt, to pick up the newspaper. I was shocked by the big headline: CZECHS AND LAOTIANS JOIN BOYCOTT. The subheadline in much smaller print read: CHINA CONFIRMS IT WILL TAKE PART IN SUMMER OLYMPICS. I cursed headline writers the world over.

There were two Czech athletes competing in the discus that afternoon at a track meet at UCLA and I wanted to meet them. Richard Perelman was a graduate of UCLA who helped organize press relations at UCLA track meets in his spare time. He arranged for me to meet Imrich Bugar and Geza Valent, two of the best discus throwers in the world. Bugar was favored to win the gold medal at the 1984 Games. Since they spoke no English and I spoke no Czech, Perelman also arranged for a friend, Doug Thomson, a Russian linguist, to interpret in that language—both Czechs spoke Russian.

After introductions, I asked them how they were enjoying southern California. They'd been in the area eight days prior to the meet and said they liked it very much.

"We are through competing for the day," Bugar said, "and we are going to go to the beach."

"I saw you both throw and I hope you're able to return this summer to repeat your fine performances," I said.

"We would like to come back; there is no reason for us not to," Valent added.

"Do you feel safe here?" I asked.

They both nodded and Valent said, "Yes."

The two Czechs walked away. They looked safe. There were no bodyguards. Nobody was hassling them. I was sure they'd have a great afternoon at the beach.

It was time to get tough with the Soviets.

Gramov's news conference in Moscow turned out to be the final straw. Cable News Network made room for us and the reporters in a small studio, and placed several television monitors around the room. Usher, Natasha Berenchko, our Russian interpreter, and I were seated on a platform facing approximately forty reporters who were crammed into the room. Another thirty were scattered in offices on the floor. During Gramov's hour-long diatribe, I noted three or four familiar faces on the dais. I didn't see Vitaly Smirnov or Constantin Andrianov and wondered, since they were the IOC members, where they were.

Most of the rhetoric was predictable, and from time to time I found myself shaking my head in disgust over the familiar complaints.

Gramov, however, crossed the line of decency when he said, "U.S. security services have infiltrated the organizing committee with members of terrorist and extremist groups. Methods have been devised for the abduction of Soviet people, for compelling them not to return to their motherland, for treating them with special drugs, including psychotropic preparations which destroy the nervous system."

One reference Gramov made puzzled me. He said the NOC had decided to boycott following an April 27 meeting of USSR embassy and State Department officials in Washington, where the State Department repudiated the positive steps that were made at the Lausanne meeting three days earlier. I could only surmise he was referring to a meeting Ed Derwinski, counselor to the secretary of state, had held with USSR embassy officials. I was furious with Derwinski over this. When he advised me he was planning to meet with the Soviets, I asked him not to do so unless Jay Moorhead or someone else representing the committee was present. He ignored me and held it while Moorhead was out of town. Subsequently, I had been assured that nothing of consequence had transpired. I had thought nothing more of it. Until now.

Gramov concluded his remarks by saying the decision by the USSR to boycott was irrevocable.

So be it. I told the reporters as much. I admitted I didn't know what State Department meeting Gramov was talking about. I didn't want to guess and said it would be looked into immediately. I was, however, damned if I would let them get away with the absurd charges. "This is an insult to the American people and inexcusable," I countered. I was convinced the boycott was for real, and I put Gramov on notice that the world wouldn't tolerate their attempts to coerce other nations to follow suit.

The State Department was quick to cover its tracks. The next day, it uncharacteristically released a transcript of Derwinski's April 27 meeting with Viktor F. Isakov, minister and counselor of the Soviet embassy, and Moorhead's embassy contact, Viktor I. Cherkashin. It didn't take much reading between the lines to conclude that Derwinski had hung the LAOOC out to dry. He'd rendered the IOC Charter meaningless by using cold war rhetoric. In case anybody had been wondering who was boss—like the Soviets, the IOC, or the LAOOC—Derwinski made it clear it was the State Department. He had excluded Moorhead from the meeting to show the Soviets the LAOOC was powerless.

Derwinski played word games with the Soviets. He claimed the State Department had adhered to the letter of the Olympic Charter and praised the Soviets for reducing the level of their rhetoric at the April 24 IOC meeting. Then he did an about-face and escalated the rhetoric to new heights. He referred to the Soviets' "spurious" charges and specifically instructed the USSR NOC to go through the U.S. embassy on certain matters.

According to the transcript, he said, "Your committee and media have condemned the Department of State for alleged 'interference' with the LAOOC. However, since the LAOOC is not a government body, it has neither the authority nor the competence to commit the Federal government. Thus, it has legitimately turned to us to provide the necessary commitments that lie within our jurisdiction."

The sheer insensitivity of language by Derwinski played into the hands of the Soviets and gave them—in case they needed it—the ultimate reason to boycott the Games.

I was so angry that not even news that a day had gone by without another country pulling out cheered me up. (To no one's surprise, Afghanistan had joined the boycott the previous day to bring the total to eight countries.)

On the way to Lausanne for the meeting of the Commission on the Olympic Movement, I thought it would be a good idea to stop in Washington. Ginny went with me on a late-night flight from Los Angeles. This was also an opportunity to spend time together and to see Keri and Heidi.

I had lunch with FBI Director William Webster and had a list of questions for him. Did the boycott increase the potential for terrorism? Would the Soviets create an incident to fulfill their prophecy? Webster said it was a wash. He didn't have any hard information that a Soviet conspiracy was in the works. He noted that terrorist threats from the right had been virtually eliminated.

The White House was the next stop for a meeting with Secretary of State Shultz and Mike Deaver. Shultz was pretty much oblivious to the Olympics. He was unaware that State Department interference was one of the primary reasons given for the boycott. Since State had inserted itself in the process, however, I requested that a high-level official appear in Lausanne to explain State's policies and procedures to the Commission on the Olympic Movement and be available to answer questions.

Kenneth Dam, a man I respected by reputation, was my choice. He was already in Europe and could easily get to Switzerland, but Secretary Shultz had other ideas. He offered two minor functionaries who possessed the diplomatic clout of Tweedle Dee and Tweedle Dum. What's more, Shultz said they couldn't attend the meetings and were available to me only. I could just see myself telling Samaranch, Gramov, and the others, "Wait a minute, I have to run upstairs and get the answers from Mr. Dee and Mr. Dum." I told Shultz thanks, but no thanks.

By the end of the ninety-minute meeting, I was disgusted

with the U.S. government and the Russians. We'd been whip-sawed by both and I didn't expect anything to change. I called the Soviet pullout absurd and reprehensible at a press conference. "We don't need the Soviets in Los Angeles to have one of the best Olympic competitions in history." But I had to suffer my frustration with the federal government in silence.

Ginny and I hooked up with Jerry Walsh and Amy Quinn that evening at Dulles for our second red-eye in as many days. I had sworn off red-eyes long ago; now they'd become a wretched fact of life. To make matters worse, we missed connections in Paris and arrived in Lausanne late, weary and cranky. Fortunately, Ginny and I had a few hours to ourselves, and we welcomed a long walk around the hotel to stretch our cramped and sore legs.

Along the way we ran into Henry Alfaro, Leslie Ward, and Mary Ann Milbourne, three hardworking reporters from Los Angeles, each of whom was making a first overseas Olympic trip. We had a pleasant chat at an outdoor café next to the Lausanne Palace Hotel and I introduced them to key Olympic officials as they walked by. All of us were surprised to see two of the most important, Marat Gramov and Vitaly Smirnov. I had been told they'd been holed up in their suites since their arrival the day before.

Gramov embraced me like a long-lost friend and, with Smirnov serving as interpreter, invited me to his suite for cocktails within the hour.

Ginny, realizing that work was about to begin, kissed me for luck and went off in search of Heidi. I excused myself to the reporters and enlisted Welsh's help.

A lavish array of caviar, smoked fish, a half dozen brands of chilled Russian vodka, and boxes of Cuban cigars were laid out for us in Gramov's suite. The entire Soviet delegation was present. Gramov obviously had something to say. He hadn't put this feast together in the last sixty minutes. That was fine; I had an agenda of my own.

Gramov toasted our friendship "despite the recent decision" and assured me once again the reasons for not participating were not personally directed toward me.

"Is there any chance the decision will change?" I asked.

Nyet," all four said in unison. Welsh and I smiled at each other, and I thought of asking him if Mel Brooks had produced this scene. I half expected a troupe of Cossacks to fly through the doors, kicking out their legs and singing the "Internationale." It was not to be.

Gramov said he understood many other NOC officials had the same concerns about Los Angeles as he.

"I hear the opposite," I told him. "In fact, I understand several NOCs that have followed your head are reconsidering." The number of countries boycotting had reached ten with the additions of Hungary the day before and Poland that morning.

He didn't respond to my gambit, so I reminded him that tampering was a charter violation. Despite his effusive assurances that the Soviets wouldn't stoop to such a trick, it was common knowledge within the Olympic Movement that they were vigorously encouraging Third World countries to boycott.

Each time Gramov cited the same old charges, I pressured him for specific examples and got nowhere. He ducked and dodged. Welsh and I finally excused ourselves to attend a dinner hosted by Mario Vázquez Raña.

Ginny caught up with me there, as Heidi had to work at the IOC secretariat to prepare for the next day's meeting. Vázquez, as always, was a terrific host. I remembered a particular feast about a year earlier when Ginny, Joel Rubenstein, and I had attended a wedding party for Vázquez's daughter at his estate in Mexico City. We were among 1,600 of his closest friends.

While showing us the sumptuous grounds, he'd led us past his own private soccer field and tennis courts toward a large, caged area. Inside, we were shocked to see a huge bear.

"A gift from the Moscow Organizing Committee," Vázquez had explained nonchalantly. Suddenly my gift of a handcrafted Wetherby rifle to the father of the bride seemed less impressive.

Vázquez, one of the wealthiest men in Mexico, is a communications magnate and owns more than forty newspapers and several radio and television stations. His brothers run other facets of the family business, which includes a furniture-manufacturing plant and airplane-leasing company. He always travels with a large entourage and picks up all expenses.

On one such occasion, at a Pan American Sports Organization meeting in Los Angeles in 1982, Vázquez's retinue panicked when the peso plummeted overnight and the hotel management called for immediate payment. Vázquez took it in stride, however, and persuaded the hotel to give him a day's grace. The next day, one of Vázquez's assistants presented a suitcase filled with American dollars to the manager of the hotel as collateral. He'd had the money flown in from his bank in Mexico City by his pilot.

We laughed over that story at dinner. Afterward Vázquez had more current business to discuss.

"There is still a chance for Cuba," Vázquez said, as we chatted privately. "I am not hopeful, but their silence is a positive sign."

"What can we do to help them stay in the Games?" I asked.

"Fidel Castro is a personal friend of mine," he said. "Since he is a fan of baseball, maybe he would like to meet with you."

"Can you arrange a meeting?"

"I can try," he said.

I wanted to meet Castro, and not just to keep Cuba in the Games, which was a slim possibility. I wanted him to say he was boycotting because of solidarity with the Soviet Union and not because of security fears.

Also, considering his great influence in Latin America and Africa, an assurance from him to stay out of the boycotting business would be a major step in holding the Games together. I was particularly worried about Africa, where, I was told, the USSR was exerting intense pressure, despite Gramov's phony pledges to the contrary. So far, however, the African nations had resisted. I didn't know how long they could hold out, particularly if the Soviets encouraged Castro to flex his muscles. I feared this because Smirnov had told me in Lausanne that a Soviet-led boycott could include seventy countries and ruin our competition.

Back home, Bill Hussey and Anita DeFrantz were working the phones to ensure maximum African and Third World participation. DeFrantz, the LAOCC's second in charge of the USC village, was also a bronze medalist in rowing at the 1976 Montreal Games and an outspoken critic of the 1980 Carter boycott. A talented and skillful attorney, she became a self-made expert on African sports affairs and was our point person in all matters dealing with that continent. DeFrantz had spent years developing excellent contacts with African sports leaders and those contacts were paying off.

Rubenstein arrived with David Simon and Ed Best later that night and called as soon as he got to the hotel. I asked him to my room.

I brought him up to date on Cuba. "Begin working on it from our end right away," I said. "Work through Guerra and make it happen soon."

The next morning, United States Olympic Committee President William Simon and Executive Director Col. F. Don Miller joined the LAOOC delegation in my suite for coffee. Simon, former secretary of the treasury under President Richard M. Nixon, is a high-powered businessman who became USOC president in 1980. Miller had been involved with the Olympic Movement for much of his life and ran the day-to-day operations of the USOC.

"Peter, I'm here to support you in any way I can," Simon said. "I'll make a few handwritten comments; otherwise, it's your show."

"In that case, why don't I introduce you first?" I asked.

"Perfect," he replied. "I've got to get back to New York. I'll have a plane waiting right after the morning session."

Simon made more than a few remarks. He recommended sanctions against boycotting countries and proposed a Soviet-U.S. bilateral agreement banning future boycotts. It was a good suggestion, but bad timing. It was poorly received by those in attendance, particularly by Lord Killanin, who reprimanded Simon severely by reminding him of the United States' role in the 1980 boycott.

Simon wasn't an easy act to follow.

The remainder of the meeting was a futile rehash of the old charges and countercharges. Having had enough of the

Soviet hypocrisy, I suggested that if they were so concerned about security they ought to leave their officials, judges, and referees home as well. This made the Eastern bloc representatives very nervous. Missing the Games would be costly in terms of political power in the IOC.

I looked directly at Yuri Titov sitting a few feet away. Titov is a Russian Mr. Gymnastics. He'd won a total of nine Olympic medals, including one gold, at the 1956, '60, and '64 Games and had served as president of the International Gymnastics Federation since 1976. He was planning to attend the Los Angeles Games.

"Why is it safe for you to attend and not your athletes, Mr. Titov?" I asked. "Doesn't your government care about your well-being, too?"

Silence as he shuffled papers in front of him. Finally, he leaned to the microphone placed on the table in front of him and said, "The athletes are youngsters. They have no experience in these matters."

That afternoon Ginny had surprised Keri at school and returned to the hotel with her. Heidi was to join us as soon as she finished work. I was excited about having a family dinner. But before we could do that I had to hold a wrap-up briefing in my room for the staff and several Los Angeles-based reporters. I was surprised to see Bella Stumbo of the *Los Angeles Times* tagging along behind Ken Reich.

Reich had told me earlier that Stumbo was in Lausanne. She was the *Times*'s best feature writer, and she'd been assigned to write a lengthy profile about me. I was flattered the *Times* would assign her. However, I wasn't eager to cooperate. She had a reputation for uncovering blemishes, and I had tried persuading the *Times* to drop the assignment as I believed it would detract from the Games and focus too much attention on one individual. Besides, I wasn't too keen on reading about my weaknesses. I agreed to meet with Stumbo on the flight home since *Times* editors had made it clear they'd do the profile with or without me.

While discussing current Olympic events with the reporters, the phone rang and Rubenstein grabbed it.

"Peter, Siperco wants to know if you can meet for a few minutes before dinner," Rubenstein said. "He says it's urgent."

"Tell him we'll be right there."

Siperco was dedicated to the movement and had often criticized the LAOCC for being less than pure in preparing for the Games. Those battles were now forgotten. He was resisting the Soviet boycott with every fiber in his body.

We visited Siperco in his room. "I think my country can hold out," he said, "but it will be very difficult."

As hard as Siperco was trying, I didn't believe Romania had the strength to withstand the pressure. One of the poorest nations in the Eastern bloc, Romania was largely dependent for its existence on its Socialist allies. Still, the Romanians pride themselves on their independence, and they saw the Olympics as being a good opportunity to demonstrate it to the world.

Siperco, being an example of this pride, was reluctant to ask for financial help, even though his country now needed it. Romania had counted on East Germany to provide the transportation for its athletes and equipment, specifically rowing shells and canoes.

We were entering sensitive waters. While we desperately wanted Romania in the Games, we couldn't have it appear that we were buying participants. The Soviets had done it successfully four years earlier—they'd picked up the tab for all competing nations—but that wasn't our style.

"Would it help if the LAOOC sent a delegation to meet with your sports leaders in Bucharest?" I asked.

"I would think so," he said. He placed a call to Haralambie Alexa, president of the Romanian NOC. Newly elected to the post, Alexa was well respected by Romanian President Ceausescu. Alexa approved our delegation visit but warned Siperco that timing was critical. The Romanians were under Soviet scrutiny and had to be careful. Siperco would pass word on from Alexa when the time was right.

"Alexandru, your people are proud and I know they don't want charity from the organizing committee," I said. "You have my word that the LAOOC will do whatever is necessary to allow your athletes to compete. If that means transportation for your athletes and equipment, we will help. If it means getting a television signal into the country so your people can watch the games, we will work something out."

I could see he was touched. "You are a very generous man, Peter," he said as he ushered us out.

I turned to him and said, "I'm not generous, just a friend."

I picked up the ladies—Ginny, Heidi, and Keri—and we walked to a quiet restaurant, the Golden Door. Their good cheer and ebullience eased the tension of the day. Groggy from four days with little sleep, I felt more like a spectator at dinner than a participant. I gladly listened to family chatter and the exciting experiences Heidi and Keri were having in Switzerland. Heidi had been treated very well by the IOC—especially by Madame Berlioux and her staff—and was making friends quickly. Her French seemed to be improving by the minute.

"Two days after I arrived," Heidi said, "Mme. Berlioux told me she'd arranged a perfect room for me with a family of one of the IOC employees. The man's wife was English and they had one small child. She assured me I'd be happy there and I moved in the next morning.

"The day I moved in, President Samaranch summoned me to his office and gave me a beautiful scarf. He said he'd found a place for me to live too. I couldn't believe it. Two days, two places to live. I thanked him but told him I had already moved into the one Mme. Berlioux had found for me. He seemed disappointed and said he hadn't known Mme. Berlioux had been looking."

We laughed. "That's typical," I said.

"What do you mean?" Heidi asked.

"You'll see. It's not unusual for them to be on different wavelengths, not to mention different floors." Samaranch occupies the first floor of Château de Vidy, Berlioux the second.

Back at the hotel, Ginny and I talked about the girls for a few minutes. It was heartening to see how much closer together they had grown. I dozed off in the middle of our conversation and barely remembered Ginny helping me to bed.

At the IOC Executive Board meeting the next morning, Saturday, May 19, Samaranch asked me to return to Switzerland the next weekend with the LAOOC sports commissioners for the IOC's meeting with the international sports federations. Necessary changes to the Games' schedule would be made there.

I was thinking about having to make another red-eye special when Siperco was abruptly called out of the room to take a phone call. Moments later he returned, gathered his belongings, and made a quiet farewell to Samaranch before leaving in tears. Samaranch said Siperco had been summoned home by his government, which was being leaned on by the Soviet Union to boycott the Games.

The meeting ended and our delegation went its separate ways. Welsh returned to New York; the rest of the staff returned to Los Angeles via Paris; and Ginny and I stayed on to spend the day with Heidi and Keri.

I had one last chance to confer with Samaranch and we discussed the Socialist ministers meeting in Prague that was set for the coming Thursday. He tried to convince me I needn't attend, because LAOOC interests would be well represented by himself, Vázquez, and Primo Nebiolo. I wasn't too sure of that.

As arranged, Bella Stumbo interviewed me the next day. It was a long session, taking most of the flight home. Ginny, understandably, felt cheated. Stumbo was a probing interviewer, and I didn't feel comfortable with some of her questions or the way they were phrased.

Bright and early, Monday, May 21, I headed straight for Rubenstein's cubicle as soon as I entered our Marina Center offices. Rubenstein was on the phone trying to raise Manolo Guerra in Cuba.

"He'll try to set up the meeting with Castro," Rubenstein said.

"Good," I replied. "What's the country count?"

"We've got a hundred eight written and twelve verbals," he replied.

"Not enough. I want at least a hundred twenty-three—all written—and I want them by Thursday." I walked away. I wanted to beat Munich's record.

It was time to go public with our scorecard. The Soviet boycott had been stalled at ten countries for the past four or five days. It was evident now they would not get eighty countries. Announcing record participation the same day as the Prague meeting could be the knockout punch.

Our damage-control task force was proving to be a smashing success. It stopped at nothing and, at times, badgered NOC officials for immediate written confirmations. In some cases, NOC officials recognized leverage when they had it and they asked for favors in return. The Italians, for example, decided they needed hotel suites instead of rooms for their soccer players. Several countries thought they could trade larger teams for more tickets and accreditations. We told them no.

The only major exception was chartering an aircraft to transport African athletes from Morocco to Los Angeles. Through reports from our envoys, we knew that many of the African nations were scraping together every last nickel and dime they could get their hands on to send their teams. We decided to help by arranging for a charter. Rabat, Morocco, was a convenient departure point because Africa's best track-and-field athletes would be assembled there two weeks before the Games for an all-Africa meet.

We suffered a blow on May 23 when Cuba pulled out. I still hoped to meet Castro—that was important—and Rubenstein continued efforts to schedule the meeting.

The next day, following the Socialist sport ministers' revival meeting in Prague, Siperco announced Romania would defy the boycott and participate in the Games. I had already decided to announce the boycott had failed, but now that Romania had offset Cuba, I did so with greater conviction. Since we had no written commitment, we intentionally left Romania off our list of 123 NOC confirmations rather than place more pressure on this courageous country.

I made plans for my last trip to Lausanne. I alerted Chuck Cale and our Romanian envoy Agnes Mura to be ready to leave for Romania at a moment's notice. As vice-president of sports, Cale could address all Romanian questions and Mura had lived there and could serve as interpreter.

I put together for the international sports federation meetings a delegation of sports commissioners whose competition schedules were most affected by the boycott. They were to meet with the heads of the international sports federations and make final arrangements. By this time, we knew there wouldn't be a great many changes. We planned to ask the federations to add teams where necessary, approve the addition of a solo event in synchronized swimming, and increase the size of the baseball competition.

I stayed out of the federation business, leaving it all to the commissioners who got most of their items approved, and had a chance to spend more time with Heidi and Keri who'd surprised me at Geneva Airport when I arrived Sunday afternoon, May 27.

The most significant development there was Romania's approval for us to send a delegation to Bucharest. En route, Cale and Mura stopped in Lausanne for a final briefing and I added judo commissioner Willy Reich and Michael Jaecke, LAOOC's gymnastic technical expert, to the delegation. Each one knew the sensitivity of the mission and the extreme importance of Romania's attendance. My last instruction was to keep in contact. I wasn't leaving Lausanne until I had assurances that discussions were going well.

While waiting for word from Romania, I took Heidi to Girardet, a famous restaurant about twenty minutes outside of town. Hoping this would be a memorable evening, I purchased a rose from a passing vendor and had the maître d' place it in a vase for her. I surprised her between courses with an elegantly wrapped small package and beamed as she opened it. Inside was a pair of gold earrings.

"Now I know what you were up to wandering around Lausanne all afternoon," Heidi said. While shopping for the gift, I had run into Heidi and told her I was stretching my legs between meetings.

"You almost caught me in the act," I said.

Heidi, new to the Olympic business, kept asking me

about Olympic issues. I didn't want to talk about the Games. We had all had too much of that lately, so we switched to another topic.

Ginny and I had written the children a few weeks earlier warning about Olympic overload to help them through the final few months. Basically, we wanted to make sure they knew how much we loved them, even though we might not have much time to show it. Heidi said the letter had caused a stir and they'd talked about it among themselves.

"Dad, it seemed so gloomy," she said.

"I apologize for the tone of the letter," I said, "but Mom and I were compelled to write it. We're so busy and we wanted you to know it would soon be over and we'd be a family again."

"I know you miss us as much as we miss you," she said. That led to lengthy conversations about life before and after the Games and those talks were good.

Mura had called while Heidi and I were at dinner and left a number. I couldn't get through and I figured she'd try again in the morning. I also had a message from Samaranch to visit him in his suite.

He said he was still hoping to meet Chernenko in Moscow and was dead set against me going with him. Although he never said so, I had the distinct impression he feared I'd be a threat to his leadership. He also cautioned me against going to Cuba with Mario Vázquez Raña—probably for the same reason. It was his job to deal with heads of state, not mine.

Mura contacted me the next morning, twenty minutes before I was to leave Lausanne.

"We have written confirmation from the Romanians and they have expanded their team from fifty to a hundred thirty athletes," Mura said happily.

On June 4, the Monday after the deadline, we announced that 142 nations would attend the 1984 Olympic Games. We hadn't just broken Munich's attendance record—we had shattered it. The boycott had been contained to fourteen nations, the last to fall being South Yemen, Ethiopia, and North Korea. Half of those had barely competed in the Games.

We had learned two days earlier all hopes of a Soviet

reversal were nonexistent. Samaranch finally made his trip to Moscow, but instead of meeting with Chernenko he met with Deputy Premier Nikolai V. Talyzin, described in news reports as a minor figure in the Soviet hierarchy. Knowing Samaranch, this Soviet snub was a great blow to his dignity. For a man of Samaranch's stature, it was like traveling across the world only to meet the doorman at the Kremlin. Knowing the Olympic players, I wasn't surprised that Samaranch described the meeting as "long and fruitful" while Primo Nebiolo, who accompanied him, characterized it as "abrupt."

I got a call from Harry Usher early the next evening while I was wrapping up an interview with Australia's Channel Nine at its studio in Hollywood. He asked me to hurry to the Hyatt Wilshire Hotel for a 7 P.M. meeting with the Rev. Jesse Jackson. This was the day of the California primary and Jackson, as one of the presidential candidates for the Democratic nomination, had been campaigning in Los Angeles. City Councilman Robert Farrell had suggested Usher and I get together with Jackson because Jackson's imprimatur on the Games would help the LAOOC in the black community. Jackson already had a brief history with the 1984 Olympics. As soon as the boycott hit, he met with Soviet Ambassador Dobrynin and tried to persuade him to get his countrymen to reconsider.

His hotel suite at the Hyatt Wilshire swarmed with supporters and campaign aides. In our talk, he compared the Olympics to his campaign theme—the Rainbow Coalition—and how both were potential forums for a more peaceful world.

"I'm planning to go to Cuba for other reasons," Jackson said. "Maybe I can talk to Castro on behalf of the Games."

As I was anticipating an invitation from Castro at any moment, we agreed whoever went first would carry an Olympic message for the other.

Jackson stopped by the LAOOC Marina Center headquarters on his way to the airport the next day and delivered a stirring address to the entire staff at an outdoor rally at noon. Earlier Joel Rubenstein had advised me the meeting with Castro was on and Jackson, as promised, composed a letter for me to deliver on his behalf to Castro. Jackson wrote in summation: "I, therefore, appeal to you, first to hear Mr. Ueberroth, who has supported my own attempts to make the participation of all countries possible; second, to reconsider the question of Cuban participation in the Olympics."

Accompanied by LAOOC linguist José Gonçalves, I flew to Mexico City to meet with Vázquez and briefly confer with the president of Mexico, Miguel de la Madrid Hurtado. On the flight I read a comprehensive dossier on Castro that Bill Hussey had miraculously prepared in less than twenty-four hours. It was interesting reading, particularly the items about Castro's personality. For example, Hussey reported: "The key to successfully meeting with him is to remember that he is a monologuist, often non-stop for an hour or two. He loves to lecture and will do so on any subject, sometimes not the one which is the particular subject for the meeting.

"If it is clear that he is in a monologue mood, let him go, don't interrupt. Sometimes, he is open to dialogue at once. You have to be the judge of the situation. Flattery is useful with anyone, but particularly so with him—his own sports prowess, the strength of his athletes under his leadership, etc."

Upon landing, we were whisked away from the airport and through Mexico City's heavy traffic by a police escort to the El Camino Real Hotel where President de la Madrid was hosting a luncheon for the Mexican press. There I was seated at Vázquez's table and waited for de la Madrid to finish making a few remarks. When he did, Vázquez and I were hustled outside and put on de la Madrid's private luxury bus. This was no ordinary bus; it was a nicely furnished mobile living room and office suite.

Another couple was present and everybody, it seemed, was talking at once. But nobody was speaking English. I sat just a few feet from the president and waited to be introduced. I knew he'd been educated at Harvard and assumed he spoke English. Since nobody else was going to do it, I stood up and introduced myself. De la Madrid spoke excellent English and began making introductions to the rest of the traveling party. He was laudatory about Vázquez and I didn't argue.

He thought Castro might be amenable to a plan whereby Cuban athletes stayed in Mexico, along the U.S. border, during the Games. Transporting Cuban athletes from Mexico to southern California Olympic sites could have been accomplished but was an unacceptable alternative as far as I was concerned. He wanted to be helpful, though, and I appreciated that.

David Israel was waiting for us at Vázquez's private airplane hangar and we took off to meet Castro. Vázquez told us on the way that railroad tracks ran across the runway at the Havana Airport and that flight traffic was sometimes delayed for the passing of a train. When we bounced over the railroad tracks on our way to the gate, I smiled.

As we pulled to a stop, Vázquez leaned over a window seat to peer through the windows, anxious to see who was there. You find out how important you are in Cuba by who meets you at the gate. He was having difficulty seeing because the humid weather had steamed up the windows. Suddenly, he shouted with glee when he saw it was José Ramon Fernandez Alvarez, a vice-president of the council of ministers and the commanding officer in the Bay of Pigs.

That Fernandez was there to greet us meant we were visitors of state and would be welcomed by Castro. Had our greeter been someone else, it would have signified we probably never would have had the meeting.

Fernandez greeted Vázquez warmly and wished him a happy birthday. He then put our delegation into several Soviet-manufactured sedans and had us driven through the city. There were few people on the streets, which I found strange. Our guest house, located on a large, lush estate, was surrounded by beautiful gardens and had a magnificent swimming pool. Before the revolution, the mansion had belonged to a wealthy family; now it was owned by the state and was used for entertaining visiting dignitaries.

It was midnight when we arrived, but the time of day obviously didn't matter to our Cuban hosts, who had a lavish feast ready and were eager to celebrate. There were tables lined up with whole suckling pigs, a variety of meats, poultry, and fish. They even had a birthday cake for Vázquez and passed out his favorite brand of cigars. Russian vodka and Cuban rum—the best in the world—flowed like water. Waiters circulated with sumptuous trays of Cuban delicacies, one of which was whole oysters in a yogurt sauce. I'm sure it was delicious but I kept refusing it, which disturbed my hosts. Everybody else tossed them down like shots of whiskey in a display of bravado. Even Israel was enjoying it. I apologized, explaining I didn't wish to insult them by not sampling the delicacy, but I was dangerously allergic to oysters and hoped they would understand.

After a while, two cars zoomed up to the front of the house and I was told Castro was anxious to meet us. Hussey was right about Castro being a nocturnal person. It was after 1 A.M.

Castro's office building was an undistinguished cement and stone structure. His office, however, was less severe, and was comfortable and attractively paneled. Castro's presence was immediately felt. He strode in, followed by Fernandez, and was obviously pleased to see his old friend Vázquez. Another gentleman then appeared and stood by silently. Later, Vázquez told me he was Castro's doctor and closest friend. According to rumor, he watches Castro like a hawk and even tests his food.

As soon as NOC President Manolo Guerra and Minister of Sport Ciro Perez Habra joined the meeting an instant later, the customary Cuban social amenities—cigars and drinks—commenced. Castro was proud of his new Scotch, which his countrymen had learned to manufacture from the Irish, and insisted we try it. He broke open one of only a dozen bottles in existence and predicted it would be as popular as Cuban rum.

"Commandante," said Vázquez, "to be able to introduce two of my very dearest friends, two men who are like brothers to me, makes this a very proud moment in my life. It is important that you know each other." Vázquez added a rather effusive description of me and concluded the introduction.

Since Cuba had announced it would not participate in the

Games, I proposed Castro send a team to participate only in the demonstration sport of baseball, which was not part of the official Olympic program. Guerra surprised me by vehemently opposing the suggestion. I had always had a good relationship with him and suspected he'd been cast in the bad guy role.

Castro listened intently. He is a very direct listener. He turns toward the speaker, fixes his eyes, and listens carefully until the person is finished. He doesn't hurry the speaker or lead the conversation.

I asked him to consider the possibility. He then recounted the story of how Cuban athletes had been banned from competing in most countries of the world during the early days of the revolution. Only the Soviet Union and the Eastern bloc nations competed with his athletes and helped them train for many years. Castro was grateful for their support and hadn't forgotten.

When we discussed security he voluntarily conceded it wasn't a problem. I asked him if he would say that publicly and he said he would. This was the best defense against the possibility of the Soviets or somebody else fulfilling its prophecy of massive security problems.

The conversation drifted toward African participation and rather than accuse him of influencing those countries to boycott, I appealed to his ego. I noted that Cuba had a great many troops on the African continent where he was hailed as a great leader. Given that respect, I told him I had hopes he wouldn't discourage African participation in the Games. He pledged he would not disrupt the Games and would say so.

Castro reemphasized that Cuba's sole reason for boycotting was to stand in solidarity with the Soviet Union and other Socialist countries. He repeated how Cuban athletes had learned sports from their Socialist brothers.

"Commandante," I said, "but not baseball."

He smiled at that and reflected on his own baseball career. If a Cuban team ever played a baseball game in Dodger Stadium, he said, his entire nation would stand still.

I spent four interesting and memorable hours with him. Castro had obviously done his homework as he asked me about skin diving, a sport we both enjoyed. Pictures were taken, cigars were smoked, and more rum was drunk. Before leaving Castro presented us with gifts of Cuba's best cigars and rum.

We returned to the guest house at 4 A.M. where a party was in full swing. I stayed a few minutes and wandered off to bed.

The next morning, Fernandez and I had a private talk on the lawn behind the guest house. Speaking on behalf of Castro, he said the commandante was intrigued with the idea of sending a baseball team and wanted more time to think it over. I interpreted that to mean he had to check with Moscow. I didn't believe Cuba would do it, but I was delighted he had agreed to leave Africa alone.

Later that morning, Fernandez made that point at a press conference. Castro had silenced the rest of the world. The Soviets never again cited security as a reason for their boycott. That gave our security planners confidence that there would be less pressure from the Soviets to make their prophecy of a security nightmare come true.

I left Cuba a happy man.

CHAPTER FIFTEEN

COUNTING DOWN

AFTER CUBA, I turned my attention to Los Angeles. Our international diplomacy was working, and we had contained the boycott. We also had the money, the stadiums, the supplies, the permits, the staff, the volunteers, and the know-how. Nonetheless, I was worried. Could we implement the planning?

If Los Angeles had yet to feel Olympic, by the first of June it began to look it. We took a paint brush to the city and began spreading the hot colors of our design concept, festive federalism, for the Olympic arts festival. I had worried the colors were too bland and wouldn't come alive, but I was wrong. Although the magentas, vermilions, and aquas had earned some derision within the LAOOC, they attracted the positive attention of the citizenry.

I congratulated Usher, who had gone out on a limb for the look. Now he had to let others go out on that limb. He had masterminded the planning by consolidating all authority within his inner circle and had performed a brilliant juggling act. From the beginning, my doctrine had been to hold back as long as possible on the spending and manpower buildup. Now it was time for Usher to let go; privately, I wondered if he could do it.

We were already growing at a rate that defied all management principles. The best rate of expansion for a company is 10 percent a year, the absolute maximum being 50 percent. But we had gone from one thousand employees to two thousand in six months and would reach seventy-two thousand by July 28. Staffing the Olympic Games would be the largest and fastest mobilization of people during peacetime. Most experts said we'd self-destruct.

Our secret weapon was volunteers. They were not deterred by management principles and were committed to making the Games a success and presenting Los Angeles as a gracious host city. To attract the number of staff and volunteers we needed, Usher and I decided to abolish our long-standing policy against nepotism. We wanted our workers to create networks and bring in people like themselves—including friends and family.

The managers Harry had restrained represented the best horses that could be found. Some were skittish, some were shy, but all were ready. We had to open the gates and see what happened. The fate of the Games rode with our Thoroughbreds and Usher had to let them run. He assured me he had them under control, and I breathed easier when he began delegating authority as we moved into the villages and the venues.

Contractually, depending on the venues, we had anywhere from two to six weeks to set the stages for the Games according to a complex rolling schedule. But even before the move-ins, as we called them, Ed Keen, our vice-president of architecture and construction, had begun transforming existing facilities into Olympic ones.

When he was the executive vice-president for site development and operations at the 1982 Knoxville World's Fair, Keen had come to the rescue of our department, first as a thirty-day consultant and then later as a full-time employee in 1983. We had learned about his abilities from other Knoxville veterans who had stepped forward when it became obvious our architecture and construction department was floundering. After Knoxville, Keen had landed a good job with the Bechtel Corporation as manager of operations at its Oak

Ridge, Tennessee, office and he didn't want to leave it when we first contacted him. Keen's background was as impressive as his size—six feet eight inches tall.

During his initial thirty-day hitch, he filed a report confirming our worst fears: We were way behind. Worse, there were no comprehensive implementation plans to fall back on. We needed Keen. I asked him to dinner at Mr. Chow's in Beverly Hills the night before he was to leave Los Angeles. I was determined that he remain with the committee. Over dumplings and seaweed, we struck a deal that I drafted on the back of the tab.

He wanted complete control. That was easy; I gave it to him. I never have any qualms about giving control to the right person. I also put the look of the Games under his authority as he requested. Finally, he demanded the staff—sixty of Bechtel's finest.

That was difficult. Robert Fluor, whose Fluor Corporation was the second largest construction and engineering firm in the world next to Bechtel, was a member of the LAOOC's board of directors and gravely ill at the time. I explained it was only right that we use as many local firms as possible. I offered to divide the manpower force into thirds among Bechtel, Fluor, and Ralph M. Parsons, another large company located in Pasadena. Keen agreed, providing he had the authority to return unsatisfactory employees. He started work full time on December 1, 1983.

One of Keen's priorities was to lengthen the time needed to complete the necessary permanent and temporary construction at most sites. Take UCLA. According to the contract, we weren't allowed access until July 1. That gave Keen less than two weeks to prepare the UCLA village. He needed more time, so he went out and got it by making friends with university officials and by convincing them to give him early access. Keen had to do some fast talking, because all venue operators feared the Olympics would move in like gangbusters and completely disrupt their operations. In UCLA's case, Keen personally assured Chancellor Charles Young that the construction of fences wouldn't interfere with his morning jogging around the university's perimeter.

During the week of spring vacation, Keen and his workers installed the underground electrical system and fencing at Pauley Pavilion, the site of Olympic gymnastics. Since this was accomplished unobtrusively, the university allowed him to keep working there, and he never left. With this as precedent, Keen invaded every village and venue early.

Security was only a step behind as soon as Keen started a job. Guards were brought in to monitor access to the site and protect the equipment. Then Mike Mount's technology group entered the picture and Keen began installing everything from telephone lines to Xerox machines, which also needed guarding. As the physical shell neared completion, our material logistics people began moving in supplies.

Equipment was delivered to individual sites from seven material distribution centers, the design center warehouse, and outside vendors who maintained their own warehouses and distribution systems. Much of the goods provided by outside vendors were first sent to our material distribution centers for processing, sorting, and final disposal.

Greg Wagner, a retired U.S. Navy commander, brought twenty years of naval supply experience to the committee in 1982. He traveled to Montreal, the Pan American Games in Caracas, the World University Games in Edmonton, and the National Sports Festival in Colorado Springs. He compiled detailed lists of all supplies and equipment needed for every sport at every venue and then began the long process of acquiring, processing, and storing.

He once described his job, saying, "It's like provisioning a fleet of ships going to sea. In the navy, ships have to be self-sufficient for as long as ninety days. In the Olympics, each venue has to be able to get along on its own for three to four weeks." He treated the larger, more complex venues such as the Coliseum like aircraft carriers; the smaller ones such as El Dorado Park like destroyers.

Starting with a rented space of only ten thousand square feet in 1983, Wagner had accumulated close to a million square feet of warehouse space for the Games. The largest was a three-hundred-thousand-square-foot facility in Bell, California. He stored material by venue and distributed it as each facility was turned over to our control. He instructed each commissioner that the distribution was a one-time-only deal. He wasn't in the resupply business, but he had found local suppliers as contacts for emergency situations.

The Olympic arts festival, which had opened to critical acclaim June 1, had logistical problems that Wagner promised would not be repeated. He hadn't realized until it was too late that the LAOOC was to function as the festival producer. As a result, Wagner's crew worked overtime to provide such items as electrical saws, spray-paint machines, tool kits, special theater lighting, and wood for backdrops and scenery. Because of this breakdown we became even more sensitive to the necessity of matching all the pieces of the puzzle.

Despite the bad start, the arts festival immediately generated excitement within the cultural community. A huge undertaking on its own, the festival came with the Olympic package as mandated by Rule 34 of the Olympic Charter. Like many Olympic rules, it was bogged down by numerous restrictions. One specifically limited the program to cultural expressions of the host country. We bent the rule to meet our needs and created an international program of dance, music, and theater that mirrored the multiethnic diversity of Los Angeles.

There was something for everybody. In dance, nineteen different dance companies performed, including eight foreign ones ranging from Pina Bausch Wuppertaler Tanztheater of West Germany to Sankaijuku of Japan. Britain's Royal Opera Company gave its first American performance and was among four international music groups and seventeen groups overall. Fourteen nations sent theater groups to the festival. Among them were the Royal Shakespeare Company of Great Britain, Poland's Cricot 2, Italy's Piccolo Teatro di Milano, France's Le Theatre du Soleil, and the U.S.'s Flying Karamazov Brothers.

Festival Director Robert Fitzpatrick had complete creative control and rarely asked for my input, which was just as well. When I was late for the dedication of the Robert Graham sculpture at the entrance to the Coliseum on June 1, the art world understood why I stayed out of it.

Besides being a connoisseur of theater and art, Fitzpatrick's good taste was also reflected in his clothing. He looked at me with shock when I arrived and I assumed he was upset because I had missed the formal ceremony.

"Did you dress in the dark this morning?" Fitzpatrick asked quietly, pulling me aside.

"What do you mean?" I responded.

"The suit's nice, but it doesn't match."

I inspected it closely and was mortified to realize I had, indeed, worn a mismatched suit. It was close but no cigar. I tried to explain I was color blind.

He said that was obvious.

Here I was, ready to deliver a few words to the scions of L.A.'s cultural elite, and I looked like a clown. I rarely get embarrassed, but I was on this occasion. I didn't know what to do. I didn't have another suit to change into and taking my jacket off was unthinkable. All I could do was grin and bear it.

During the luncheon, as I watched Fitzpatrick expertly work the crowd and thank the guests, I remembered our first meeting in the summer of 1980. He had been recommended by Mayor Tom Bradley, Paul Ziffren, and several LAOOC board members. He was president of the California Institute of the Arts in Valencia, and had developed a reputation as a leader in southern California's growing cultural awareness.

We weighed the merits of a cultural festival while strolling along the beach at Laguna Beach one afternoon. Fitzpatrick had studied previous festivals and didn't like the results.

"At Montreal," he reminded me, "the festival director reported to ninety-nine vice-presidents and was stuck in a corner and treated like a bastard child. Everything he did was scrutinized and watered down by the layers of bureaucracy. The poor guy wound up with a boring program and a nervous breakdown."

"I can guarantee that the director of our festival will be in complete charge of all creative elements," I told him. "Also, I'd rather tell the IOC to forget it if we can't do something special."

The $2 million budget didn't thrill Fitzpatrick, either.

"It isn't enough, Peter," he said. "I've been to all the great European festivals—Edinburgh, Spoleto, Avignon—and they spend that much on backdrops."

"I can't guarantee you any more than two million dollars at this time," I replied. "But maybe we can find a corporate sponsor to help us out with funding. I promise that as our prospects rise, so will yours."

"If there is artistic freedom, an adequate budget, and direct access to you, I'll do the job," he said.

We shook hands. My only demand was to make it damn good. He had free run. One of the few times he needed my support was when he canceled the Joffrey Ballet just before the start of the festival. The Joffrey had violated the exclusivity clause that Fitzpatrick had inserted in all performer contracts by scheduling other performances in the area during the festival. I got a lot of calls from government officials and leaders of the cultural community complaining of Fitzpatrick's harsh disposal of the Joffrey Ballet and requesting that I lean on him heavily. I refused.

One of those Fitzpatrick greeted with his usual warmth that day at the Graham statue ceremony was Robert Erburu, president of the Times Mirror Company, the sponsor of the festival. Erburu had already badgered me about the Times's ticket locations, and he had a right to be angry: Their $5 million commitment had earned them the worst seats in the house. I commiserated with Fitzpatrick, who had nothing to do with the Times ticket allotment, but nonetheless was getting an earful. I decided I had better return to our Marina headquarters and rectify the situation, *and* change my suit.

Next to security, tickets had always been my greatest concern. Ed Smith, vice-president for ticketing, had worked for two years on a system specifically created for the Games by Arthur Young and Company, one of the nation's big eight accounting firms. Arthur Young had had previous success with the computer hardware for the Los Angeles Dodgers' ticketing system. Smith, who had worked on that project, joined us in 1979, first as an Arthur Young consultant and then as a staff employee. He took over ticketing in late 1981.

Aided by Arthur Young resources, Smith had created a concept for distributing seven million tickets, 70 percent via mail order; the remainder was reserved for purchase by the Olympic family and sponsors. It was the largest computerized ticket-distribution system ever conceived.

As always, I was skeptical of anything that had to do with computers. This program really scared me because it had never been done before and any mistakes could devastate the Games. Smith eventually sold me on the idea by convincing me there were features built into the system that would make it the fairest ever.

It was designed to give a gas station attendant in Montana the same opportunity to get Olympic tickets as the president of a New York bank. Among the features were random selection for sold-out events, waitlisting, second- and third-choice options, and numerous checks to prevent ticket scalping. The first time Smith showed me the ticket brochure, I looked it over and tossed it back at him. "You have to be a calculus major to figure this out," I said to him in despair. I had told him to keep it simple, but it was too late. It was June 1983 and we were set to announce that tickets were going on sale. He assured me that people would understand.

Now, a year later, that didn't matter. Delivering the tickets in June 1984 as promised did. After some scary moments, Smith had most of the tickets in the mail. Still, if he encountered problems similar to those he had with the Olympic arts festival, we were in deep trouble. The system had distributed 95 percent of the festival tickets in three days. That was fantastic. But the remaining 5 percent took two weeks. Extrapolating those numbers to the Games' tickets, we'd still be distributing tickets at Christmas. Smith assured me modifications to the system had been made and would work.

Usher and I had met in my office late one night back in April and he'd briefed me on ticketing. He had called it a nightmare.

"Peter, I don't know if we can get the tickets out," he'd said.

"How far behind are we? A few days? A few weeks?"

"I'm afraid to estimate." Harry explained that the computers were overloaded and bugs were continually popping up.

"This is our Achilles heel," I said. "You live with the tickets or we die with the tickets. I don't care what you have to do. Stay on top of it. This is top priority. Throw everything we have at it—people, computers, money."

We had three IBM System 38s, two at the Marina Center for personnel and accreditation and the other at the ticket-data center in downtown Los Angeles. The two at the Marina Center were underutilized and Usher combined the two work-loads on one computer and delivered the other to Smith. That eased the crunch.

We shut down the mail-order system in early May and opened nine ticket and information centers around the city on June 7. We still had more than one million tickets remaining. This was another logistical horror, since the personal comput-ers used at the individual ticket centers didn't have access to the full ticket inventory and could only sell their daily allot-ments. This meant a ticket buyer could be refused for a par-ticular sports ticket at one center and buy twenty at another. Also, it took about five minutes to process each order and we had lines of angry people outside each center. And, speaking of angry people, our telephone lines handling ticket informa-tion complaints were overloaded at the Marina Center, forc-ing us to open an additional phone bank at our Westwood office. The first few days were madness, but once we worked the bugs out we sold a lot of tickets.

By the end of June, Smith had distributed 80 percent of all the mail-order tickets by registered mail and those that remained were not far behind. It was a great accomplishment. Now we worried about the accuracy of the seating assign-ments, some crazy person bombing the ticket-data center, counterfeiting of tickets, and what to do about the small per-centage of undeliverable tickets. Smith's solution was to open a will-call office.

Then there were the seventy-two thousand people who would work the Games. The volunteer concept had worked. To help it work, I had given up my salary at the start of the year and become a volunteer. I thought it was necessary to show solidarity with our largest corps of workers, about whom there were questions. Yes, they had volunteered, but would they stay or quit after spending two days in the hot sun? How well would they complement the paid staff? Usher and I once again took turns stoking the engine.

Beginning in May and continuing through June we held general orientation meetings at each of the venues. We told our volunteers how important they were, how they were playing a part in history, how they were representing their neighborhoods, their city, and country. We told them it was an opportunity for all of them to make friends from around the world.

"The success of the Games," I said, "rests on your shoulders, your willingness to work for long hours under difficult conditions over a period of several weeks. This won't be easy, but you'll never duplicate this once-in-a-lifetime experience. The Games can't go on without you."

One very hot and humid Saturday, David Wolper and I watched volunteers rehearse opening ceremonies at the Coliseum and El Segundo High, not too far from the airport. It was heartening to see volunteers of all ages participating—particularly the two dozen small children dancing and singing in one of the auditoriums at the high school. To me it was like a patchwork quilt; I couldn't transfer what I was seeing onto the Coliseum floor. It seemed disorganized, and I was particularly troubled by the incessant squabbling among Wolper's lieutenants. Wolper, having lived through preproduction jitters throughout his career, welcomed me to Hollywood.

There were now two or three Olympic stories running every day in every local newspaper. Southern Californians were getting an Olympic education. More than a month had elapsed since Bella Stumbo of the *Los Angeles Times* had interviewed me and I was wondering what had happened to my request that the profile run immediately. I had heard scuttlebutt that I wasn't going to like the story and this was hanging over my head. I like my bad news right away.

I was finally assured it would run on Sunday, June 24. The powers that be at the *Los Angeles Times* had made it a page-one story.

I flew that Saturday on one of the committee's helicopters from my home in Laguna Beach to the Coliseum for the U.S. Track-and-Field trials. There, Amy Quinn handed me the early "bulldog" edition of the Sunday *Times,* which contained Stumbo's profile. I read it in a trailer behind the Coliseum and although certain passages were painful, my skin had thickened over the years and I knew I could deal with the emotional backlash. One passage, however, was untrue and would cause me a lot of trouble.

I remembered Stumbo had taped the entire interview and took notes assiduously. Toward the end, while discussing Los Angeles Police Chief Daryl Gates, whom she had profiled a year earlier in a three-part series, she asked me what I thought of him. I replied, "You know him better. What do you think?" She said some people called him a Nazi. To which I responded, "Tell me, is he really a Nazi at heart? You tell me, you're the one asking the question." The first part of my reply appeared on its own in the story without clarification. I was horrified: first that it would appear at all and secondly that it had been taken out of context.

I called Gates immediately and apologized. He hadn't seen the story yet, but said he understood how comments were often twisted. He told me his wife had cried for three days after Stumbo profiled him.

Back in Laguna Beach that afternoon, the entire family had gathered for the weekend, which I knew would be one of the few times we'd have together until the Games were over. Ginny was excited with the reunion and invited several of our closest friends to a barbecue on the beach. That was several hours away. I wandered down to the beach and sat with Vicki. I noticed a copy of the *Times* tucked under her towel.

"What did you think of the story?" I asked her.

"Shy and ruthless, huh?" she said.

I shrugged and smiled. "It could have been worse."

"I think it's awful. It makes you sound mean and inhuman. Why don't they ever give you credit for all the good things you do?"

"What bothered you most?"

"I don't know. I can't give you one specific example. It's

just so one-dimensional. I don't get the impression the story is about you."

"If it will make you feel better, I wasn't knocked out about it, either."

"What angers me the most are the nasty comments from the unnamed sources. Why be cowardly and not allow your name to be used?"

Vicki was a senior at the University of Colorado and had some news experience, having spent the previous summer working for ABC News in New York. I was thankful it hadn't jaded her. If she chose a career in journalism, I knew she'd make it a better profession.

We took a talk along the beach and discussed it further. Gates never came up. It did four days later, though, on June 27, when I was in New York for press interviews and to meet the staff of the baseball commissioner's office on Park Avenue. Gates had called a news conference and demanded an apology for calling him "a Nazi at heart." He threatened a libel suit and implied my alleged comment was a ploy to bulldoze him into signing a final security contract. As far as I was concerned, I had already apologized. I ignored it.

The next morning on *Today,* Bryant Gumbel pressed me for further comment. I told him what had transpired and explained how Stumbo had phrased the question. Gates fueled the fires for a few more days and I continued to ignore him, figuring either the reporter would release her tape and transcript of the interview, which would require my response, or it would just die on its own. It died when the *Times* released a statement saying it stood by Stumbo, even though she couldn't produce the tape of that conversation.

After *Today,* I hooked up with Samaranch and Berlioux at Butler Aviation and flew to Washington. Samaranch had been edgy for weeks over rumors that the Soviets were planning to turn their fears into reality by creating an incident. He'd requested a meeting with Secretary of State Shultz to outline his worries and pass on information. Berlioux had accompanied Samaranch, but her main purpose was to resolve a whole host of Games-related issues with me.

As he had done the day of the boycott, Jay Moorhead

arranged a working suite at the Hay-Adams Hotel. We were scheduled to meet Shultz that afternoon. Over lunch, Berlioux began clearing her agenda, starting with television rights. While ABC had a provision for arbitration in the event of a boycott, other international networks had begun pressing for refunds. The IOC had received one third of the broadcast revenues and Berlioux was as adamant as we were about not returning any money.

The European Broadcasting Union had threatened to withhold its final payment of $1.9 million, and I told Samaranch and Berlioux I had thrown one of the leaders of the Japanese consortium out of my office when he asked for money back. We knew the final $500,000 payment from the Eastern European broadcast union—OIRT-TV—was lost, and we agreed not to press URTNA-TV, the African consortium, which had no means to pay the small amount it owed.

Berlioux began badgering me about the IOC's Biltmore Hotel bill and a slew of petty accreditation demands. The more petty she got, the more I steamed. When she balked at our plan to honor Olympians by having them carry the IOC flag into the stadium, rather than soldiers during the opening ceremony, I told her we were going ahead with it anyway.

"That comes as no surprise, Peter," she said. "You have been violating the charter for five years."

It was one thing for the Russians to cry foul over the charter; it was another for Berlioux to do it. I was standing behind an antique, straight-back chair that had to be worth a few dollars. I gripped the arms and angrily stared at Berlioux.

"Where the IOC is concerned, you have no regard," she added.

I picked the chair off the floor a foot or so and slammed it back down, breaking the back two legs. I raged. I didn't know what to do with the chair, so I just let it fall.

"You're out of line," I snapped. "We've been sitting here for two hours saying yes to every damned petty request you've made. Is it in the Olympic Charter to give accreditations to children of the prime minister of Iceland or to the children of the head of state of Luxembourg? Where does it say in the charter that the president of UNESCO and his guests get accreditation? We've followed the damned charter down the line and I resent your accusations."

"Your plan has been approved," she said. "That does not mean I have to agree with it."

I growled and let the issue drop. I noticed that Samaranch was enjoying the show.

"Jay," I said, turning to Moorhead, "have the hotel bill the chair to the IOC."

At the State Department, Ed Derwinski, State's protocol director, met us at the front door and escorted us upstairs to pose for photographs with Shultz. We were then shown into a large meeting room where twenty chairs had been arranged in a large circle.

"I want to assure you that we will do all the U.S. government is obligated to do for the 1984 Olympic Games and at the same time we will not interfere with the organizing committee's responsibilities," Shultz said.

For once Derwinski had done his homework. At least this time he'd brought everyone working on the Games together and had briefed Shultz on Olympic protocol. Samaranch outlined his two concerns. "The risk of problems at the Games is much higher because of the Soviets' decision not to attend," he said. "Because the athletes are not happy in Czechoslovakia, Hungary, and the GDR, the Soviet Union may feel a need to do something to justify its decision."

"A major security effort is under way," Shultz said. "Seventeen thousand people are involved and we have a large budget. We believe a good job can be done. We are conscious of the problems that you raise."

Derwinski added, "Total coordination between the agencies exists. We've had very effective dry runs. We are possibly going to be overprepared."

"I was told by the Mossad," countered Samaranch, "that its mistake at Munich was having two main security groups working together. Who has ultimate authority in this country if a major threat were to occur?"

"If there were a threat of such a nature," said Shultz, "the Federal Bureau of Investigation would be the lead agency. . . ." Shultz also explained, "History shows that the way to prevent something is to have extensive preventive capacity in place. That is the strategy. Concerning the Israeli comment, it is routine for the FBI to coordinate with state and local law enforcement bodies. This is not a new thing; we do this on a continuing basis."

Samaranch then pursued his second area of concern: defections. "What will happen with the defections of minors?" he asked.

Shultz deferred the question to an aide, Elliott Abrams, the assistant secretary of state for human rights and humanitarian affairs, who described the process. The Immigration and Naturalization Service, he said, handled defections on a case-by-case basis. He said defection decisions are not based on age.

Shultz went on to say, "We don't want people to ask asylum during the Games. Our problem is that too many people want to come to the United States."

Samaranch brought up the uncertainty of Bolivia's attendance, which nobody took seriously. Shortly, after we had announced Bolivia as one of 141 NOCs attending the Games, it pulled out for economic reasons. A few days later, it reversed its decision. Between the two announcements, Tony Kornheiser, a witty sports columnist for the *Washington Post,* wrote a tongue-in-cheek commentary suggesting Bolivia raise funds by either passing the hat or, in the spirit of the 1984 Games, getting a commercial sponsor. He suggested Budweiser. This column escalated into an international incident. The Bolivian government took great umbrage and pulled out for the second time in less than a week. Kornheiser apologized, saying he meant no disrespect to the Bolivian people. But that apology didn't stop the death threats he was receiving. Bolivia eventually came around once more.

Shultz offered State Department support and followed it up with a pitch for special treatment at the Games for guests of the U.S. government. I was amused by Shultz's newfound support. We were no longer pariahs. We had tickets. Now we were looked upon as partners in protocol.

There were times when I thought running the Olympic

Games was like the movie *Jaws*. And this was one of those times. Just when I thought it was safe, *bam!*

Our personal mini-State Department had labored so hard to gather the greatest contingent ever of African athletes to participate in an Olympic Games, and just as we thought we had Africa locked up, we forgot to lock up Julian Roosevelt, the IOC member representing the United States.

Roosevelt announced out of the blue his support for South African reinstatement to the Olympic Movement. Worse, upon returning from a trip to South Africa, he noted with surprise the high caliber of the country's black swimmers because "blacks generally don't like to swim. They don't like the water."

Those comments were picked up by the wire services and printed in newspapers around the world.

Roosevelt had never been particularly helpful. He was fifty-nine years old, a grandnephew of President Theodore Roosevelt, and an Olympic yachtsman. We were quick to disassociate ourselves from him and harshly denounced his comments. Fortunately, few within the Olympic Movement paid any attention to what he said.

By the Fourth of July, the Marina Center began to look empty. As each day passed, more people were deployed to the villages and venues. The torch relay was scheduled to pass through Wenatchee, Washington, on the holiday and I was tempted to go. I'd been hearing and reading about its success for nearly two months and was anxious to see it again. Instead, I decided to stay close to home and make the rounds of the venues.

One of my first surprise visits was to the Coliseum, the centerpiece for the Games, where I was greeted by Ed Keen and H. D. Thoreau and Bill Bedford, the cocommissioners for athletics. Although the Coliseum wasn't completely ready yet, one couldn't help but be impressed with the $15 million face-lift it had received.

Besides the new track, which had been tested to rave reviews a few weeks earlier at the U.S. trials, Keen and his crew had constructed new shot put, high and long jump pits, resodded the field, installed a new public address system, refurbished the restrooms, replaced 1,500 seats, repaired escalators, constructed a 6,000 foot storage building, rebuilt all the concession stands, remodeled the press box, renovated the dressing rooms, opened a tunnel that had been sealed shut for decades, replaced all the lamps and existing light fixtures, and replaced the entire stadium's electrical system. Outside the stadium in Exposition Park Keen had repaved a circular road that could accommodate twenty buses at a time, installed new fencing, renovated the plaza area, resodded the park, resurfaced streets and walkways, and installed a new lighting system.

I had one question for them. "Are you ready?"

"Yes," they replied.

At every venue I visited during that time I asked the same question. The answer of the commissioners, the staff, the volunteers, and the security guards was always an enthusiastic yes. At those venues where competition would end early, such as cycling, modern pentathlon, shooting, weightlifting, yachting, and baseball, I followed up with, "Would you be willing to be redeployed?" Again, the unanimous response was yes.

As energetic and committed as everyone was, and as prepared as the venues were, we began to have problems when we started issuing staff uniforms. Not everyone liked the way they looked and many volunteers resigned because they thought they looked like clowns.

Meanwhile, the LAPD continued to be a millstone around my neck. Our agreement with the City of Los Angeles had a loophole large enough to drive an eighteen wheeler through, and Daryl Gates was an expert driver. It gave Gates final approval over the level of staffing at the villages and the venues within the LAPD's jurisdiction. Not surprisingly, he rejected our plans and wanted $9.5 million in additional funds to cover the costs of officer deployment that he determined were necessary. Included in these costs were $425,000 for hot lunches, $20,000 for golf carts, massive public relations expenditures, and a questionable formula for overtime payments to officers.

He had us over a barrel. Criticism of security planning

was the last thing we needed. If Gates didn't get what he wanted, he'd have an excuse for anything that went wrong. Plans called for LAPD officers to begin staffing the villages on July 7, one week before athletes would move in. Given our recent public battle, the "Nazi" controversy would have been resurrected had I jumped into the negotiations. I left that to Usher. I remained involved in the strategy behind the scenes. On Friday, July 6, Usher went downtown to wrap it all up. We planned to give Gates what he wanted. Usher offered to put the full amount requested into an escrow account as protection against disputed items subject to arbitration. He even turned over a check for $4.38 million as a goodwill gesture. All we asked in return was that this was a ceiling on LAPD costs. The offer was rejected by the city council.

Usher further angered the LAPD later that day by claiming the LAPD wanted us to pay for its "caviar lunches." By Monday, we agreed to limit arbitration only to selected costs amounting to a maximum of $6.7 million. Within hours LAPD officers were on their posts at the villages.

That same day, we were embroiled in a conflict with the White House advance people, who lobbied for a larger speaking part for the president in the opening ceremony. Accustomed as Ronald Reagan was to a script, he was equally accustomed to a starring role. The Olympic Charter, however, was specific about the script, and limited Reagan's remarks to: "I declare open the Games of Los Angeles, celebrating the Twenty-third Olympiad of the Modern Era." That wouldn't even warm Reagan up—certainly not in an election year.

Things were moving quickly. I decided to play hooky July 10 and attend the All-Star baseball game in San Francisco. It felt strange being in a non-Olympic atmosphere, but it was relaxing and gave me a chance to catch my breath. The next day Ginny and I took the kids to see the premier of the Chengdu Acrobatic Troupe at MacGowan Hall at UCLA. Fitzpatrick had labored hard to bring the troupe over from China and insisted I attend and meet the performers. They were sensational and the kids loved the show.

Meanwhile, some selected national Olympic committees

were being threatened by mail. Zimbabwe, Sri Lanka, South Korea, Malaysia, China, Singapore, and Nigeria had all received similar vile letters, all postmarked from the Washington, D.C., area suburbs, and allegedly from the Ku Klux Klan. For example, the one to Nigeria printed on plain white paper had a KKK logo in the upper-left-hand corner and a headline across the top: THE OLYMPICS—FOR THE WHITES ONLY! Below there was a box around the following message:

AFRICAN MONKEYS!

A GRAND WELCOME AWAITS YOU IN LOS ANGELES!

WE HAVE BEEN TRAINING FOR THE GAMES BY SHOOTING AT BLACK MOVING TARGETS. IN LOS ANGELES OUR OWN OLYMPIC FLAMES ARE READY TO INCINERATE YOU. THE HIGHEST AWARD FOR A TRUE AMERICAN PATRIOT WOULD BE THE LYNCHING OF AN AFRICAN MONKEY.

BLACKS, WELCOME TO THE LOS ANGELES OLYMPICS!

WE'LL GIVE YOU A RECEPTION THAT YOU'LL NEVER FORGET!

An ape hanging from a rope dangled from the box with a placard around its neck that read: HANG THE NIGGER!

We turned the letters over to the FBI and the State Department, whose investigations indicated that the letter-writing campaign was a carefully conceived Soviet disinformation plot. Samaranch and I both feared this was not the end of Russian attempts to disrupt the Games.

Bright and early Thursday morning, July 13, we held our final media briefing for the Los Angeles press corps. We had had more than a hundred briefings over the years to keep journalists up to date on all aspects of organizing the Games. Not all had been pleasant. Usher and I faced forty reporters that morning, and Usher showed up in his festive Olympic uniform—light blue blazer, tattersall sports shirt, gray slacks, gray sneakers, and a straw hat—to become the hit of the day.

We addressed many familiar issues and outlined the problems still to be faced. One was ABC and the $35 million it still owed. Another was the hate letters. Another was smog. A terrible siege of smog had descended upon Los Angeles, provoking news stories and concern about the athletes' health. All we could do was hope it would lift before the competitions began. Given my druthers, I preferred to have it at this time than during the Games. Finally, the inevitable growing pains were bound to attract notice and we took special care to describe what they might be. All in all, the mood was upbeat. I felt the media had begun to feel the pride of hosting the Games.

I had two lunches scheduled that day. The first was with commissioners and senior staff at the Olympic Village dining hall at UCLA, hosted by its LAOOC mayor Jim Easton. Everyone arrived in their blue and gray management uniforms, except for me for which I received no end of ribbing. I tried to explain I hadn't had time to pick it up, but nobody bought that.

Although an air of nervous tension hung over the room, the camaraderie was comforting and gave one the sense it would overcome all obstacles to come. As I looked around, I was impressed with the level of leadership we had assembled. I thought at that time I would never again see so many highly qualified people in one place at one time.

Willy Reich, of all people, a man who rarely shows emotion, suggested we join hands in prayer. Donn Moomaw, our weightlifting commissioner and the pastor of the Bel Air Presbyterian Church, asked the universal God for assistance and guidance over the days that lay ahead.

I left before lunch to join Madame Berlioux in Westwood. She was there with her assistant Marie Chevallier, and Charlotte Hyde and Joel Rubenstein. Berlioux had come to town for the Games and her arrival signified the invasion by the rest of the Olympic world. We chatted about the international scene and she raised Samaranch's continuing concern that the Games would be marred by Soviet-inspired terrorism.

Friday the thirteenth made me superstitious for the first time in my life. I had reluctantly approved a major crowd event in downtown Los Angeles called "The Big Picture."

The mayor, all the civic leaders, sports celebrities, and Hollywood stars were photographed along with a sea of humanity against a backdrop of the Los Angeles skyline. I feared it was a disaster waiting to happen and I was nervous throughout the hour-long ordeal.

On my way back to the Marina Center, I dropped by unannounced at the main press center to see our press operations director, Richard Perelman. He'd joined the committee just out of Loyola Law School in the fall of 1980 and was one of the success stories of the LAOOC. He was young and brash and I wondered when we hired him if he had the stamina to see the job through. Those fears proved unjustified—he was one of the most intelligent and capable people we had—but the Richard Perelman I saw that day was dead on his feet. I don't think he had slept since he'd moved his operation into the main press center the previous Monday.

"Richard, go home and sleep. Turn the work over to your staff."

"Peter, I know what I'm doing," he started to say.

I interrupted him. "I won't have you burn out when we need you most. This job is too important."

He didn't like me interfering. I respected him for that, and he grumbled all the way out the door. He was a new man when he showed up the next day.

Saturday, July 14, was all important. We opened the villages at UCLA and USC and the satellite village for the rowers and canoeists at the University of California, Santa Barbara. I attended the UCLA opening with Mayor Bradley who, appropriately, had graduated from UCLA. Usher opened USC with City Councilman John Ferraro, one of the early supporters of the Games and a graduate of USC.

It was a magnificent day—the smog had broken and UCLA looked sensational. A beautiful woman wearing a blue hostess uniform escorted the dignitaries to their seats. When she took me to mine, I wrapped my arms around her.

"You look great," I whispered in her ear.

"Thank you, sir," she added in a very official voice.

"Vicki, I think I'm the proudest father in the world today," I said.

"You ought to be," she said. Then she smiled and added, "By the way, my feet are killing me. These Olympic shoes are terrible."

I hugged her again and she went off to greet and escort Mayor Bradley to his seat.

The ceremony was fun. Jim Easton had selected a Chinese triple jumper, Zou Zhenxian, to cut the ribbon and enter the village. It went off flawlessly and I toured the village with pride. The Games were on.

LIGHTING UP AMERICA

THE CUSTOM IN ancient Greece was to employ runners called Spondophores who raced through the countryside to alert the populace that the Olympic Games were about to begin and that athletes should begin their journey to Olympia.

In 1984 we had better communications, but we still needed that old-fashioned touch to get the message across. That touch was the Olympic torch relay as the message of the flame passed from hand to hand.

By the time we opened the Olympic villages on July 14, the torch relay was nearing Sacramento. The California media had joined the caravan, reporting on its progress to Los Angeles: It was seven days away.

The torch relay had been a hit from the beginning, but after that first day its progress had been overshadowed by the Soviet boycott. Locally, it was an extraordinary experience for its citizens. In Boston, it drew a crowd of thousands at Fanueil Hall and then it traveled along the historic Freedom trail. In south Philadelphia, a blind torchbearer followed in the footsteps of the movie character Rocky Balboa, and up the steps of the Philadelphia Museum of Art as a band played the stirring music from the film.

President Reagan greeted Olympian torchbearer Kurt

Thomas on the south lawn of the White House on May 14. Thomas was America's best gymnast in 1980 and had been hurt as much as any athlete by the Carter boycott. He ran on behalf of all 1980 athletes.

Wally McGuire, the logistical genius behind the relay, found the White House staff difficult. Reagan officials had one overriding concern—to make network news in scheduling the event. That was fine except the White House plan was to put the relay in the middle of Washington rush-hour traffic, creating a nightmare for the local police and playing havoc with McGuire's schedule. McGuire was dead set against it. To accommodate the White House he'd either have to speed up or eliminate portions of the route. He considered eliminating Annapolis but that was an Olympic soccer site and we needed the relay to inspire public interest there.

The White House had its way and McGuire worked it out by running longer days and accelerating the pace so it arrived at the nation's capital in the early afternoon in time for network news deadlines.

I watched the White House event on television that night. Reagan made a few remarks. He called it a great day for America and said the Olympic Games in Los Angeles would be a great Games.

I tried to keep in close touch with either McGuire or Jim Suennen, the trip director and McGuire's right-hand man. Suennen was an advance planner for our press department who previously had worked on the staff of Governor Edmund G. Brown, Jr., and he'd traveled with the torch caravan 95 percent of the time. When he wasn't with the caravan, McGuire monitored it from his office in San Francisco or from our Marina Center headquarters. Occasionally, he'd report on its progress in person.

One of those occasions was Monday, June 11, when the torch, on its thirty-fourth day, was making its way through Missouri on its way to Oklahoma and Texas. From the nation's capital, it had moved west through the Virginia countryside, over the Blue Ridge Mountains, through the industrial areas of western Pennsylvania, Ohio, and southern Michigan. It passed through Detroit and Chicago and then turned southeast, going through Indiana, the blue grass country of Kentucky, Tennessee, North Carolina, and Georgia. From Atlanta, it headed west across Alabama, Mississippi, and Arkansas, and turned north again to Missouri, where it passed Gateway Arch in St. Louis.

The day before, Andrew H. Malcolm in the *New York Times* became the first journalist to write for a national audience about the great impact the relay was having on millions of Americans. In a story datelined Loose Creek, Missouri, Malcolm wrote, ". . . it seems to be igniting some special feelings tied less to the Olympics and more to patriotism."

"It's a combination of both," McGuire told me when we were having lunch outside in the Café de Coubertin on that warm, beautiful southern California afternoon. All of the outside tables were taken by committee staff members. McGuire had been discussing the phenomenon of the relay that Malcolm had captured so well in the *New York Times* feature.

"The Olympics are definitely a big part of it," McGuire continued. "As the torch passes—whether through big city streets or along lonely roads—people who gather chant, 'Go, USA! Go, USA!' It's really an uplifting experience."

"Why are people turning out?" I asked. "Is it the boycott?"

"The boycott has something to do with it," McGuire answered. "I'm sure the overwhelming support of the torch is an unconscious and collective response to the Soviets. Americans are saying: 'To hell with the Russians. We don't need them in our Olympics.' But that's not all of it."

"I believe the patriotism has always been there," I said, "lying dormant for so long—decades, really. The torch is the catalyst."

"You're right," McGuire said. "Wherever it goes, it draws people out of their humdrum lives and gives them something different to do, something exciting; it gives them an excuse to go out and cheer by the roadside and feel good about themselves."

"What kinds of crowds are we getting?"

"All kinds," said McGuire. "Huge crowds in the big cities. In the small towns, everybody turns out. I've had old men tell me the relay is the best thing that's happened since the troops came home from World War II.

"Then in the country, in the wide open spaces where we're twenty, thirty miles from the nearest town, we'll find a half dozen or so people standing along the roadside waving small American flags and sometimes singing the national anthem or 'America the Beautiful.'

"I have no idea how they get there, but they do. They come out in their work clothes; some get dressed up in their Sunday finest. At night, some women are wearing night dresses and have curlers in their hair and men, carrying small children piggyback, are in pajamas. I've had men and women of all ages grasp my hand and thank me. So has everybody else on the caravan. Remarkable."

I felt chills go down my spine. I also felt a great deal of pride.

"What moved you the most?" I asked.

He thought for a long while. "There have been so many," he said. "But Atlanta stands out."

He told me about the proud struggle of a disabled child who had carried the torch along Peachtree Street in the middle of downtown. People were lined four and five deep on the sidewalks and were captivated by the determination of the boy moving slowly, concentrating on holding the torch aloft. Uniformed police were stationed about every twenty yards. Initially, the boy was frightened of the flame. He held it away from his body and it unsteadied him even more.

"He stumbled several times," McGuire continued, "and each time I could hear the crowd gasp. There was one, huge, bear of a policeman who was crying like a baby. As the child struggled past him, he wiped tears from his eyes and quietly said, 'C'mon, kid. You can do it.' It was as if the crowd knew its support would help the boy finish and when he did the crowd began cheering like there was no tomorrow. I cried and I doubt if there was a dry eye in the city of Atlanta."

One by-product of the torch relay mentioned in the *New York Times* article, and confirmed by McGuire, was how it was making heroes of people who'd never before been heroes. But that didn't deter legitimate heroes from participating.

Muhammad Ali, the former heavyweight champion of the world who had gotten his start by winning a gold medal in the 1960 Rome Olympics, ran a kilometer before thousands of fans in his hometown of Louisville, Kentucky. Appropriately, his kilometer ended at Muhammad Ali Boulevard.

When Ali accepted the torch, he said to those nearby, "If I don't make it, if I fall on my face, I want you to promise not to take my picture." His fans responded by shouting, "Go get 'em, champ . . . looking good, champ." Grown-ups and children alike ran alongside him. Everybody wanted to talk to the champ and touch him. One man kept yelling, "Hey champ," trying to get his attention. Ali finally looked over at him and said, "Oh, you said 'champ.' I thought you were saying 'hey tramp.'"

Two days later, the relay ran into trouble as it approached the Kentucky-Tennessee border. A thunderstorm with severe lightning stopped the runners in their tracks for three hours several miles from Pineville, Kentucky, which was their overnight destination. Expecting to find the small community shut down for the night when they arrived at two in the morning, the caravan was shocked when greeted by several hundred townspeople, many wearing nightshirts and robes, holding candles to light the way.

Once the *New York Times* article appeared, everybody seemed to jump on the bandwagon. It wasn't uncommon for people to drive hundreds of miles to see the torch. From Missouri, it passed through southeastern Kansas and headed south to Oklahoma and Texas. There it turned west and went across northern Texas, through the panhandle, to New Mexico.

I watched another touching episode on videotape that occurred in Kansas City, Kansas. A small retarded girl, pretty as a picture, valiantly ran her kilometer on a slight incline. It was painful to watch and I asked Jim Suennen, who'd been there, why she had been assigned to run uphill. He explained that her parents had specifically requested that kilometer because an incline made it easier for the child to maintain her balance. She had trained for weeks by holding a hammer aloft as she ran. Still, she had a difficult start. About halfway through, you could see the confidence surge in her. She lifted her head and beamed with pride. Her entire class was standing by the road holding balloons and cheering, "Run, Amy, run." I asked Suennen how many boxes of Kleenex they used up that day.

Suennen had hundreds of stories. He told me that in Chicago a runner was so excited he was high-fiving people on the sidewalks. "Out of nowhere," Suennen said, "a kid popped out just in time to get the high-five along the side of his face. He didn't know whether to laugh or cry. Another time, a kid was running alongside the torchbearer and, not watching where he was going, ran smack into a light pole. He was dazed but got up and continued to run along."

The relay turned north when it reached Albuquerque and passed through historic Santa Fe. From there it entered Colorado, where Dick Sargent was representing the LAOOC as a featured speaker at a ceremony in Colorado Springs. It was June 22 and more than twenty-five thousand people, many from Wyoming and Nebraska, filled the stadium of a local high school for one of the most picturesque of all the torch-relay events.

At the precise moment that a young, blond-haired girl passed it to a black boy on the track of the stadium, the Colorado Springs Philharmonic Orchestra played ABC-TV's Olympic theme while a vivid red sun peered brilliantly from behind majestic Pikes Peak.

A few days later, the people of Craig, Colorado, a depressed Rocky Mountains mining town of ten thousand, rolled their celebrations for the Fourth of July and the town's centennial into one big party timed to the arrival of the torch relay.

Town officials had arranged to have four air force jets buzz the relay caravan as it arrived and set off the fireworks they had been saving for the Fourth at a giant barbecue the night of June 25. First thing the next morning, on the field of the local high school, the townspeople prepared a mammoth pancake breakfast for everyone. Then the torch was gone, heading northwest.

The *Los Angeles Times* finally caught up with the torch in Utah, but long before the *New York Times* ran its story, I'd been urging *Los Angeles Times* reporters and editors to catch up with the relay. I wanted to see some good news in my hometown paper. Also, I knew the relay was a prairie fire spreading from coast to coast and it was only a matter of time before some publication or network made it a national story. Instead, the *Los Angeles Times* ignored my appeals and assigned Maura Dolan, a cityside reporter, to investigate how the LAOOC had devised its method of assigning the kilometers that sponsors had paid for.

At that time, two thirds of nearly three thousand total kilometers statewide had been sponsored; southern California was all sold out. To accommodate as many runners as possible, McGuire had already laid out a criss-crossing route through Los Angeles and parts of Orange County. When we announced the plan a year earlier, we promised to assign runners as close to their desired location as possible on a first-come, first-served basis. By March 15, we'd informed the public that there weren't any more kilometers south of Santa Barbara.

One runner was unhappy with her kilometer assignment in Adin, California, a tiny community along the Oregon border, and complained to Dolan at the *Times*. The runner, a seventy-year-old grandmother, had sponsored a kilometer so her grandchildren could see her run in Huntington Beach, her community. But she was one of the last to enter the program. She told Dolan she had heart trouble and couldn't run in the high altitude of Adin. We were sympathetic when Dolan called, but told her it wouldn't be fair to arbitrarily replace somebody who had entered the program earlier. We offered to refund money to the grandmother or to anyone else unhappy with an assigned location and to make switches if other sponsors stepped forward.

Fortunately, only a few people had been assigned kilometers so far away, And on the day Dolan's story ran, several sponsors—including Tom Celorie of the LAOOC staff—offered to switch. I gave him a day off to take his family to Adin.

Before entering California, the torch wound its way through northern Utah, Idaho, and across Washington to

Seattle, where it turned south and headed down the coast through Oregon. Adin, like Craig, Colorado, went all out. The people there treated Celorie and his family like royalty and managed just fine without the grandmother from Huntington Beach. More than two thousand people turned out for a barbecue—four times the town's population—and the citizens hung a huge banner at the town limits that read: WELCOME TO GOD'S COUNTRY.

Celorie stopped me in the office when he returned. "The best part was my daughter got to see me run," he said. "She's only two, but we got plenty of pictures and she'll be able to appreciate that day when she's older."

"How was it?" I asked.

"They were incredibly friendly," he said. "We stayed in one of the ranchers' homes. At the town barbecue celebrating the torch relay they gave me a key to the city and a gilded horseshoe."

My worries about a lackluster reception in California proved groundless. Californians went wild—even more so than in other parts of the country. From the mountain area of Adin and Honey Lake, the torch made a short swing through Nevada. As it skirted around part of scenic Lake Tahoe, former vice-president Walter Mondale and Geraldine Ferraro, whom Mondale had just selected as his Democratic running mate, took time out from their busy schedules to join other well-wishers along the roadside. The torch went through the beautiful California gold country, through Sacramento, and arrived on July 16 in San Francisco, which was preparing for the Democratic national convention.

McGuire and I had breakfast the next day. He'd been on the torch caravan when it arrived in San Francisco but had returned to L.A. to pave the way for its arrival there. The event in downtown San Francisco, McGuire said, drew several hundred thousand people, much larger than the crowd Mondale and Ferraro had drawn at the same time a few miles away. He expected far greater crowds in Los Angeles and wanted to make sure the final logistics were perfect. He was worried. The great majority of relay runners in southern California were Youth Legacy Kilometer runners and not the tried-and-true cadre of AT&T runners who had filled the gaps between Youth Legacy Kilometer runners across the country.

AT&T had more than lived up to its commitment. Aside from financing the relay, it helped staff the 37-vehicle caravan and allowed 250 employees to take a week off from work to run those kilometers that hadn't been sponsored. Each runner was carefully selected and each ran roughly seven miles a day to keep the relay on schedule. The AT&T runners also caught the spirit of America and along the way they showed tremendous warmth and a lot of heart.

In Kansas one cadre runner, having learned that a child suffering from cancer was hoping for a glimpse of the torch from his bedroom window, took an impromptu detour to show the child the torch up close.

The caravan was led by a Buick convertible followed by the torchbearer and two sedans providing immediate security, support personnel and equipment. The rest of the caravan consisted of a forty-three-foot mobile chuckwagon; a forty-five-foot dining car; a forty-eight-foot refrigerator/freezer; four specially designed motor homes to house the cadre runners; another four motor homes for relay-support personnel, two more for press and VIPs; a mobile relay-control center; and an emergency services vehicle. A pair of fourteen-foot GMC Magnavans followed. One held repair equipment and spare parts and the other the torches, extra miner's lamps and, at night, the flame itself.

Given L.A.'s traffic, plus the high percentage of youthful runners and a tight schedule, McGuire had plenty to do. Then a new problem arose: The people of Los Angeles had finally caught Olympic fever. That fever manifested itself in an overwhelming demand for tickets—any tickets.

Ed Smith had no sooner closed the remote ticket centers and had mailed out the last few tickets to customers when he convinced Usher and me to put more than a hundred thousand tickets on sale at a three-day Ticket Faire at Santa Anita Race Track. For those three days, Santa Anita dispensed Olympic tickets rather than pari-mutuel tickets. The remaining tickets were a combination of those we had set aside for boycotting countries and returns from other national Olympic committees and sponsors. We were initially reluctant about the plan, because again this was unprecedented and we didn't want a riot. To reduce the risk, we invited only those from southern California who had previously ordered tickets. We had an overflow crowd. People were clamoring to attend the Games.

Meanwhile, the torch was at our door. It stopped overnight at Pepperdine University in Malibu on July 20 and entered Los Angeles the next day. I started the morning at the UCLA village with an early operations committee meeting. From there I had to hustle to the Biltmore Hotel in downtown Los Angeles for the IOC Executive Board meeting. By then I was using a helicopter all the time. As we lifted off the pad at UCLA, I asked Joe Allen, the pilot, to get clearance to buzz Malibu. It had been seventy-five days since I'd seen the torch off in New York and I was eager to see it again on the open road.

From the air, I could see the lights of the caravan break through the early morning haze along Pacific Coast Highway. People had already begun gathering on the road. It was impressive. We hovered overhead briefly and then headed downtown, where I would see it arrive at city hall later that day.

Usher was among the thousands present at the top of the California Incline, a long hill that leads from the Pacific Coast Highway into Santa Monica and greater Los Angeles. O. J. Simpson ran it up the incline. There was a brief ceremony at the top and then O.J. transferred the flame to Michael Bailey, a seven-year-old boy who suffered from cerebral palsy.

"Peter," Usher told me later, "it was one of the most moving experiences of my life. This little boy could barely walk. He had a specially designed walker with wheels and a socket to hold the torch and he pushed it along real slow. You could see the determination in his face. O.J. walked along with him, offering encouragement. People in the crowd were cheering and crying. It took him fifteen minutes and I don't think anybody will ever forget it.

"I was beside myself. I was crying—like everybody else. I didn't want to let go of the moment, so I jumped the press truck and followed it for a few more miles. The whole thing is really something else. People are on a high and it's going to carry over into the Games."

THE GAMES

I WAS IN the eye of the storm.

The torch was moving south to San Diego where it would make a U-turn and return in time for the opening ceremonies. The Ticket Faire at Santa Anita had raised more than $5 million, and Olympic fever was running rampant. The so-called laid-back people of southern California were anything but. They even went crazy over Olympic pins. Marketplaces appeared spontaneously all over the community, and prices for these small, inexpensive pieces of metal—or plastic, in some cases—soared out of sight.

Los Angeles looked great. We had installed 20,000 street banners; more than 60 specialty tents; 20,000 signs; 3,500 spiral tubes; 200 canopies; 24 thirteen-foot helium-filled balloons; and more than 2,000 national flags. We'd constructed approximately 1,500,000 cubic feet of scaffolding at the villages and venues. We'd used 400,000 containers of annual flowers, approximately 35 miles of decorative fabric for fences, and more than 11 miles of glitter strips to decorate scaffolds, stages, and award stands.

While people enjoyed the hot colors hanging from light poles and draped on fences, Olympic workers continued to balk at the uniforms. Usher had assured me they would look terrific and predicted they'd become prized possessions. Mike Morphy, the commissioner for equestrian events, couldn't understand the fuss. He had a set of official's uniforms—orange polyester jacket with gray polyester slacks—delivered to Prince Philip at Buckingham Palace so he could have them altered.

Dick Sargent, meanwhile, had brought in the African charter. As soon as he landed at LAX, he called.

"Anything go wrong?" I asked.

"Nope," Sargent said.

"Okay. Thanks." I hung up.

Bomb threats became a fact of life. We called in the bomb squad an average of twice a day but, luckily, never found one.

Uniformed officers, though plentiful, were unobtrusive and polite. Fears that petty jealousies and overstaffing would interfere with their work proved unfounded for the most part. When the Israeli and Turkish delegations arrived, the appropriate law enforcement agencies provided coordinated ground and air protection from the minute each delegation departed the airplane to the minute it entered the village. Sargent had observed both arrivals and called me as soon as the athlete buses left the airport.

"Any problems?" I asked.

"Nope," Sargent replied.

"Okay. Thanks." I hung up.

While the rank and file were standing shoulder to shoulder, Police Chief Daryl Gates opened an old wound by questioning the motives of the FBI in forming a hostage rescue team specifically for the Games. Gates wondered aloud—to a reporter, no less—if the hostage rescue team, a specially trained force of fifty, was a step in the direction of a national police force. The FBI ignored Gates and promised his comments wouldn't adversely affect the policing of the Games. I hoped not.

That same day, July 17, one of our private security guards—the Blue Berets as Ed Best called them—was arrested for carrying a concealed weapon into the USC village. It turned out the guard had an outstanding warrant for a minor traffic violation and the incident raised suspicions about the quality of our background checks. Law enforcement had been critical of our extensive use of private security all along, and this gave them a perfect opportunity to fire off a salvo. It didn't. But I began to worry about the caliber of people hired by our security guard consortium. This guy had apparently slipped through the net. How many more had?

The great majority of athletes were perfect guests, but some caused problems—a few humorous. One group of African runners didn't like the stop-and-go city street traffic, so they tried training on the Harbor Freeway in downtown Los Angeles during rush hour and brought commuter traffic to a standstill.

Other athletes had serious problems, like the two female athletes who failed the mandatory gender verification test as prescribed by the IOC medical commission and were benched for the Games. The LAOOC medical team, headed by our medical director, Dr. Anthony F. Daly, examined the competitors' chromosomes by taking a cell sample from inside the cheek.

Drugs and doping were big concerns. The last thing we wanted was a repeat of the fiasco at the 1983 Pan American Games in Caracas, where a series of drug violations took center stage and overshadowed the competition. We had warned athletes to expect even more sophisticated testing in Los Angeles and hoped they would heed the warning and compete fairly.

Athletes had their social obligations as well. One of the most prominent functions took place at the Los Angeles Zoo where the city hosted a reception for the Chinese delegation. The zoo was exhibiting two rare Chinese pandas that Dr. Armand Hammer and Mayor Bradley had obtained. It was a beautiful event—a western-style barbecue—and well run except that the PRC team arrived more than two hours late. It was an LAOOC foul-up. The dispatch orders had somehow gotten lost and the team members were forced to cool their heels while waiting for another bus at the UCLA village.

But that was minor compared to the payroll problems our transportation department was having. Alan Epstein, vice-president of transportation, had brought on five thousand drivers, mechanics, fuelers, and cleaners over a ten-day period at the end of June. In the rush, about two hundred names had been incorrectly entered into the payroll system and, as a result, many weren't getting the right paychecks. Tempers flared; we had threats of resignations, even strikes. Epstein raised cash immediately and distributed partial payments amounting to nearly $500,000 over several weeks until the payroll system caught up.

Epstein resolved another problem by dispatching motorcycle riders to pay $3 in lunch money to transportation personnel at venues where box lunches were unavailable. Each rider carried a satchel filled with $1 bills and I worried about muggers.

Ginny and I had moved into a large five-room suite at the Biltmore Hotel on July 16, the same day IOC President Samaranch arrived in Los Angeles. Joel Rubenstein, who ran the Biltmore operation, had arranged duplexes for both Samaranch and Monique Berlioux.

The suite was my command center. Sherry Cockle had an office next door and Lucie Gikovich, another assistant, had a room down the hall.

It felt more like home when Heidi and Keri joined us a few days later. Both were working for the LAOOC in the hotel and had rooms in the hotel. Vicki was staying at the house in Encino and Joe, who was traveling down the state on the torch-relay caravan when we moved into the Biltmore, was staying with our oldest and dearest friends, Jane and Jim DeVore, in Beverly Hills.

It's not enough to say that the DeVores are friends; they're family. Whenever Ginny and I were away during the Olympic years, and those times were many, the DeVores always filled the breach and opened their arms and homes for the Ueberroths left behind.

Jim DeVore had joined the LAOOC and was handling a very sensitive ticket assignment. It's customary at sport, theatrical, and musical events that a ticket allotment be set aside for the discretionary use of the event organizers and managers. In our case, a relatively small amount was allocated for me, Harry Usher, and Paul Ziffren. This reserve was to cover on-site ticket emergencies and special last-minute needs of the IOC and other officials. I needed someone I trusted implicitly to handle the funds and the tickets. DeVore was the one.

To enable me to monitor the Games from the suite, our technology people had installed a wall of twenty-three televisions in the living room, each with a direct feed to a different competition site. I also had a giant screen in the room and three telephones, one a direct line to Roone Arledge and another to Usher at the Marina Center.

Samaranch was having technological problems on the floor below me. He couldn't get the Associated Press, United Press International, Reuters, and EFE, Spain's wire service, hooked up in his suite. His problem was the tip of the iceberg.

Nine thousand members of the media had begun descending on Los Angeles and it was our job to provide them facilities to do their work and file their stories. Gaps in the telephone lease lines that connected Los Angeles to other parts of the world were preventing this. Several international news agencies were affected. AT&T had promised to put this together, but its recent divestiture may have been the reason for the delay.

Rather than relying on one company to handle the U.S. portion of this technological relay, we had to rely on each AT&T affiliate involved. While the affiliates tried to connect the lease lines, Reuters, Agence France Presse, Sports Information Dienst, Deutsche Press Agentur's photo bureau, European Press Photo Union, and others suffered and threatened to fashion a boycott of their own. By July 24, Agence France Presse was totally exasperated and made plans to pack their pads and pencils and return to Europe.

I paid a a visit to each of the agencies at the main press center and promised relief. I contacted one of AT&T's senior officials, Bill Higgins, and told him very simply that AT&T was facing a huge international image problem. The agencies understood AT&T was at fault. AT&T had the lease lines connected within forty-eight hours.

Otherwise, the technology was impressive and we created

an electronic Olympic connection throughout southern California. The technological star by far was EMS—Electronic Messaging Service—by AT&T. Besides providing a wide range of Olympic information and up-to-the-minute results, it gave Olympic family members the ability to send and receive instantaneous messages. Those with alpha-numeric pagers could also send and receive messages through EMS. Throughout the Olympic network, we had 1,700 EMS terminals; 300 EMS printers; 1,500 alpha-numeric pagers; 300 radio telephones; 100 car-mounted cellular telephones; 20 portable cellular telephones; and 4,000 hand-held two-way radios.

My pager beeped incessantly. And when Usher and I were together, our beepers invariably sounded in harmony. One of those times was at Mayor Bradley's reception for the IOC at city hall the night of July 24. While talking with IOC and city officials, my pager signaled and an instant later Usher's went off. We had the same message: NADIA HAS ARRIVED.

Nadia was Nadia Comaneci, the Romanian gymnast who had dazzled the world with a string of perfect 10s at the Montreal Olympics eight years earlier. She was fourteen then; now she was recently retired from active competition and was aspiring to become a coach. But she wasn't experienced enough to coach Olympic gymnasts. When I invited her to the Games, Alexandru Siperco and Haralambie Alexa thought it would be a great opportunity for her to work with the team and get to know members of the International Gymnastics Federation. We found her a place in the USC village with the Romanian team.

We tried to do everything we could for the Romanians. I don't think there was an LAOOC employee or anybody in the City of Los Angeles, for that matter, who wasn't aware of the risk they had taken in defying the Soviet Union. We helped fund their transportation and arranged for a special television feed into the country so the Romanian people could see the Games. The Romanians arrived on July 22 and two days later hosted a wonderful reception for the LAOOC. They had brought with them Romanian wines and delicacies and drove Agnes Mura crazy while perfecting preparations.

Reporters were on the scene when Nadia arrived in Los Angeles. There had been rumors for more than a week that she would run the final leg of the torch relay. It was untrue. Rafer Johnson had been selected the week before, but it was a tightly kept secret and the rumors about Nadia heightened the suspense.

Rafer was the ideal choice. He was an Olympian and had won the decathlon silver medal at Melbourne in 1956 and the gold at Rome four years later. He represents what the Olympics are all about—honesty, integrity, good sportsmanship, and commitment—and he brought all of those ideals to our organizational efforts as a member of our board, spirit team, and speaker's bureau. There was never a time when we asked Rafer for his help that he didn't deliver.

I broke the news to Rafer in my office one afternoon at the marina center. By then our headquarters was virtually deserted and nobody noticed Rafer being escorted upstairs. David Wolper was there. He'd been hounding me for a month to name the runner because he needed him for rehearsals. David insisted that the run required lengthy training. I kept putting him off to build the suspense, which he said drove him insane. Finally, I invited both to the marina center.

"People have been speculating for months about the identity of the final torchbearer," I told Rafer. He and Wolper sat silently. I detected a slight smile playing at the corners of Wolper's mouth.

"I'd like you to run it," I said to Rafer.

Rafer was stunned—and ecstatic. "Thank you," was all he could say.

Wolper didn't miss as beat. "It's a bitch," he said to Johnson. "We're talking a lot of stairs, Rafer. You've got to run a lap around the Coliseum track, climb the stairs leading up from the floor of the stadium, and then the real backbreaker—ninety-six steps up the hydraulic slip stair to the top where you'll face the crowd and light the torch.

"We had a college football player try it and he fell flat on his face, but I know you can do it."

On the morning of July 25, I woke up in complete agony. My left eye was puffed up and throbbing and I looked like I'd lost a fight. I vaguely remembered that something had irri-tated my eye at the opening session of the IOC's eighty-eighth congress the night before. It ached all through the operations committee that morning, and afterward I finally called Dr. Daly for help. He sent me to an ophthalmologist at the USC village clinic who removed a sliver of glass that had somehow lodged there. Relief. The pain ceased almost immediately.

But there was another kind of pain I had to endure. Joe was scheduled to run a torch kilometer in Laguna Beach that evening and wanted Ginny and me to be there. We wanted to go, but it was impossible.

"Will I see you later down at the beach house?" he had asked while stopping at the hotel before heading south.

Ginny and I exchanged unhappy glances. She'd tried to persuade me to drop everything and go. I was tempted. But I had a report to deliver to the IOC, a meeting with Mario Vázquez Raña, and had promised to be at the LAOOC's re-ception honoring the IOC that evening.

"Joe, you know I'd rather watch you run than do any-thing else," I said. We were in the bedroom. I sat next to him on the bed and put my arm around him. His face fell. "You know that thousands of people are pulling me in different di-rections. I have to be there for them."

I felt like hell. I should be there for Joe. It didn't make me feel any better knowing that his sisters and the Devores and other family friends would cheer him on. Watching tears fill Ginny's eyes made it unbearable. She was torn too, but felt she should be by my side.

Vicki called later that night.

"Joe was sensational," she said. "He was so proud. The neighbors all showed up and we had a beach party after-ward."

"Did you take pictures?" I asked.

"Everybody took pictures and we got it on videotape."

Ginny was on the extension and said, "Good. We'll watch it after the Games and have our own party." Vicki knew we'd miss her run also. She was scheduled to carry the torch in downtown Los Angeles a few hours before opening ceremonies.

First thing the next morning I met with Samaranch. Three Libyan journalists had been denied visas into the United States, and the small Libyan delegation had threatened to pull out unless they got an explanation.

Bill Hussey and Ed Best reported that the FBI had investigated the so-called journalists and recommended that their requests for visas be rejected. The implication was that they were suspected terrorists. There were also reports about a Libyan plan to unfurl a PLO flag during the opening ceremony. All things considered, I wouldn't miss the six-member Libyan delegation, and I told Samaranch that.

Later that morning, Nadia Comaneci met the world media at a press conference at the main press center. More than six hundred journalists attended, making it the largest news conference to date. It was my first meeting with Nadia and I found her charming. She spoke very little English and relied heavily on Agnes Mura's language skills.

As soon as she was introduced, reporters asked her if she was in Los Angeles to run the torch into the Coliseum. Through Mura, she said, "I would be very honored, but I have not heard anything of the sort. Mr. Ueberroth has the final decision on it."

When asked if the runner might be someone who would embarrass the boycotting nations, I replied, "No. We would not do anything to hurt anyone's feelings. It will be someone everyone will recognize."

Nadia was nervous at first, but rose to the occasion. With Mura's expert help, she handled most questions well, including those about Bela Karoly, her former coach. Karoly had defected to the United States after his success with Comaneci and was currently coaching America's best gymnast, Mary Lou Retton. This was a touchy subject because there had been reports that Karoly's defection caused Nadia much anguish. A movie that had recently aired on television depicted her as overweight and depressed to the point of suicide.

A question about the movie disturbed her and she inhaled deeply before answering. Mura tried to console her.

"Smile, Nadia," she said. "Make those cameras click away."

Comaneci regained her composure and said, "I haven't seen the film. From what I have heard, it contains a lot of things that aren't true."

Toward the end of the news conference, reporters began pressing me about problems we faced on the eve of the Games. I explained the Libyan matter and shifted to other African team problems. A group of African athletes had attended a pre-Olympic training camp in Georgia and lost much of their equipment when their bus caught fire. We had replaced their uniforms. At the UCLA village the day before, our security people thought they had their first defection—an athlete from Mali. It turned out the athlete merely wanted information on how to become an exchange student.

More serious was what happened to the playing floor at the forum. It had been damaged when a careless worker who was lowering the huge scoreboard neglected to stop it before it crashed into the middle of the basketball court. We shifted training schedules and repaired the floor.

After the press conference, a $2 million drug testing facility, which we paid for and turned over to UCLA, was dedicated in honor of Paul Ziffren. This was the fifth IOC certified drug-testing laboratory in the world. The others were in Cologne, Moscow, Montreal, and London. From there I dropped in on Richard Bretzing, special agent in charge of the Los Angeles FBI office, for more information on the Libyan journalists.

David Wolper, in the meantime, had the final dress rehearsal for the opening ceremony at the Coliseum. He had opened it to the families of the nine thousand volunteers, some twenty thousand people. We excluded members of the media and were roundly criticized for it. Many had demanded a preview.

Back at the Biltmore, I noticed something very familiar showing on the bank of televisions.

"Is that what I think it is?" I asked the staff people who gathered there. The answer was yes.

I picked up the hot line.

"Roone," I said, "could you cut the cord to the press center?"

ABC's live feed was being shown all over town, including the press center where I was told several thousand reporters were getting a preview of the ceremony.

By July 27, the day before opening ceremonies, I planned to announce our deal with ABC. We had verbally agreed to refund $20 million of the $35 million ABC still owed.

But, first, at a meeting of the commissioners and senior staff that morning at 6:15, Usher and I announced we had several thousand opening ceremonies tickets to distribute to deserving staff and volunteers.

Usher and I had debated this for days. He feared people would take their eye off the ball; I insisted it would boost morale and encourage people to work even harder. Those at the meeting were thrilled and I knew it would send waves of happiness through our army. Our only condition was that everybody had to be in uniform.

Before leaving, I briefed Mike Mitchell, our vice-president of venue development, on the ABC talks so he could finalize the deal later that morning. All it required was a handshake and I asked him to page me when the deal was ready for signature.

By 2 P.M. we still didn't have a deal with ABC. I had received two important messages: The ABC session was still in progress, and the six-person Libyan delegation had left for Tripoli. I called John King, president of First Interstate Bank, while waiting for the press conference to begin at the main press center. Since it was Friday afternoon and banks would soon close, I asked him to cut a $20 million cashier's check made out to ABC Sports.

I was handed a note during the middle of the press conference. It read: "No deal." I was angry and managed to bluff through the rest of the press conference and an interview with Howard Cosell. Then I made a beeline to the hotel.

"What the hell happened?" I asked Arledge as soon as I got him on the hot line. "Why did your people screw up the deal?"

Arledge hemmed and hawed. ABC had reneged. He told

me ABC refused to go with a ceiling. They wanted insurance against a ratings disaster.

People within the Olympic Movement had told me for years that ABC would turn on the organizing committee at the last moment. Naïvely, I thought we had a solid relationship and ABC would stick by us.

"I'll talk to you after the ratings are in." I slammed down the phone and picked up another.

"Paul," I said to Paul Ziffren, "whatever you do, don't go to the ABC dinner tonight." This was tough for Ziffren. The dinner at Chasen's, a fashionable Beverly Hills restaurant, was for ABC's board of directors, many of whom were clients and friends of Ziffren's. He protested but once I explained what had happened, he understood.

I was expected at the pre-Olympic gala at the Hollywood Bowl that evening, but I was too keyed up to go. There was also the opening ceremonies speech I had to write, so I asked Ginny to go in my place. She had entertained the wives of national Olympic committee members at Lawry's California Center all afternoon and was exhausted. I didn't envy her. She had been escorting Juan Antonio Samaranch's wife, Bibis, all week and, along with Jo Usher and Mickey Ziffren, had organized entertainment and tours for Olympic family wives.

While composing the speech with David Israel and Amy Quinn, Ed Best called with tragic news. A maniac driver had run down dozens of people on the sidewalks of Westwood, just a few blocks from the entrance to the UCLA village.

"Some athletes may have been involved," Best said. "LAPD is on the scene. I'll get back to you when I have more information."

My heart stopped. We turned on each of the networks to await further word. I wondered if this was related to the massacre in San Diego County, where some lunatic gunned down men, women, and children at a McDonald's restaurant. Even though the San Diego police chief had denied any connection between that incident and the Olympic Games, local authorities feared it would inspire a rash of copycat episodes.

Best later reported that no athletes were among the injured, but a few members of the Olympic Marching Band were hurt and had been admitted to the hospital—all but one with minor injuries. The band, comprised of youngsters from colleges and universities from around the country, was to perform in the opening ceremonies. I watched the late-night news with horror. The debris and confusion in Westwood were chilling.

Best called shortly after midnight with an update. According to Chief Gates, he said, the incident wasn't related to the Games or to the McDonald's massacre. Nonetheless, for that and for many other reasons, sleep was difficult. I tossed and turned all night. So did Ginny. At the crack of dawn, we were up having coffee and watching a spectacular sunrise. I watched from the window.

"This is it," Ginny said.

"I can't wait for it to be over," I said.

"It's still exciting," she said. "It'll be great. Wait and see."

"I hope so. It's nerveracking. The pressure is almost unbearable."

Ginny joined me and we watched in silence for a moment. "At least we have a beautiful day," she said.

One by one the staff began to trickle in. You could sense the tension. No one could sit still.

"Joel," I said to Rubenstein, "do you have more information about last night?"

"No," he said.

"Get an update from Best. David," Israel was next, "make sure the Reagan event works perfectly. The schedule's set, no changes. Don't let them thug you. Who's in the box this evening, Lucie?"

"I don't know, Peter, who?"

"Very funny," I laughed. It cut through some of the tension. Lucie Gikovich then produced a seating chart, which I checked.

"Amy, have you and Perelman distributed tickets to the press?" I asked.

"Perelman has taken care of the international press and I covered the locals," she replied.

Since we had held back a surplus of opening ceremonies tickets, we offered a few to each of those who had covered us regularly. It was a gesture of appreciation—nothing more. Being sensitive to the media's wariness of gifts, we made it a point to explain to each that we neither expected nor wanted anything in return.

I asked David Simon if Governor George Deukmejian would join us in the president's box.

"No," he replied. "He's adamant about sitting in the stands with his family."

Rubenstein returned. "One band member is still in the hospital," he said. "She'll be okay but won't make the ceremony tonight."

"Send her flowers from the LAOOC and make sure everything is done to make her comfortable."

"What do you want me to do with Samaranch?" Rubenstein asked.

"He needs more tickets. Make sure he gets them and everything else he needs. The same goes for Monique."

"Monique has plenty of tickets for the secretariat," Rubenstein said. "But she'd holding back—she doesn't want everyone to go, only her favorites."

"Joel," I said, "why do I need to know that?"

Rubenstein shrugged.

I looked around for Dick Sargent. "Where's Dick?"

"He's with his family," Israel said.

"Page him," I said, "and have him check in. I may need him."

By 11 A.M. I was checking on preparations and practicing my speech at the Coliseum where Wolper took me through my paces. As we walked through the stadium, I noticed hundreds of young kids taping plastic bags to seats. There was a box of bags at the end of each row.

"What are they doing?" I asked.

"They're distributing the stunt cards," Wolper said. "Our stunt's going to make Moscow's look like chopped liver."

In Moscow, the army had practiced months to pull off more than a thousand different card stunts. It was a marvelous demonstration of military discipline. We knew we couldn't duplicate their stunts, so Wolper decided, in his words, "to blow them away with one giant card trick."

Just then I noticed a youngster accidentally knock over an entire box of cards.

"Take your time," I called to him.

"It's okay, mister," he yelled back. "Nobody will know the difference."

"I'm sorry, David. What did you say about chopped liver?"

"You don't know what I've been through with these damn cards, Peter," he said. "Come with me."

In his trailer, he showed me one of the bags. Inside was a bright-red plastic pull-out with handles.

"I've got a hundred thousand of these, all different colors," he said. "Look at the wrapper."

On one side were directions in six languages; on the other, near the bottom, were printed the words "Made in Israel."

Wolper said he'd told the company that it could only print directions. As always, we were sensitive to the IOC rule forbidding commercialization at Olympic sites.

"I went berserk when I saw it," Wolper said. "I could see a section full of Arabs creating a scene over this. Or worse, Monique."

Wolper had received the cards too late to tape over the identification. When he threatened to withhold the balance of the fee due, the company agreed to a settlement: He paid only half the balance.

He smiled, "A deal's a deal."

A microphone on the floor of the Coliseum reminded me of my speech. Wolper must have read my mind.

"What are you going to say tonight?" he asked.

"I'm going back to the hotel to figure that out," I said. The speech was weighing heavily on my mind. Speaking before ninety thousand people and a television audience of half the world's population was intimidating. I had two minutes to dedicate the Games to the athletes and set the right tone for the next sixteen days.

I arrived at the suite just as Vicki returned from her run with the torch. She was wringing wet.

"It's the most exciting thing I've ever done," she said.

I was sorry I'd missed it. She was one of the last runners. She'd received the flame from Bill Simon and had passed it to Anita DeFrantz.

Ed Best called again. The FBI and the LAPD had reports that nasty elements were going to seize the torch before it arrived at the Coliseum. Both agencies were ready to roll— over each other. The FBI's hostage rescue team had moved into the LAPD's command post near the Coliseum and didn't wait for an invitation. Best knew the flame had arrived at the Coliseum around noon but checked to make sure it was still there. He then notified the agencies and tensions eased. Everybody was wired very tight.

Meanwhile, Harry Usher joined President and Mrs. Reagan at the USC village where the president wished the U.S. team well. Setting this event had been a month-long hassle. The White House staff had wanted Reagan to address the team just before the opening ceremonies. Wolper nixed that. He wanted all the athletes in the sports arena, the athletes' staging area, two hours early. If Reagan had his way, the U.S. team would have arrived last, which would have been interpreted as special treatment for the U.S. athletes. "As the host country, they should be first to arrive," Wolper had told me, "not last."

LAOOC point man David Israel negotiated a compromise and Reagan met the athletes earlier in the day.

Ginny and I had two stops on the way to the opening. One was a reception for the Games' patrons at the University of Southern California. Each patron had anted up $25,000 for two tickets per day to the events of his choice. There were about seven hundred patrons. The funds from the program enabled thousands of kids to attend the Games each day. The other was a reception hosted by Dr. Armand Hammer at the Museum of Natural History in Exposition Park.

At 3:15 P.M., while mingling at the Hammer reception, I said to Ginny, "It's time to go."

We walked hand in hand across the park, which was jammed with people. Families were camped out on the lawns having picnics. The concession stands were beautifully decorated. People stopped me to shake my hand; others waved and called out greetings. Ginny tightened her grip.

We entered the Coliseum through a special entrance. Up in the press box, which had been converted into the president's box, I made the rounds, greeting IOC people, LAOOC board members, and sponsors. I purposely avoided all of ABC's board of directors except Frank Carey who was also chairman of IBM.

There were complaints about excessive security precautions being taken at two VIP entrances. Because of Reagan's imminent appearance, unknown to us the Secret Service had stationed magnetometers for weapons detection. This created long lines and short tempers, one being Gates's. When I asked Best about it, he told me Gates had shouted over his hand-held radio, "Get those damn things out of here. We are facing panic in the entrances." The Secret Service shut them down.

When President and Mrs. Reagan made their entrance, Ginny and I greeted them and sat next to the Samaranchs. At about 3:50 the Coliseum was practically filled. We were on schedule and everything was going well—or so I thought.

Wolper came over at that point and whispered, "I don't know how to tell you this, Peter. Don't change the expression on your face. There may be a bomb in the peristyle end and we may not be able to light the torch. The LAPD bomb squad is on the scene."

A knot formed in my chest and I asked Wolper to keep me posted. Ten minutes later he gave me the thumbs up and on cue church bells all over Los Angeles began chiming. A voice boomed over the loudspeaker: "Ladies and gentlemen, welcome to the Games of the Twenty-third Olympiad."

I later found out that an ABC technician had opened an electrical control box to make last-minute changes in the wiring, and in the process he'd severed one line and added one.

When another technician spotted the rewiring, he alerted security. The LAPD bomb squad was on the scene almost immediately and inspected the wiring without alarming the crowd. Considering the circumstances, they did a helluva job.

Wolper's production was everything he had promised—an emotional outpouring of friendship and the story of America set to music. It was the perfect way to welcome the greatest athletes in the world. It was Hollywood at its best: glamorous but not glitzy; patriotic but not corny.

After the church bells, trumpeters and typanists played the Los Angeles Olympic theme. As those notes faded, five skywriting airplanes formed the word "welcome" across the southern California sky. Young women passed out flowers, each bearing a note of welcome. Out of the peristyle end a man in a jet pack electrified the crowd by flying through the air and landing on the floor of the Coliseum.

While a 1,000-member choir and a 60-piece orchestra performed "Welcome," specially written for the ceremony, more than 1,200 of the Olympic drill team danced a routine using five-foot-tall white and gold helium balloons as props. The balloons were released when the number ended.

The eight-hundred-member Olympic Marching Band entered the Coliseum through the crowd, signaling the beginning of "Music of America." This spectacle was the part that brought to life America's history through its music.

At the conclusion of that presentation, the announcer instructed the audience to locate the plastic stunt card at their seats. "Five," he said, "four, three, two, one." More than ninety thousand people raised their cards on cue and the stadium was transformed into the flags of 140 nations.

The president's box was bulletproof, so the sounds of the music were muffled and it was hard to get a feel for the crowd's enthusiasm. Ginny and I went to the other side of the box where the windows were open. It seemed to be a different ceremony.

We were standing behind Lord and Lady Killanin when eighty-four white baby grand pianos magically rolled out of the peristyle end for George Gershwin's "Rhapsody in Blue."

Killanin, who had attended every Olympics since 1948, turned to me and said, "This is simply the best I've ever seen."

Then came the athletes' march, and when the team from the People's Republic of China entered the stadium, the audience erupted in cheers. The entire crowd of 92,665 stood and applauded. It was a grand welcome.

Nadia Comaneci sat in the open section of the box with Agnes Mura. When it was Romania's turn, I grabbed each of their hands and held on through another standing ovation. Nadia isn't known for showing emotion, but she did that day: Tears streamed down her cheeks. She was proud of her country and I was too. I was also proud of the way the people of southern California embraced all the athletes. The last team to enter was the United States—and the crowd went wild.

That was my cue. Samaranch and I walked onto the field to deliver our remarks. I spoke of peace and friendship.

"Before you stands the finest group of young men and women ever to assemble in the history of sport," I said. "They represent the best that this world has to offer. They represent the best hope for the future of mankind. Athletes from one hundred and forty nations gather here today to honor their own countries and the Olympic Movement. . . ."

A mention of the torch relay brought spontaneous applause. "The success of this torch run has exceeded our fondest dreams. Millions and millions of our fellow Americans stood along the roadsides, cheering the runners and thereby becoming part of the Olympic Movement. These Americans had two messages to give to the world. The first was an enormous rekindling of pride in our own country, the United States of America. And more important, these millions and millions of people turned out along the way to express a friendship and a love and a caring for all nations of the world. . . .

"We wish to make no political statement. We wish only to show hospitality and friendship and make a better world if we can."

Samaranch noted the record number of nations participating in his remarks and thanked the volunteers. The crowd heartily applauded when he said, "Our thoughts also go to those athletes who have not been able to join us." I thought his statement was a very dignified way of recognizing those who had been hurt most by the Soviet boycott.

Reagan then declared the Games open. He was the first U.S. president to do so. Charles Curtis, vice-president to Herbert Hoover, opened the 1932 Games; then-Vice-President Richard M. Nixon opened the 1960 Squaw Valley Winter Olympics; and Vice-President Walter Mondale did the same at Lake Placid in 1980.

Ten U.S. Olympians and Bill Thorpe, Jr., carried the Olympic flag into the Coliseum. The Olympians were Bruce Jenner, Dr. Sammy Lee, Pat McCormick, Billy Mills, John Naber, Parry O'Brien, Al Oerter, Mack Robinson, Richard Sandoval, and Wyomia Tyus. This was new. In the past the flag was accompanied by a military escort. Four thousand homing pigeons were released as the band played the Olympic hymn and the flag was raised.

Then out of the tunnel sprinted Gina Hemphill, holding the torch high. It was electric. She was radiant. The music was triumphant. I was frozen and held my breath. Ginny held my hand, and I prayed that Rafer Johnson would make it. As Gina entered the home stretch of her lap around the track, athletes crowded the lanes and slowed her progress. Rafer waited patiently. When she reached him and passed the torch, the crowd, recognizing who he was, raised the decibel level another notch. I thought my heart would stop.

Three days earlier, Johnson had told Wolper he was hurting. He'd overtrained and had shin splints. Wolper beseeched him to try the run one more time. The next day, Johnson did and made it all the way up the ninety-six steps—for the first time. When he finished, he embraced Wolper and wept in his arms. Wolper, however, had a back-up for everything, even for Rafer. If he faltered, Bruce Jenner was prepared to assist.

As Rafer started up the 50-degree incline, I counted each step. Not once did he falter. He was magnificent. He turned and faced the crowd when he reached the top. I wondered what the view was like. He raised the torch and ignited a fuse that propelled the flame through the Olympic rings to the caldron high atop the Coliseum. Incredible. A twenty-one-goosebump salute, as Wolper had promised.

To end the show a young, aspiring singer, Vicki McClure, a supermarket checker, sang "Reach Out and Touch" while the athletes and fans joined hands in celebration of the moment and the moments to come.

I left a message on EMS for each sports commissioner before the day ended. "The first commissioner has come through. Now it's your turn. Good luck." I signed it "PVU."

Finally the athletes took center stage. On the first day of competition, July 29, Samaranch and I attended the first gold medal ceremony at the shooting competition at Prado Recreation Area in San Bernardino. It went to Xu Haifeng of China, the winner of the free pistol competition. It was China's first gold medal ever and a perfect way to start the Games.

The commissioner of shooting, Robert Petersen, had joined the committee late but had caught up quickly. He's a publishing giant and also owns one of Los Angeles' finest restaurants, Scandia. As I looked at the lavish buffet in the VIP lounge, I wondered how the restaurant was faring since Petersen had moved Scandia's chef to the shooting site. Once the secret was out, Olympic officials made it a point to visit shooting just to sample the cuisine.

It didn't take long for the U.S. team to win its first gold medal. In Mission Viejo that afternoon, about 80 miles south of the shooting venue, Connie Carpenter-Phinney barely beat teammate Rebecca Twigg in the first women's cycling road race in history. It was also the first gold medal the U.S. had ever won in cycling. This event, conducted along 79.2 kilometers of public thoroughfare in Orange County and far from commissioner Pete Siracusa's base of operations at the velodrome at California State College, Dominguez Hills, had worried me. But Siracusa had a long reach and ran it well.

Our only problem was a lack of telephones for reporters. Since it was off the beaten track, we had underestimated the media interest and were caught short. However, Rich Perelman's venue press chief, Judy Stolpe, reacted brilliantly and arranged for reporters to make calls from private homes. That was the kind of ingenuity which was bound to make the Games a success.

The next morning a local columnist wrote I had intentionally kept Mark Spitz from participating in the opening ceremonies. Although Spitz was never quoted directly in the story—that came later—it was implied we had snubbed him because he'd been involved in a licensing dispute with us.

I was flabbergasted and instinctively knew this story would travel around the globe. I had fought Monique Berlioux for months to have Olympians carry the IOC flag. Now one had turned it into a *cause célèbre*.

David Israel and Jeanne D'Amico, one of the first LAOOC employees who ran our speaker's bureau, had compiled a list of prospective Olympians. Our only criterion was that flagbearers be chosen from those who'd helped us along the way, either as members of the Olympic spirit team or as part of the speaker's bureau.

Spitz was superb as an athlete. He'd won seven swimming gold medals and was the hero of the 1972 Munich Games. He had also won two golds, a silver, and a bronze at Mexico City in 1968. But Spitz never made our list. He wasn't a member of the spirit team and never gave a speech on behalf of the LAOOC. I'd been told by our swimming people that whenever we asked his help, he demanded a fee. The licensing dispute had nothing to do with it. According to our lawyers, a business partner of Spitz's was involved in litigation with us, not Spitz.

One of the things I most admired about Rafer Johnson was his desire to give something back to the Olympic Games. The same can be said for those who carried the flag. One Olympian as deserving as any was Donna DeVarona, another swimming gold medalist. She had worked for the LAOOC and had conceived the spirit team. She'd also testified before Congress on our behalf for the coin program legislation. She was a tireless and dedicated volunteer. But as an ABC commentator she was eliminated to avoid a conflict of interest. Unlike Spitz, who also worked the broadcast booth for ABC, she didn't complain.

The best news that morning was no traffic. The feared traffic gridlock didn't materialize. Monday morning rush-hour traffic was a breeze and probably smoother than it had been for decades. The only congestion appeared around Hollywood Park in Inglewood, where we held our second Ticket Faire.

With a hundred thousand Games tickets remaining, lines a quarter-mile long wrapped around the clubhouse creating a few traffic problems for those attending basketball across the street at the forum.

At swimming, Richard Perelman feared a photographers' revolt over the poor vantage points specified by the fire marshal. Perelman said the photographers had a valid complaint, so that afternoon Ginny and I took in the swimming competition and invited the fire chief as our guest. Our seats were in the middle of the photographers' section and it didn't take long for the fire chief to understand the problem. He immediately freed an area on the deck that was ideally suited for photographers. Within minutes the photographers had scattered to their new positions and we were sitting alone.

Jay Flood, the swimming commissioner, showed Ginny and me around the venue and pointed out where Ed Keen had reinforced the spectator stands beyond code specifications. As the U.S. team began building up its collection of medals, the stands shook and I was grateful for Keen's foresight. Flood, as expected, had the competition under control.

"Can your people hold out?" I asked, a question I would repeatedly ask over the next two weeks.

"Absolutely," Flood replied.

As Ginny and I left the venue, I made it a point to thank every law enforcement officer on site.

We celebrated Lord Killanin's birthday that evening with champagne cocktails. Killanin was in good humor and said he was just glad to be alive. At a reception a few nights earlier, he'd choked on a piece of food and was saved by the quick reflexes of an LAPD officer who administered the Heimlich maneuver.

Killanin, who had been president of the IOC when Los Angeles was awarded the Games, was a great friend and supporter. To show our gratitude, we broke an IOC rule and awarded him a Games gold medal. He had tears in his eyes when he saw the gift.

"This should be between us," I said with a smile. "I wouldn't want to incur Monique's wrath."

"I wouldn't either," Killanin replied.

While the athletes were hitting their strides, the LAPD got a serious workout on the fourth day. An alert Blue Beret became suspicious of a car doggedly trailing an athletes' bus on the freeway and notified the LAPD. LAPD officers were on the scene within minutes and took the driver into custody. The driver was armed and had explosive devices and martial arts weapons stored in the trunk. The suspect was a self-proclaimed "warrior of the people."

The LAPD was called out in force again on August 1 to provide heavy security for a memorial service honoring the eleven Israeli athletes murdered in Munich. The Jewish community in Los Angeles had petitioned the IOC to recognize the Israeli dead before the Games. But the IOC wanted no part of it, claiming the request was political and would disturb certain factions of its membership.

LAOOC board member Stephen Reinhardt, a federal judge, didn't buy that explanation and, with our help and that of Mayor Bradley, arranged a service at city hall, attended by several hundred leading citizens and twenty-five members of the Israeli delegation. It was a poignant tribute to athletes who'd arrived at an Olympic Games to compete but had returned home in coffins. Such a tragedy should never be forgotten and, as I watched police helicopters hover overhead, I knew it wouldn't. I counted the days until the end of the Games.

Ginny and I had a regular routine by this time. After breakfast and an early morning staff meeting, I'd head off to the marina center for the operations meeting and visit a venue or two during the day. Ginny would visit other venues with Jo Usher. The object of the venue visits was to boost morale and stoke the volunteer furnace. I could never underestimate the value of the volunteers and from day one I worried about burnout.

From the marina center command post, Usher fixed every problem that came his way. Before the Games we thought we'd be inundated with all sorts of nightmares. By the middle of the first week, the operations meetings were light. And it wasn't long before Usher could get out and visit venues on his own.

After the operations meeting on Thursday, August 2, I visited old friends at the water polo site at Pepperdine University in Malibu. This had to be one of the prettier Olympic sites of all time. Raleigh Runnels pool, overlooking the Pacific, sparkled in the summer sunshine. I knew many of the volunteers from my water polo days at San Jose State and the Olympic Club. Some didn't recognize me, but not because I hadn't seen them in a long time: They didn't expect to see me in the blue and yellow driver's uniform.

From there I traveled down the coast by helicopter to Loyola Marymount University to visit the weightlifting competition. As I approached the entrance, I saw my son, Joe, working inside the public information booth, giving directions to a confused spectator. He was surprised to see me.

"What are you doing in that uniform?" Joe asked.

"The same thing you are," I said. "Working."

Joe wore a green and yellow service uniform, which he loathed. He'd pleaded with me to get him a blue and gray staff uniform, but I had turned him down.

"Can you take a break?" I asked.

"I can't right now," he said. "I'm the only one here. If I can I'll meet you inside."

"Are you getting tired?" I asked. Joe, like everybody else, was working long hours.

"No," he said, shaking his head. "I'm going strong. I feel like the designated hitter. They put me in a different place every day and I love it."

Donn Moomaw, a former UCLA all-American football player, greeted me at the door. We sat with Al Oerter and his wife. Oerter had won gold medals in the discus at four straight Olympic Games and had hoped to compete in Los Angeles before being forced out by injury. He was a track-and-field buff and looked forward to the competition beginning the next day.

"I'm afraid there's going to be more competition on the freeways than in the Coliseum," I said. Friday, August 3, was Doom's Day, or Black Friday as the media had called it ever

since we printed the first schedule years before. It was the first
day of track and field. Boxing and swimming were also in full
swing in the Exposition Park-Coliseum area and everybody—
traffic planners, law enforcement officers, reporters, and residents—predicted gloom and doom.

"I plan to make it a point to get there early," Oerter
said.

"If I were you, I'd get there tonight."

Later that day I expressed worry over traffic to several
local reporters. Traffic up to this point had been practically
nonexistent and I wanted to keep it that way. I didn't want
the public to get complacent and revert to normal driving pat-
terns on our busiest day. I had hoped by hyping Black Friday,
it would keep motorists out of their cars.

We had had a ticketing problem the day before at the
morning session of the modern pentathlon. Shooting and
cross country were scheduled for the final day. Since few spectators ever attend the shooting, we coupled the two events for
ticketing purposes, figuring that two people and a rattlesnake
would show up for the shooting session. We only had seating
for several hundred. Roughly eight thousand people had
stormed the gates and we weren't prepared for them. We ac-
commodated as many as we could.

At the briefing, Mary Ann Milbourne of the *Los Angeles
Daily News* asked what we'd do for the angry ticket purchasers and I told her we would refund their money. I told
them I was shocked by the turnout at Coto de Caza, where
modern pentathlon was held.

"If you think that's bizarre," I said, "we had to fire an
employee for scalping field hockey tickets." They laughed,
but it was true.

Ken Reich of the *Los Angeles Times* had heard a report
that the IOC had protested ABC's chauvinistic coverage of
the Games, which I confirmed. Samaranch had received complaints from several team attachés about ABC's emphasis on
the U.S. team. By this time, the United States was running
away with the medal count.

We'd made a mistake by not providing the international

feed into the villages. Athletes there could see only the ABC feed, the same programming that went to the U.S. public. Many of the foreign athletes complained of ABC's U.S. bias. International broadcasters were featuring their athletes in the same way, but their feeds were unavailable to the athletes. Samaranch and Berlioux realized this when they visited the international broadcast center and said so.

In a conversation with David Wolper, he said, "For two hundred twenty-five million dollars, they can show damn well what they please." ABC was obligated to show the U.S. public what it wanted to see—Americans winning gold medals. The ratings had gone through the roof. I was glad ABC had reneged on the deal. It had made its August 1 installment of $20 million and only owed $15 million more. There would be no refund.

Dr. Tony Daly came by my suite after the briefing to report on the medical side of the Games. The volunteer doctors, nurses, and other personnel were doing great. His concern was doping. The first athlete to test positive was a Japanese volleyball player whose test showed ephedrine, a substance banned by the IOC. He'd been administered the substance in an herbal tea by his trainer.

"I don't question the test," Daly said, "just their methods. The IOC medical commission conducts its interview like an inquisition."

"How so?" I asked.

"The commission decided the trainer was at fault rather than the athlete and banned him for these Games and the next two. The trainer insisted the cold remedy was a common one and was unaware it contained a banned substance. They treated him like a criminal. It was tough to watch."

Daly had a running feud with two of the medical commission's leading advocates of drug testing, Dr. Manfred Doenike and Dr. Arnold Beckett, whom he referred to as the "hunters." Although Daly opposed the use of any illegal drugs as much as anybody else, he objected to their vigilante methods.

"Do you think there'll be a lot of positives?" I asked.

"I don't think so," he said. "Fifteen at the most and that

certainly won't distract from the Games. No matter what, it's out of our hands. Prince de Merode, the chairman of the IOC medical commission, runs the show. He's a dictator about it and controls all the results."

Unbelievable. No traffic on Black Friday. It was a miracle. The traffic organizers all deserved gold medals. For our part, Alan Epstein and Bill Forsythe kept the athletes and Olympic family moving smoothly around the city. Epstein, a young lawyer from New York, was an operations planner when he first joined us in the early years. He moved up the ladder swiftly and when we needed a leader in transportation I didn't hesitate to put him in charge. Forsythe, his second in command, provided the nuts and bolts and coordinated our planning with the public agencies.

Early that evening, Ginny and I attended a reception at the French consul general's home at the urging of Charlotte Hyde, our liaison to Monique Berlioux and a Frenchwoman to the core. I had been selected to receive the French *Légion d'honneur* and Hyde demanded I be there personally to accept it. This was a great honor and I wished I'd had the opportunity to enjoy the moment more.

The best part of the evening was yet to come. Ginny had put out an all-points bulletin for the kids to meet us at Pauley Pavilion for the women's all-around gymnastics finals. As it had been since Olga Korbut burst onto the scene in 1972, women's gymnastics was a hot event. This time the featured stars were two adorable teenagers—Mary Lou Retton of the USA and Romania's Ecaterina Szabo. They were spectacular.

During a break I introduced my daughter Heidi to Nadia Comaneci in the VIP lounge. Nadia excused herself after a few friendly words and dashed off to watch Szabo perform her final floor exercise. While I chatted with Hyla and Dick Bertea, co-commissioners of gymnastics, the entire stadium went dark. The crowd held steady and didn't panic for those few minutes. Wayne Ichiyasu, our driver and security guard, quickly ushered Ginny, Vicki, Keri, and Joe outside. Competition resumed when the lights went on. I felt bad for Szabo because the momentary power shortage would surely affect her routine. (Szabo won the silver medal, losing narrowly to Mary Lou Retton.)

Heidi and I caught up with the others outside and we went to Peppone's for a late dinner. We spent the rest of the evening talking about our move to New York.

Over the weekend—the midway point—I continued making the rounds of venues. On Saturday, it was handball at California State University, Fullerton, and track and field at the Coliseum. I would have been lost without a helicopter. As it was, I arrived at the Coliseum just in time to see Carl Lewis win the 100 meter, the first of his four gold medals that equaled the great Jesse Owens. Lewis would attract much criticism during the next week. It started after the 100 meters when a spectator handed Lewis a gargantuan American flag to carry on his victory lap. The media speculated that the spectator had been planted and reprimanded Lewis for show boating.

What *was* spontaneous was Myrella Moses' emotional outpouring during her husband's spectacular victory in the 400-meter hurdles. Filmmaker Bud Greenspan later showed me his film of Myrella crying and wringing her hands throughout Edwin Moses' race. Next to her, IAAF president Primo Nebiolo provided consolation.

"How did you get Myrella next to Primo?" I asked Greenspan.

"It wasn't easy," he laughed. "At first Primo didn't want to do it. I told him she was a basket case and would have a nervous breakdown unless somebody with his strength was there to comfort her. That didn't work. Then I told him it would be good for sport. 'No,' Primo said shaking his head. I finally laid it on the line. 'Primo, millions of people will see this film and you will be prominently featured.' Without hesitating, he said, 'Well, if it will be good for the film.'"

The next day I headed north with Ginny for the final day of rowing at Lake Casitas to join the Ushers and Samaranch. They had left Los Angeles first and early morning fog in Ventura County had prevented their helicopter from landing at the site. Rather than return to Los Angeles, the pilot had landed in someone's large backyard. Then the owner of the property had graciously given them a lift to Casitas. Ginny and I were more fortunate and didn't have any landing problems.

Eight gold medals were awarded that day to eight different countries—Canada, Great Britain, New Zealand, Federal Republic of Germany, Italy, Romania, USA, and Finland. Rowing was one of the sports most affected by the Eastern bloc pullout, as the East Germans and Soviets were expected to dominate. I had always thought more countries would win medals because of the boycott and this was proof positive.

After the competition, Peter Jordano, mayor of the University of California, Santa Barbara, village, took us on a tour of the beautiful campus overlooking the Pacific Ocean. No wonder the rowing and canoeing athletes resisted rejoining their delegations in Los Angeles after the competitions.

Wherever I went old friends were in charge and were making the Games successful. They were in the trenches, their sleeves rolled up, willing to take the first bullets. Jordano, like most of the commissioners and envoys, was one of them.

While wandering through the village, Ginny and I caught a glimpse of Joan Benoit on television winning the women's marathon with a wide grin and easy stride. She had overcome a serious knee injury to win this race. But the biggest winners were women long-distance runners who'd been kept out of the Olympics far too long. One of the LAOOC's greatest achievements was convincing the IOC to include this race in its program at its Executive Board meeting in February 1981.

I found out a few hours later about the tormented finish of Gabriela Anderson-Schiess, a Swiss entrant who made her home in Colorado, and wondered if it would undo the good Benoit had done earlier. Her ordeal was a picture shown repeatedly throughout the day and it wasn't pretty.

Suffering from exhaustion she maneuvered and stumbled across the racing lanes on the final lap. It took her more than fifteen minutes to finish the lap. It was difficult to watch and like many viewers I questioned the decision of the doctors to allow her to finish the race.

"How is she?" I asked Tony Daly that evening.

"She's fine," he said. "She was given intravenous fluids and was up and around thirty minutes later."

"Was letting her finish the right thing to do?"

"Without a doubt." Daly said. "Osher was on the spot. She was sweating, which showed she wasn't in danger of hypothermia, and she shied away each time somebody from the medical team approached her."

Dr. Eugene Osher, the chief medical officer for the marathons, was a partner of Daly's and well respected. Daly invested the same trust in the people he brought on that I had with those I selected for key roles.

Entering the final week, boosting staff and volunteer morale became top priority. It had been a long haul. So far we'd been successful and I knew the tendency would be to let down. I was reminded of the phrase "Feet, don't fail me now."

With this in mind, I warned law enforcement about the curious early departures of Eastern bloc officials at the August 7 meeting of the Olympic Law Enforcement Coordinating Committee at Piper Tech in downtown Los Angeles. A few days earlier, International Cycling Federation President Valery Syssoev had wished me continued success and farewell. It seemed odd that a federation president on a junket to one of the greatest cities in the world would leave early. Also, I told the group that IOC member Vitaly Smirnov waxed poetic about the Games and our hospitality in a thank-you note before he left on August 1.

"Are they leaving for a reason?" I asked.

They got the point that maybe the Soviets were leaving for a reason and maintained the level of security that had worked up until that time.

Competitions continued to lead the news and I continued on the venue circuit. Things had been going so well, but I still waited for the other shoe to drop. Every time someone of-

fered congratulations, I said, "So far, so good." It was like
living on the razor's edge.

During lunch with Prince Philip and equestrian commissioner Michael Morphy at Santa Anita on Thursday, August
9, I asked His Royal Highness how the competition was pro-
ceeding.

"So far, so good," he said. We all laughed. He had read
my standard response in the newspaper.

Morphy had an excellent rapport with Prince Philip. He
had hosted the prince and his daughter, Princess Anne, the
week before, at his home in Carlsbad, California, a beachside
community near Fairbanks Ranch, site of the middle day of
the three-day equestrian endurance event. Morphy and the
prince had gone for a swim when they arrived, which had
caught Scotland Yard off guard, as it is responsible for the
prince's safety. According to Morphy, the prince laughed as
he dashed into the surf and Morphy and the prince could see
the guards' discomfort.

Morphy smiled as he told me the story. "The prince said,
'This is bloody wonderful.' Then he took off and started
swimming away from shore. I'm a strong swimmer and it took
everything I had to keep up."

At a commissioners' meeting that night, Usher and I reminded a roomful of tired people that while the end was in
sight there was still a lot to do. In some sports the physical
wind down had begun. We'd already torn down cycling, modern pentathlon, shooting, and baseball and were in the process of dismantling weightlifting and yachting. We asked those
commissioners who were finished to help their colleagues.
There were three days left, ample time for catastrophe to
strike.

We had a close call at handball later that night. As spectators leaned against a railing to catch bouquets of flowers
being thrown by the gold-medal-winning women's Yugosla-
vian team, the railing collapsed and twelve people fell about
eight feet to the floor. Daly's medical team responded instan-
taneously and, fortunately, there were no serious injuries.

Mary Decker's collision with controversial South African
runner Zola Budd, who was competing for Great Britain,

made headlines around the world. It came during the finals of the 3,000 meter. Fans had been waiting for this matchup since the Olympics began. IAAF investigators on the track initially blamed Budd for the accident and disqualified her. They later reversed the decision, following a protest by the British team and a review of the films. I had watched the race from my seat in the president's box and felt bad for both Decker and Budd. But my heart really went to the winner, Maricica Puica of Romania, whose victory was overshadowed by the collision and it was a shame. She was a great runner who could have won the race regardless of the misfortune to Budd and Decker.

Those last few days passed agonizingly slowly. As closing ceremonies approached, we began receiving political pressure from the Democratic party, demanding equal time. Vice-presidential candidate Geraldine Ferraro's staff wanted her to appear at the ceremony. The Games weren't a political football and nobody needed the extra security hassles at that point. I spoke to Ms. Ferraro directly and explained our position. I invited her children or anybody else she might want to go. She understood and withdrew the request.

By August 12, I was running on empty. The support and understanding of Ginny and the kids provided the last shot of adrenaline that kept me going. If I paced, Ginny paced beside me. If I needed a lift, Vicki, Heidi, Keri, or Joe was there with a hug. Gestures, not words, pulled us all through.

Closing ceremonies were a great celebration for the athletes. I tried to celebrate with them but couldn't. Their party was over; ours wouldn't be over until the last athlete was safely on his way home.

That instinct to carry on came into play the next night, Monday, August 13. Ginny had packed our belongings and was preparing for a farewell dinner in our suite with the Samaranchs and Monique Berlioux when Ed Best called. He reported that a pipe bomb had been located in the wheel well of a Turkish athletes bus at the airport. My adrenaline began pumping like mad.

"Where are the athletes?" I asked.

"They're safe," he said. "The bomb was defused by an LAPD officer on the spot."

"How did it get by our checks?"

"It's being investigated now."

"Something isn't right," I told him. "I don't see how this could happen. Get out to the airport immediately. Take somebody from the press department with you to make sure it doesn't get blown out of proportion."

"I'm on my way," Best said.

I relayed the news to Ginny, then turned on the television for up-to-date reports and worried. I still didn't understand how it could have happened. The buses were swept for bombs before and after every trip. The only place a bomb could be planted would be en route or at the airport where security was very tight.

Usher called from the marina center.

"The bus was completely swept at UCLA," Usher reported. "I don't like it."

"I agree," I replied. "Do you have any other details?"

Usher explained that three buses transporting the Turkish athletes arrived at the airport without a hitch. The athletes had already left the buses when the officer said he heard ticking and noticed a suspicious object in the wheel well of one of the vehicles. He disarmed the bomb by pulling off a wire.

"Gates is out there now," Usher said. "We'll see what he has to say."

Meanwhile, television reporters were on the scene describing the evacuation of approximately a thousand travelers. The airport began receiving other bomb threats and pandemonium was setting in.

I called news directors and implored them to wait until all the information was in before escalating the story. It was too late. I watched Gates cite Officer Jim Pearson for heroism on the spot. When Best called back, he was even more suspicious. The airport was back to normal by midnight.

The next morning, moments before IOC President Samaranch presented the silver medal of the Olympic Order to Mayor Bradley, LAOOC Chairman Paul Ziffren, and Harry Usher at city hall, Chief Gates confirmed our suspicions at a news conference: Pearson had planted the bomb himself.

The last athletes—two Italians—left Los Angeles Wednesday, August 15. It was over.

The family gathered that evening in Laguna Beach. We were weary, but happy. As I watched Ginny in the kitchen, I tried to remember when we had last sat down for a dinner at home. I couldn't. The kids were off by themselves in various corners of the house. Outside the sun was going down. Dinner wouldn't be served for another hour or so. I grabbed Ginny.

"Let's go for a walk," I said.

We wandered down to the beach. There was a slight chill in the air and we wrapped our arms around one another as we watched a bright red sun sink into the Pacific Ocean. I felt relaxed for the first time since May 8. We strolled through the sand arm in arm.

We were silent, both lost in our own thoughts. Mine raced through five years of confrontations and headaches. I thought of the sacrifices I had made and those I had demanded of my family. I glanced at Ginny and she smiled back.

I remembered what Horst Dassler had told Ginny and me about the fates of Olympic organizers. It was that evening we had had dinner with Monique Berlioux in Lausanne more than two years earlier. "The day after the Games," he had said, "each was left out to dry on the dock like yesterday's fish."

Just then a jogger sprinted toward us, a young man with the stride of a long-distance runner.

"Congratulations, Mr. Ueberroth," he said.

"Thanks," I said. I smiled at Ginny.

When he was well past, I heard him shout, "Hey, Mr. Ueberroth."

We turned around. "Would you do it again?"

I hugged Ginny and looked her in the eyes.

"Maybe."

EPILOGUE

Los Angeles basked in the immediate glow of the Olympic Games for several weeks. I understood the reluctance to let go—I felt the same way.

City officials, all of whom were now our friends, wanted to keep the colors of festive federalism flying and beseeched us to leave the banners in place, which we did.

If it had anything to do with the Olympics, people wanted it and that included the banners, freeway signs, pins, and a lot of equipment we used to stage the Games. More than ten thousand people showed up at the Los Angeles Convention Center two weeks after the Games to swap pins. That market thrived for another two months.

We auctioned off award stands, flagpoles, massage tables, typewriters, office furniture, stadium cushions, binoculars, posters, television sets, and much more. Harry Usher even sold the uniform off his back to kick off the week-long sale in October.

We also donated more than $1 million worth of equipment and supplies—$700,000 to Los Angeles County, and the remaining to the University of California, Santa Barbara. We gave local law enforcement radio communications equipment and motorcycles.

The Olympic torch relay had netted $10.9 million, which we distributed to the YMCAs, Boys Clubs of America, Girls Clubs of America, and the Special Olympics. It was the largest fundraiser of its kind ever held.

All this was in addition to the millions of dollars' worth of facilities we left behind: the nine new Olympic tracks throughout the area; the office building and drug-testing facility at UCLA; the velodrome at California State College, Dominguez Hills; the shooting range in San Bernardino County; and the Olympic swim stadium at the University of Southern California.

In keeping with our promise of a full accounting as soon as possible after the Games, we announced on September 15 that our preliminary audit projected a surplus of $150 million. That surplus was revised to $215 million three months later. All of the surplus, as mandated by our by-laws, was distributed to youth and sports in the United States—60 percent to the United States Olympic Committee for its program and the remaining 40 percent for southern California. The Los Angeles Organizing Committee Amateur Athletics Foundation was formed by the executive committee of the LAOOC Board of Directors to administer the funds.

The size of the surplus shocked the world. Our mandate was to stage the Games at no cost to the taxpayer. That was priority number one—to have a *surplus* not a *deficit*. This required fiscal conservatism as well as prudent and responsible management. We had a detailed contingency plan covering every possible problem and cost.

Because of unknown factors, including everything from terrorist attacks to labor strikes, we never knew before the Games precisely what they would cost.

Through the years, I consistently predicted a small surplus. Had I publicly foretold larger than expected revenues early in the Games' planning, the consequences would have resulted in heavier expenses and gouging by suppliers and vendors. Every Tom, Dick, and Harry we were doing business with would have demanded a contract renegotiation.

An example of Olympic financial drain occurred at the Winter Games in Lake Placid. A week or two before the

Games, organizers predicted a $1 million surplus. However, unforeseen problems during the Games turned that projection topsy-turvy and caused Lake Placid to go $6 million into debt. This was an unexpected $7 million swing in less than a month. Factor this by ten and you get an idea of the scope of our potential downside. The only solution to problems at that late date was to throw money at them. We were lucky: Nothing happened—no massive security problems, no labor strikes, no transportation breakdowns, and no natural catastrophes.

Moreover, in almost every case our commissioners and managers came in dramatically under budget. Another unknown was the American people, whose support of the torch relay and the Games led to the phenomenal television ratings enjoyed by ABC. On the eve of the Soviet-led boycott we placed $70 million in reserve to cover potential nonpayment by ABC.

Our spring 1984 projection of $110 million in ticket revenue was $40 million short. Ticket sales and attendance skyrocketed because of public support. Almost 6 million spectators attended the Games, and they cheered 7,078 athletes from 140 nations. It was the largest Games in terms of spectators and countries represented in the Olympic Movement's history.

I find it ironic that after refusing to spend one cent on our Games, the United States is spending lots of dollars on the 1988 Olympics in Seoul, Korea, to augment the billions the Koreans plan to spend. While I wish the Seoul organizers all the luck in the world, I regret that while their Games may be paid by America, their Games won't be made in America.

Because of the size of our surplus, which I attributed greatly to the cooperation of national Olympic committees—many of which increased the size of their teams at our request to compensate for the boycotting nations—I initiated a plan to reimburse them for their stay in Los Angeles. The cost would have been $7 million, a small fraction of the surplus and a nice way to say thank you to those who made our Games great.

I felt strongly about this. To explain my position I wrote a commentary in the fall that ran on the editorial page of the *Los Angeles Times:*

Many share the credit for the success of the 1984 Games, but a large portion of it must go to those countries that responded to our call and made an investment in our ability as a nation to host them. As a result, we had a full competitive field in every sport. When Carl Lewis ran his heat in the 100-meter preliminaries—every lane was filled. Mary Lou's gold medal is more meaningful because of the grace and dignity and competitive spirits of Romania's Ecaterina Szabo. The same is true of Peter Vidmar's silver medal, because of the talents of Japan's gold medalist Koji Gushiken and the determination of China's Li Ning who won the bronze. The examples are endless, but the snapshot that lingers is a field filled with young athletes representing 140 nations at the Opening Ceremony.

In a sense, those 140 nations paid a deposit, and the time has come to return those monies as our way of saying thanks for having faith in our nation, faith in our ability to host the world's best athletes and in some respects faith in the future of our globe.

The final estimate of what those nations saved all of us cannot be calculated. How could we possibly put a price tag on the face we saved as a nation? How much is the rejuvenated and enhanced image of this country as friendly and hospitable worth? . . .

The time has come for this last goodwill gesture to be made, for us to say "thanks" and to recognize our debt to those countries who stood up for us and by us to make the Games of the XXIIIrd Olympiad worthy of remembering.

The plan was approved by the LAOOC Board of Directors in December but rejected by the United States Olympic Committee two months later.

As for the LAOOC, it was time to let go and as difficult as it was Olympic workers began moving on. On August 17, the first and largest wave of permanent employees departed the marina center, the old helicopter-assembly plant. We threw a huge party outside the Café de Coubertin to see them off. Usher had the area festooned in the trappings of the Games, and it was a warm and emotional farewell. Usher and I tried our best to thank each and every person for his efforts, devotion, and loyalty.

We had climbed the mountain together. It was long and hard and as we approached the top the air became thinner; it became painful for everybody. Coming down was equally painful. I knew many would want to stay there; others would look for other mountains. I wished them all well but warned each that there would never be another mountain like organizing and staging the Olympic Games.

Before leaving for New York and my new job in baseball the afternoon of September 27, I made a round of farewells to those staff members who remained behind to wrap up LAOOC business. I told each of them that the Tahitians don't say goodbye, they say "See you soon." On the airplane, I reflected on the people who worked on the Games. I don't think there had ever been so much ability in one place as there was those final months at our headquarters at the marina center. It was a privilege to have been a part of it.

Ginny was waiting in New York. She'd leased an apartment on Fifth Avenue across the street from Central Park. The children had returned to school: Vicki to finish her senior year at the University of Colorado, Heidi to begin her sophomore year at Vanderbilt University, and Keri and Joe were back at Cate School in Santa Barbara. Each, I knew, was a better, stronger person for having played a part in history.

Before I could unpack my bags, I had an umpires' strike to resolve. I rolled up my sleeves and studied all the issues. I sat down with Richie Phillips, the general counsel of the Major League Baseball Umpires' Association, and promised him fairness as the arbitrator between the parties if he'd bring the professional umpires back for the final games of the National League championships. That's all there was, a promise of fairness. No contracts. No witnesses. Just trust.

Phillips kept his end of the bargain and I kept mine. I intervened and ruled that the owners should award the umpires a better contract, which they got just before the start of the 1984 World Series.

I brought the same kind of trust to the table a few months later in resolving the television superstation issue. Superstations—Ted Turner's WTBS in Atlanta and the Tribune Company's WGN in Chicago—were broadcasting games into other teams' markets, peeling away potential team revenues.

When two parties negotiate, it's important that each walks away with something substantial. In this case, each did: the superstations with the blessing of the teams to continue broadcasting; and the teams with a cut of the superstations' broadcast revenues.

Larger and more complex problems continue to unfold. During my first year as commissioner of baseball, I've had to confront the financial decay prevalent among many of the teams in the major leagues. It is a serious threat.

Equally serious is drug abuse and it is imperative that we rid baseball of it for the sake of our youth, who look to baseball for role models, and the future of our country. Someone somewhere has to say "Enough is enough" to drugs. And I've done that.

Since the 1800s youngsters have grown up idolizing baseball players, and I'm determined to see that continue. Baseball must take a stand against illegal drugs, which are attacking the underbelly of our society.

This has not made me the most popular person in the game, but practicing good leadership and striving for excellence are not popularity contests. If I've learned one lesson from the Olympic experience it is that when you take risks, you inevitably ruffle feathers. When you're as committed as I am to baseball, you go ahead and ruffle them.

Last August, a labor dispute between 650 major league players and 26 owners threatened to interrupt one of the most exciting seasons in baseball history and shut down the sport that touches 30 million fans across the United States and Canada. This simply did not make any sense to me and I took the appropriate steps to curtail it, none of which pleased either side. But baseball resumed, made up the few games that were missed, and the fans once again paid rapt attention to Pete Rose's assault on Ty Cobb's record and the excitement of the game.

Baseball is an important part of the fabric of our country. People care about the game, more so than any other sport, amateur or professional. They care about the people who play it and they care about the overall welfare of the game itself. As commissioner of baseball, it's my job to make the sport better, not only for the players but also for the owners, managers, coaches, minor leaguers, and, most important, the fans.

In conclusion, I would like to repeat the philosophy with which I started this many pages ago. It is my opinion that we live in the greatest country on earth. If the people believe in our country and our fellow citizens, we can accomplish almost any worthy goal. That includes becoming more of a world citizen and bettering relations with such nations as Cuba and the Soviet Union. Those doomsayers who say "impossible" don't pay much attention to history. When I was growing up, the enemies I was told to hate were Japan and Germany. Today, they are among our staunchest allies.

Nothing stays the same. Things either progress or retrogress. We seem to sometimes underestimate the qualities of our fellow citizens. If we pull together, we can effect progress and make this a better world for our children. I'm an unabashed patriot and I'm proud of it.

THE SUPERSTARS

ALTHOUGH IT TOOK seventy-two thousand people to make the 1984 Olympic Games a success, there were many who performed exceptionally well and they deserve special mention.

At the risk of leaving somebody out—for which I apologize in advance—I asked key executives at the Los Angeles Olympic Organizing Committee to help me compile the following list of superstars.

Our criterion was to include only those who were involved with the committee and the staging of the games for at least a *full year*. Not to do so would have resulted in a list five hundred pages long.

On this list are volunteers, employees, leaders of law enforcement, key corporate sponsors, government officials, outside vendors, and sports leaders. Each person at some time during the preparation or operation of the Games stood very tall in his attempts to make the Olympic Games of 1984 a special moment in sports history.

Evelyn Hall Adams	William Anthony
Ray Aghayan	John Argue
Jennifer Chandler Ainslee	Roone Arledge
Tamas Ajan	Kathryn Arnold
Carmenza Alba	Larry Arnold
Haralambie Alexa	Patricia Arnold
Bea Alford	Yrene Asalde-Brewster
Maurice Allan	Roy Ash
Howard Allen	Nick Ashford
Joe Allen	Abdelazim Ashry
Lynda Alvarez	Ruth Atkins
Andy Anderson	Lee Aurich

Angela Avery
Cynthia Avery
Randall Backus
Marv Bader
Alan Baker
Duane Baker
Monte Baker
Dr. Lailee Bakhtiar
Laurie Bakkensen
Dee Bandur
Max Bangerter
Carmen Bank
Willie Banks
Ike Baranowicz
Neil Barbanell
John Barber
Phil Bardos
Norman Barker
Julie Barnathan
Ernie Barnes
Luciano Barra
David Barrett
Dr. Arthur Bartner
Ken Bastian
Dr. Eric Bates
Rolf Baumann
Bob Beamon
Charley Bear
Le Comte de Beaumont
Bill Bedford
Lillian Beim
Steve Beim
Ross Bell
Melissa Belote
Joann Belsey
Robert Belsey
Roy Bence
Bruno Beneck
Jeff Benjamin
Marje Bennetts
Walter Beran
Natasha Berechko

Cynthia Berentson
Dick Berg
Harvey Berg
Bess Bergmann
Barry Berkus
Monique Berlioux
Ernani Bernardi
Hal Bernson
Dick Bertea
Hyla Bertea
Alyse Best
Ed Best
Jerry Best
John Bevilaqua
Ben Biaginni
Judy Biggs
Dr. Perry Binder
Larry Binkley
Ed Birch
Ric Birch
Chuck Bittick
Dallas Bixler
Boyd Black
Jim Black
Karin Blaskowitz
Joseph Blatter
Donn Bleau
Jeff Bliss
Maury Blitz
Edward Bloch
Sherman Block
Frances Bloore
Tracey Bluhm
Shelley Blumberg
John Boesch
Thierry Boucquey
Sandy Bourne
Jim Bradley
Tom Bradley
Marvin Braude
Steve Broudy
Cathy Ferguson Brennan

John Bretza
Samuel Bretzfield
Richard Bretzing
Jack Brick
Keith Bright
George Broder
Paul Broussard
Carroll Brown
Earl Brown
Willie Brown
Phil Brubaker
Jane Bryan
Angela Buchanan
Gail Bugliosi
Bill Burke
Gene Burke
Yvonne Brathwaite Burke
William Burke
Martha Burns
Hal Burson
August Busch III
Barbara Busch
Jean Bush
Dr. Jerry Buss
Bill Butcher
Suzanne Byard
Chuck Cale
Anton Calleia
Peter Caloyeras
Doug Calvert
Scotty Campbell
Warner Canto
Miguel de Capriles
John Carlos
Franco Carraro
Carol Carruthers
Hannah Carter
Claude-Roger Cartier
Itzhak Caspi
Jeanne Castanzo
Leo Castanzo
Mike Castine

Mary Cavella
Tom Celorie
Stella Cendejas
Joseph Cerrell
Rudy Cervantes
Pierre Chabloz
Otis Chandler
Lindsay Chaney
Pam Chang
Philippe Chatrier
Marie Chevallier
Douglas Chirchick
Annie Cho
Man-Lip Choy
Warren Christopher
Owen Churchill
Fred Claire
William Closs
Ruth Clough
Ray Cobel
Sherry Cockle
Herbert Cohn
Lela Cohn
Ruth Coine
Phillip Coles
Wayne Collett
Keith Comrie
Olga Connally
Maureen Connally-White
Gloria Conroy
John Cooper
Greg Cornell
Jorge Corralejo
Gerald Corrigan
Ben Cowitt
Rob Cranny
Kay Crawford
Don Crivellone
Beppe Croce
Jim Cross
Lance Cross
Dan Cruz

Arpad Csanadi
David Cunningham
Virginia Cushman
Bill Dahlman
Douglas Dailey
Dr. Tony Daly
Jeanne D'Amico
Deane Dana
Carol Daniels
Justin Dart
Horst Dassler
Terri Daubner
W. L. (Pete) Davidson
Alison Davis
Grace Davis
Michael Deaver
Jim De Bello
Richard Decker
John Dee
Anita DeFrantz
Gigi Delamestro
Don Delliquanti
Dr. Evie Dennis
Russ Derek
George Deukmejian
Donna DeVarona
John Dever
Barry Devine
Jane DeVore
Jim DeVore
Peter Diamond
Manny Diaz
Ken Dickman
Nan Diesen
Barry Diller
Don Dixon
Julian Dixon
Brad Donovan
James Dougherty
Ginger Douglass
George Dowding
Wanda Dowding

Leigh Drolet
Jerry Drum
Dr. Fred Dubick
Charles Ducommon
Charlie Dumas
Hazel Dunbar
Walter Dunn
Mary Duque
Gregory Easton
Jim Easton
Jeri Gonzales Eckert
Mary Edgert
Barbara Farrell Edmonson
Bill Edwards
Dianne Edwards
Gene Edwards
William Edwards
June Ehrlich
Barbara Eich
Joe Eich
Fred Eisman
Lucy Eldridge
William Ellinghous
Jack Elliott
Jane Ellison
Cynthia Emmets
Rolf Engen
Alan Epstein
Bob Erburu
Maggie Erickson
Patrick Escobar
Rene Essomba
Sophia Estrada
Larry Estrin
Audrey Etkins
Harold Ezell
Jack Farber
Margaret Farnum
Robert Farrell
Donna Fenchel
Nancy Ferber
John Ferraro

Dick Ferris
Richard Ferry
Margy Fetting
Jeff Fick
Ron Field
Donna Figueroa
Joel Fishman
Bob Fitzpatrick
Jay Flood
Priscilla Florence
Robert Fluor
Sir Dennis Follows
Gib Ford
Mary Lou Forster
Bill Forsythe
Dennis Fosdick
Jerry Foster
Barbara Fouch
Ann Frame
Victor Franco
Tony Frank
Tracy Frank
Mike Frankovich
John Fransen
Arturo Franz
Angelia Fraser
Ed Freu
Conrad Freund
Camilla Frost
Marti Frucci
Carlos Fuertes
Ingrid Fuhrmann
Tak Fujii
Jimmy Fukuzaki
Craig Fuller
Bruce Furniss
Alan Furth
Raymond Gafner
Lee Galles
Bob Galvin
Mimi Gan
Yves Gandillon

Judy Garland
Art Gastelum
Moonyean Gatanela
Brad Gates
Daryl Gates
Bob Gaughran
Roy Gavertt
Pape Gaye
Randi Gelfand
George Gerber
Walter Gerken
Hal Gershowitz
Lew Gerstner
Dr. Jim Gerth
George Gibbs
William Gibbs
Traci Gibson
Lucie Gikovich
Joan Gilford
Carla Giuliani
Philip Glass
Jules Glazer
Francesco Gnecchi-Ruscone
Shep Goldberg
Robert Goldstein
Frank Gomez
Jose Gonçalves
Alma Gonzalez
Manuel Gonzalez Guerra
Brian Goodell
Melanie Goodman
Gail Goodrich
Anita Gosha
Kevan Gosper
Gary Gossard
Dr. Todd Grant
Bob Graziano
Ramona Green
Randy Green
Bud Greenspan
Cappy Greenspan
Dr. Richard Greenspun

Michael Greenstreet
Dan Greenwood
Dorothy Griffard
Tom Groppel
Jim Gross
Don Guinn
Louis Guirandou-N'Diaye
Jan Gulbrandsen
Walter Gundy
Melanie Gurk
Dave Gustafson
Louis Gutierrez
Lili Guttenberg
Horst Habeler
Nigel Hacking
Kenneth Hahn
Tom Halleran
Cliff Halsey
Thornton Hamlin
Marvin Hamlisch
Dr. Armand Hammer
Bert Hammond
Kate Hanlon
Pirkko Hannula
H. H. Hanson
Kelly Hardwick
Jim Hardy
Maggie Hardy
Greg Harney
Elihu Harris
Juanita Harris
Jackie Harrold
Randy Hart
Susie Hartwell
Jim Harvey
Frank Hathaway
Yoichi Hattori
Joao Havelange
Ingrid Havens-Zomber
Philip Hawley
Redha Hazourli
Carol Head

Michael Helin
Robert Helmick
Gina Hemphill
Alan Henderson
Jackie Henderson
Ed Hennessy
Ramona Hennesy
Harold Henning
Debra Henry
Ike Herbert
Virginia Hernandez
Ron Hertel
Ray Hervy
Maurice Herzog
Freddi Hess
Bonita Hester
Jim Hetherman
Phil Hettema
Natalie Hill
Mike Hillis
Darcea Hiltz
Robert Hinchberger
Zelona Hinchberger
Ted Hinshaw
Dr. Charles Hirt
Donna Hirt
Larry Hitchcock
Becky Hitchman
Karen Hobel
Russ Hodge
Laura Hoffman
Cheryl Holmes
Niels Holst-Sorenson
John Holt
Judy Horton
Tom Horton
John Hotchkis
Larry Hough
Barbara Hounsell
Mike Howard
Vaclav Hubicka
Harry Hufford

Susan Huhndorf
Tom Hurley
Bill Hussey
Linda Hwa
Charlotte Hyde
Gillian Hyde
Kathy Ichiyasu
Wayne Ichiyasu
Flor Isava Fonseca
Kim Isbister
David Israel
Carole Jablon
Chuck Jackson
Jesse Jackson
Roger Jackson
Bernard Jacoupy
Robin Jaffe
Cleon Janos
Jorge Jarrin
Kim Jasper
Kathy Jennett
Lee Jennings
John Jerde
Peggy Jerome
Jim Johanneson
Eric Johnson
J. J. Johnson
Monika Johnson
Rafer Johnson
Raymond Johnson
Maxene Johnston
Shirley Johnstone
Roberta Jones-Booker
Donna Jordan
Rena Jordan
Gerd Jordano
Peter Jordano
Peter Joyce
Russell Justice
Shafi Babu Kahn
Bea Kass
Ed Keen

Jake Keever
Lamine Keita
Dr. Thomas Kellen
Thomas Keller
Marge Kelley
Al Kelly, Jr.
Jack Kelly
Tom Kemp
Heinz Kempa
Don Keough
Stan Kephart
Cornelis Kerdel
Jack Kerollis
Steven Kibbons
Lord Killanin
Maureen Kindel
John King
Tim King
Jack Kirkwood
Steve Kittell
Masaji Kiyokawa
William Klages
Larry Klein
Christopher Knepp
Mildred Knox
Don Koll
Rich Koppel
Don Kopriva
Ken Kragen
Barbara Kranyak
Tova Krim
Syd Kronenthal
Lenny Kruzecki
Gry Kvalheim
Per Kvalheim
Andre Lacoutieur
Rene Lagler
Jerry LaMar
Ante Lambasa
Amadou Lamine Ba
Alfredo La Mont
Ron Lane

Otto Lang
Dorothy Langkop
Pearl Lanum
Dr. David Latta
Bea Lavery
Rich Lawin
Debbie Lawrence
Craig Lawson
Joe Layton
Bill Leach
Donald Leach
Julie Leach
Anne Leavitt
Charles Lee
Clifton Lee
Rich Lee
Rosalind Lee
Sammy Lee
Dr. Mark Legome
John Leisner
Larry Lemoine
Bill Lennartz
Scott Letellier
Richard Levin
Sidney Levine
Roxanne Lew
Betty Lewis
Kevin Lewis
Dr. J. Lightfoot
Bill Lignante
Mike Linkletter
Barnett Lipman
Lloyd Lipoff
Paul Lippe
William Liss
Ed Litrenta
David Little
Tony Liyarro
Duke Llewellyn
Dick Lloynd
Mary Loescher
Denny Long

George Long
Anselmo Lopez
Mike Lordanich
Dr. Michael Lubran
Linda Lucks
Pavle Lukac
John Luke
Julie Lynn
Robert McCarthy
Vicki McClure
Pat McCormick
George McDonald
Tom McDonald
Jack McDonough
Dennis McDowell
Emmet McGaughey
Skip McGinty
Wally McGuire
Don McIntyre
Dr. Allen MacKenzie
Earl McKinley
Mike McLees
Miguel de la Madrid Hurtado
David Maggard
Monica Maldonado
Rosa Mapete
Joan Marantz
Ruth March
Marc Marcussen
Howard Marguleas
Bill Marlin
Margaret Marlin
Forrest Mars
John Mars
Elsie Martin
John Martin
Lynn Marx
Julius Mason
Bud Mathis
Don Matso
John Matthews
Dr. Ronald Matsunaga

Anani Matthia
Hans Mautner
Tom Megonigal
Pete Mehringer
C. L. Mehta
Rich Mejia
Mike Mellin
Norma Mena
Tom Mendenhall
Rich Merrick
Kevin Metz
Ann Meyers
Barbara Meyers
Branko Mikulic
Arlene Miller
Bob Miller
Charles Miller
F. Don Miller
Lennox Miller
Norm Miller
Richard Miller
Rush Miller
Billy Mills
Carole Mitchell
Mike Mitchell
Arne Mollen
Raoul Mollet
Jan Montgomery
Steve Montiel
Julian Montoya
Dann Moomaw
Donn Moomaw
Bob Moore
Cliff Moore
Shirley Moore
Jay Moorhead
Luz Morales
Mike Morphy
Dave Morris
Ken Morris
Bud Morrow
Pat Morrow

Mike Mount
Lothar Muench
Julie Mulvaney
R. J. Munzer
Agnes Mura
Bob Murch
Dr. Franklin Murphy
Jim Murray
Luna Musselman
John Naber
Mary Nagano
Barbara Namerow
Dr. Norman Namerow
Julian Nava
Lucy Nazarian
Lillian Nealy
Primo Nebiolo
Clarita Neher
Sandy Neilson
Charles Nelson
Doug Nelson
Mark Nelson
Bea Nemlaha
Bruce Nestande
Joe Neubauer
Jean Shiley Newhouse
William Nicholas
Lynne Niemiec
Luc Niggli
Nikolaos Nissiotis
Pete Norregard
Tina Noyes
Parry O'Brien
Dr. Ramon Oceguera
Lisa Odom
Isaac Ofek
John Ohanesian
Mike O'Hara
Shunichiro Okano
Tom O'Keefe
Steve Okino
Maidie Oliveau

Dick Olsen
Ken Olsen
Dick Olson
Peter O'Malley
Dr. William Ommert
John O'Neil
Thomas O'Neill
Peggy Orchowski
Abraham Ordia
Ron Orr
Sergio Orsi
Richetta Osborn
Carol Osher
Dr. Eugene Osher
Denis Oswald
Carolyn Otto
Sam Overton
Paul Owens
Bill Pachal
Nelson Paillou
Dan Packer
Jan Palchikoff
Kai Palchikoff
Vilma Pallette
Charles Palmer
Richard Palmer
Leonard Panish
Jeanie Parks
Norm Passas
Patty Patano
Judy Patching
Dan Pavillard
Toni Pearsall
Wilbur Peck
John Pennel
Roberto Peper
Rich Perelman
Massimo Della Pergola
Jane Perica
Deuk Perrin
Dr. John Perry
Mario Pescante

Bob Petersen
Pete Peterson
Steve Pickell
Kathy Pickus
Fred Pierce
Lois Pinch
Burt Pines
Derek Pinchbeck
Joe Pinola
Peter Pitchess
Dean Pitchford
Hermann Ploss
Carolyn Plumley
Sidney Poitier
Paul Pollard
Alys Pollet
Paula Jean Pope
Vern Porter
Michael Portonova
Richard Pound
Chellie Powell
Mae Powell
Walter Prawicki
Paul Preza
Dallas Price
David Price
Eli Primrose
Prince Philip, Duke of
    Edinburgh
Peck Prior
Cyndi Procope
Dr. James Puffer
John Quellet
Amy Quinn
Connie Ramberg
Walter Rasic
Kosti Rasinpera
Bill Rathburn
Joe Raymond
Mary Reagan
President Ronald Reagan
Wlodzimierz Reczek

Dale Rediker
Dana Reed
Willy Reich
Ira Reiner
Stephen Reinhardt
Ray Remy
Lloyd Reuss
Robert Reynolds
Mike Rice
Victoria Richart
Lionel Richie
German Rieckehoff
Thomas Riley
Max Rinkenburger
Angie Rios
Mike Roarty
Nick Roberts
William Robertson
Jim Robinson
Mack Robinson
Christopher Robles
Douglas Roby
J. J. Rodriguez
John Rodsett
Dr. Anthony Rogers
Beatrice Rogers
Seth Rogers
Jan Romary
Rod Rood
Michael Roos
Kathy Rose
Murray Rose
John Roseboro
David Rosenfeld
John Rosenfeld
Sherri Rosenfeld
Emmett Ross
Sheilah Ross
Jeffrey Roth
Alan Rothenberg
Claire Rothman
Beverly Rothstein

Wylene Royal
Joel Rubenstein
Jeff Ruhe
Claude Ruibal
Robert Runyan
Kenneth Ryan
Margo Ryan
Othman al-Saad
Pat Saevig
Juanita St. John
Cora Salcedo
Hugo Salcedo
Dr. James Salz
Juan Antonio Samaranch
John Sandbrook
Barry Sanders
Auriel Sanderson
Dick Sargent
Linette Savage
Alice Saviez
Pete Schabarum
Bill Schmidt
John Schmidt
Rock Schnabel
Peter Schneider
Philipp Schoeller
Jamie Schoenfeld
Paul Schrage
Horst Schreiber
Bill Schroeder
Jackie Schrogin
Bill Schulz
Fritzie Schumann
Yvonne Schwartz
Eriberto Scocimara
Manita Scocimara
Byron Scott
Bob Seagren
Robert Selleck
Piero Selvaggio
Grace Seto
Beverly Shaffer

Curran Shaffer
Larry Shannon
Dr. Myron Shapero
Lynda Shatteen
Dr. Stephen Shea
Aaron Sher
Katsuji Shibata
Risa Shimoda
Eunice Shriver
Ken Shropshire
Diane Siegel
Regina Siethoff
Esther Silvas
David Simon
William Simon
Bridget Simone
Valerie Simpson
Sasha Singer
Alexandru Siperco
Pete Siracusa
Cindy Sisson
Paul Slaughter
Vitaly Smirnov
Ed Smith
Frank Smith
Jeanne Smith
Dr. Robert Smith
Tommie Smith
Jim Snyder
Murray Sommer
Dennis Song
Sandra Spector
Bill Speicher
Fay Spencer
Paul Spengler
Lou Sporrer
Laura Squair
Charles Stanford
Boris Stankovic
Bob Stanley
Shannon Steere
Ed Steidle

Valerie Steiner
Henry Steinman
Willie Stennis
Alex Stepovich
Sandy Stepovich
Joanne Sterbenz
Dick Stevens
Eloise Stevens
Dan Stewart
Doug Stewart
Dwight Stones
Dennis Storer
Andy Strenk
Jack Strickland
Dr. Alan Strizak
Anto Sucic
Jim Suennen
Barbara Sullivan
Gene Summers
Deborah Sussman
Kelso Sutton
John Svenson
June Svonkin
Don Swanson
Prince Takeda
Fumiya Tamiaki
Hank Tatarchuk
Buddy Taylor
Juanita Taylor
Bruce Tenen
General Sven Thofelt
Fred Thomas
Sandra Thomas
Jere Thompson
John Thompson
Gary Thomson
H. D. Thoreau
Bill Thorpe, Jr.
Walt Thurner
Joan Thye
Bill Timmons
Ken Tiratira

Dave Todd
Septimiu Todeo
Dr. Paul Toffel
Carolyn Tomlin
Ron Tomsic
Rosa Topete
("The Torchrats")
Art Torres
Leslie Toth
Mike Trager
Stan Trembicki
Dr. Martin Trieb
Dr. F. Joseph Triggs
Walther Troger
Hoodie Troutman
Hope Tschopik
Fred Turner
Laura Turner
Tony Turner
Wyomia Tyus
Ginny Ueberroth
Heidi Ueberroth
Joe Ueberroth
Keri Ueberroth
Vicki Ueberroth
F. Umegaki
John Underwood
Harry Usher
Jo Usher
Charles Ussery
John Van de Kamp
Adrien Vanden Eede
J. W. van der Krol
Leon Van der Wyk
Darrell Vange
Kim Vange
Dick Van Kirk
Gilbert Vasquez
Chris Vatcher
Mario Vázquez Rana
Olegario Vázquez Rana
Michele Verdier

Art Villalovos
Danny Villanueva
Shannon Vukalcic
Esther Wachtell
Fred Wada
Greg Wagner
Card Walker
Darrell Walker
Tommy Walker
Ted Wallace
Liz Waller
Debby Walsh
Ruth Walsh
Julia Wark
Luanne Warner
Lew Wasserman
Ray Watt
Ed Weatherby
Rick Webb
William Webster
Klaus Weidner
Dr. William Weil
Barbi Weinberg
Jerry Weintraub
Jerry Welch
Gail Weldon
Jerry Welsh
Steven West
Fred White
Homer White
Marilyn White
Willie White
Fritz Widmer
Paul Wiggin
Herb Wildman
Bill Williams
Frank Williams
John Williams
Linda Williams
Ulis Williams
Anne Willoughby
Glenn Wilson

P. J. Winkler
Zanne Winship
Steve Wise
Bill Wishard
Wally Wolf
George Wolfberg
Florence Wollner
David Wolper
Gloria Wolper
Lai Wong
Monique Wong
Delores Wood
Robert Wood
Joe Woodard
Waid Woodruff
Dr. Earl Woods
Lee Wookey
James Worrall
Katy Wright
Marilyn Wyatt
Tom Yanagihara

Wendy Yano
Nancy Yasoian
Shelby Yastro
Pat Yoemans
Dr. Charles Young
Shirley Young
Richard Zanuck
David Zaremba
Euphemia Zaremba
Leigh Zaremba
Judy Zeller
Marina Zenovich
Susan Zerfas
Zhenliang He
Song Zhong
Zhong Shitong
Mickey Ziffren
Paul Ziffren
Lucile Zlotek
Galal el Zorba
Dr. James Zumberge

INDEX